ASIA

A Continental Overview
of Environmental Issues

THE WORLD'S ENVIRONMENTS

KEVIN HILLSTROM AND
LAURIE COLLIER HILLSTROM, SERIES EDITORS

Global warming, rainforest destruction, mass extinction, overpopulation—the environmental problems facing our planet are immense and complex.

ABC-CLIO's series The World's Environments offers students and general readers a handle on the key issues, events, and people.

The six titles in the series examine the unique—and common—problems facing the environments of every continent on Earth and the ingenious ways local people are attempting to address them. Titles in this series:

Africa and the Middle East

Asia

Australia, Oceania, and Antarctica

Europe

Latin America and the Caribbean

North America

ASIA

A Continental Overview
of Environmental Issues

KEVIN HILLSTROM
LAURIE COLLIER HILLSTROM

A B C · C L I O
Santa Barbara, California
Denver, Colorado   Oxford, England

Library of Congress Cataloging-in-Publication Data

Hillstrom, Kevin, 1963-
  Asia : a continental overview of environmental issues / Kevin Hillstrom, Laurie Collier Hillstrom.
    p. cm. — (The world's environments)
  Includes bibliographical references and index.
  ISBN 1-57607-688-1 (acid-free paper) — ISBN 1-57607-689-X (eBook)
  1. Asia—Environmental conditions. 2. Environmental degradation—Asia. 3. Environmental protection—Asia. 4. Conservation of natural resources—Asia. I. Hillstrom, Laurie Collier, 1965– II. Title.

GE160.A78H55 2003
363.7'0095—dc21   2002156274

07 06 05 04 03   10 9 8 7 6 5 4 3 2 1

This book is also available on the World Wide Web as an eBook.
Visit http://www.abc-clio.com for details.

ABC-CLIO, Inc.
130 Cremona Drive, P.O. Box 1911
Santa Barbara, California 93116–1911

This book is printed on acid-free paper ∞ .
Manufactured in the United States of America

Contents

List of
Tables and Figures

Tables

Figures

Introduction

THE WORLD'S ENVIRONMENTS

A s the nations of the world enter the twenty-first century, they confront a host of environmental issues that demand attention. Some of these issues—pollution of freshwater and marine resources, degradation of wildlife habitat, escalating human population densities that place crushing demands on finite environmental resources—have troubled the world for generations, and they continue to defy easy solutions. Other issues—global climate change, the potential risks and rewards of genetically modified crops and other organisms, unsustainable consumption of freshwater resources—are of more recent vintage. Together, these issues pose a formidable challenge to our hopes of building a prosperous world community in the new millennium, especially since environmental protection remains a low priority in many countries. But despite an abundance of troubling environmental indicators, positive steps are being taken at the local, regional, national, and international levels to implement new models of environmental stewardship that strike an appropriate balance between economic advancement and resource protection. In some places, these efforts have achieved striking success. There is reason to hope that this new vision of environmental sustainability will take root all around the globe in the coming years.

The World's Environments series is a general reference resource that provides a comprehensive assessment of our progress to date in meeting the numerous environmental challenges of the twenty-first century. It offers detailed, current information on vital environmental trends and issues facing nations around the globe. The series consists of six volumes, each of which addresses conservation issues and the state of the environment in a specific region of the world: individual volumes for *Asia, Europe,* and *North America,* published in spring 2003, will be joined by *Africa and the Middle East; Australia, Oceania, and Antarctica;* and *Latin America and the Caribbean* in the fall of the same year.

Each volume of The World's Environments includes coverage of issues unique to that region of the world in such realms as habitat destruction, water pollution, depletion of natural resources, energy consumption, and development trends. In addition, each volume provides an overview of the region's response to environmental matters of worldwide concern, such as global warming. Information on these complex issues is presented in a manner that is informative, interesting, and understandable to a general readership. Moreover, each book in the series has been produced with an emphasis on objectivity and utilization of the latest environmental data from government agencies, nongovernmental organizations (NGOs), and international environmental research agencies, such as the various research branches of the United Nations.

Organization

Each of the six volumes of The World's Environments consists of ten chapters devoted to the following major environmental issues:

Population and Land Use. This chapter includes continental population trends, socioeconomic background of the populace, prevailing consumption patterns, and development and sprawl issues.

Biodiversity. This chapter reports on the status of flora and fauna and the habitat upon which it depends for survival. Areas of coverage include the impact of alien species on native plants and animals, the consequences of deforestation and other forms of habitat degradation, and the effects of the international wildlife trade.

Parks, Preserves, and Protected Areas. This chapter describes the size, status, and biological richness of area park systems, preserves, and wilderness areas and their importance to regional biodiversity.

Forests. Issues covered in this chapter include the extent and status of forest resources, the importance of forestland as habitat, and prevailing forest management practices.

Agriculture. This chapter is devoted to dominant farming practices and their impact on local, regional, and national ecosystems. Subjects of special significance in this chapter include levels of freshwater consumption for irrigation, farming policies, reliance on and attitudes toward genetically modified foods, and ranching.

Freshwater. This chapter provides detailed coverage of the ecological health of rivers, lakes, and groundwater resources, extending special attention to pollution and consumption issues.

Oceans and Coastal Areas. This chapter explores the ecological health of continental marine areas. Principal areas of coverage include the current state of (and projected outlook for) area fisheries, coral reef conservation, coastal habitat loss from development and erosion, and water quality trends in estuaries and other coastal regions.

Energy and Transportation. This chapter assesses historic and emerging trends in regional energy use and transportation, with an emphasis on the environmental and economic benefits and drawbacks associated with energy sources ranging from fossil fuels to nuclear power to renewable technologies.

Air Quality and the Atmosphere. This chapter reports on the current state and future outlook of air quality in the region under discussion. Areas of discussion include emissions responsible for air pollution problems like acid rain and smog, as well as analysis of regional contributions to global warming and ozone loss.

Environmental Activism. This chapter provides a summary of the history of environmental activism in the region under discussion.

In addition, each volume of The World's Environments contains sidebars that provide readers with information on key individuals, organizations, projects, events, and controversies associated with specific environmental issues. By focusing attention on specific environmental "flashpoints"—the status of a single threatened species, the future of a specific wilderness area targeted for oil exploration, the struggles of a single village to adopt environmentally sustainable farming practices—many of these sidebars also shed light on larger environmental issues. The text of each volume is followed by an appendix of environmental and developmental agencies and organizations on the World Wide Web. Finally, each volume includes a general index containing citations to issues, events, and people discussed in the book, as well as supplemental tables, graphs, charts, maps, and photographs.

Coverage by Geographic Region

Each of the six volumes of The World's Environments focuses on a single region of the world: Africa and the Middle East; Asia; Australia, Oceania, and Antarctica; Europe; Latin America; and North America. In most instances, arrangement of coverage within these volumes was obvious, in accordance with widely recognized geographic divisions. But placement of a few countries was more problematic. Mexico, for instance, is recognized both as a part of North America and the northernmost state in Latin America. Moreover, some international environmental research agencies (both governmental and non-governmental) place data on Mexico under the North American umbrella, while others classify it among Central American and Caribbean nations. We ultimately decided to place Mexico in the Latin America volume, which covers Central and South America, in recognition of its significant social, economic, climatic, and environmental commonalities with those nations.

Similarly, environmental data on the vast Russian Federation, which sprawls over northern reaches of both Europe and Asia, is sometimes found in resources on Asia, and at other times in assessments of Europe's environment. Since most of Russia's population is located in the western end of its territory, we decided to cover the country's environmental issues in The World's Environments Europe volume, though occasional references to environmental conditions in the Russian Far East do appear in the Asia volume.

Finally, we decided to expand coverage in the Africa volume to cover environmental issues of the Middle East—also sometimes known as West Asia. This decision was made partly out of a recognition that the nations of Africa and the Middle East share many of the same environmental challenges—extremely limited freshwater supplies, for instance—and partly because of the space required in the Asia volume to fully explicate the multitude of grave environmental problems confronting Asia's central, southern, and eastern reaches. Coverage of other nations that straddle continental boundaries—such as the countries of the Caucasus region—are also concentrated in one volume, though references to some nations may appear elsewhere in the series.

Following is an internal breakdown of the volume-by-volume coverage for The World's Environments. This is followed in turn by two overview maps for the current volume, one showing country locations and key cities and the other indicating physical features.

Africe and the Middle East

Middle East and North Africa:
Algeria
Bahrain
Cyprus
Egypt
Gaza
Iraq
Israel
Jordan
Kuwait
Lebanon
Libya
Morocco
Oman
Qatar
Saudi Arabia
Syrian Arab Republic
Tunisia
Turkey
United Arab Emirates
West Bank
Yemen

Sub-Saharan Africa:
Angola
Benin
Botswana
Burkina Faso
Burundi
Cameroon
Central African Republic
Chad
Congo, Republic of the
Congo, Democratic Republic of
   (Zaire)

Côte d'Ivoire
Equatorial Guinea
Eritrea
Ethiopia
Gabon
Gambia
Ghana
Guinea
Guinea-Bissau
Kenya
Lesotho
Liberia
Madagascar
Malawi
Mali
Mauritania
Mozambique
Namibia
Niger
Nigeria
Rwanda
Senegal
Sierra Leone
Somalia
South Africa
Sudan
Tanzania
Togo
Uganda
Zambia
Zimbabwe

Asia
Afghanistan
Armenia
Azerbaijan

Bangladesh
Bhutan
Cambodia
China
Georgia
India
Indonesia
Iran
Japan
Kazakhstan
Korea, Democratic People's
  Republic of (North)
Korea, Republic of (South)
Kyrgyzstan
Lao People's Democratic Republic
Malaysia
Mongolia
Myanmar (Burma)
Nepal
Pakistan
Philippines
Singapore
Sri Lanka
Tajikistan
Thailand
Turkmenistan
Uzbekistan
Vietnam

Australia, Oceania, and Antarctica
Australia
Cook Islands
Fiji
French Polynesia
Guam
Kiribati

Nauru
New Caledonia
Northern Mariana Islands
Marshall Islands
Federated States of Micronesia
New Guinea
New Zealand
Palau
Papua New Guinea
Pitcairn Island
Samoa
Solomon Islands
Tonga
Tuvalu
Vanuatu
Wallis and Futuna
Various territories
*(Note: Antarctica is discussed in a
  stand-alone chapter)*

Europe
Albania
Austria
Belarus
Belgium
Bosnia and Herzegovina
Bulgaria
Croatia
Czech Republic
Denmark
Estonia
Finland
France
Germany
Greece
Hungary

Iceland
Ireland
Italy
Latvia
Lithuania
Republic of Macedonia
Moldova
Netherlands
Norway
Poland
Portugal
Romania
Russian Federation
Slovakia
Slovenia
Spain
Sweden
Switzerland
Ukraine
United Kingdom
Yugoslavia

**Latin America
    and the Caribbean**
Argentina
Belize
Bolivia

Brazil
Caribbean territories
Chile
Colombia
Costa Rica
Cuba
Dominican Republic
Ecuador
El Salvador
Guatemala
Guyana
Haiti
Honduras
Jamaica
Mexico
Nicaragua
Panama
Paraguay
Peru
Suriname
Trinidad and Tobago
Uruguay
Venezuela

North America
Canada
United States

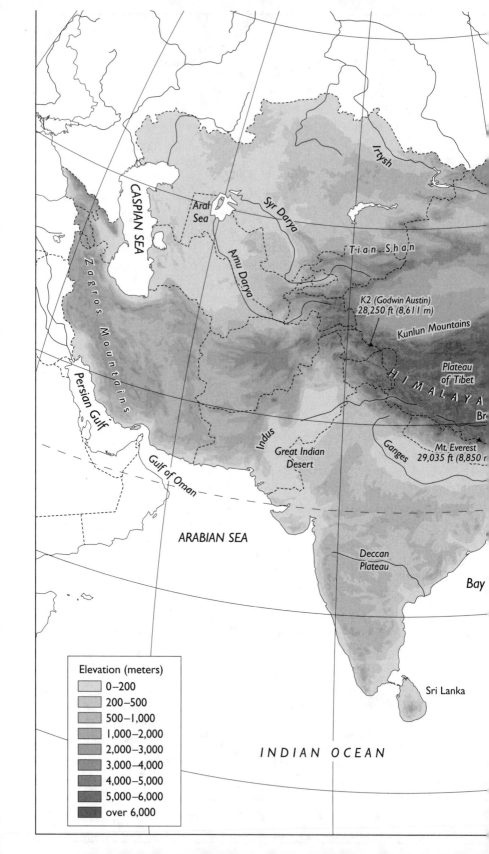

CASPIAN SEA

Aral Sea

Irtysh

Syr Darya

Amu Darya

T i a n   S h a n

K2 (Godwin Austin)
28,250 ft (8,611 m)

Kunlun Mountains

Z a g r o s   M o u n t a i n s

Plateau
of Tibet

H I M A L A Y A

Persian Gulf

Br

Indus

Great Indian
Desert

Ganges

Mt. Everest
29,035 ft (8,850 r

Gulf of Oman

ARABIAN SEA

Deccan
Plateau

Bay

INDIAN OCEAN

Sri Lanka

Elevation (meters)
- 0–200
- 200–500
- 500–1,000
- 1,000–2,000
- 2,000–3,000
- 3,000–4,000
- 4,000–5,000
- 5,000–6,000
- over 6,000

Acknowledgments

The authors are indebted to many members of the ABC-CLIO family for their fine work on this series. Special thanks are due to Vicky Speck, Martha Whitt, and Kevin Downing. We would also like to extend special thanks to our advisory board members, whose painstaking reviews played a significant role in shaping the final content of each volume, and to the contributors who lent their expertise and talent to this project.

Biographical Notes

Authors

KEVIN HILLSTROM and **LAURIE HILLSTROM** have authored and edited award-winning reference books on a wide range of subjects, including American history, international environmental issues, environmental activism, outdoor travel, and business and industry. Works produced by the Hillstroms include *Environmental Leaders 1* and *2* (1997 and 2000), the four-volume *American Civil War Reference Library* (2000), the four-volume *Vietnam War Reference Library* (2000), *Paddling Michigan* (2001), *Encyclopedia of Small Business, 2d ed.* (2001), and *The Vietnam Experience: A Concise Encyclopedia of American Literature, Films, and Songs* (1998).

Advisory Board

J. DAVID ALLAN received his B.Sc. (1966) from the University of British Columbia and his Ph.D. (1971) from the University of Michigan. He served on the Zoology faculty of the University of Maryland until 1990, when he moved to the University of Michigan, where he currently is Professor of Conservation Biology and Ecosystem Management in the School of Natural Resources and Environment. Dr. Allan specializes in the ecology and conservation of rivers. He is the author of *Stream Ecology* (1995) and coauthor (with C. E. Cushing) of *Streams: Their Ecology and Life* (2001). He has published extensively on topics in community ecology and the influence of land use on the ecological integrity of rivers. He serves or has served on committees for the North American Benthological Society, Ecological Society of America, and the American Society of Limnology and Oceanography. He serves or has served on the editorial board of the scientific journals *Freshwater Biology* and *Journal of the North American Benthological Society,* and on scientific advisory committees for the American Rivers and Nature Conservancy organizations.

DAVID LEONARD DOWNIE is Director of Education Partnerships for the Earth Institute at Columbia University, where he has conducted research and taught courses on international environmental politics since 1994. Educated at Duke

University and the University of North Carolina, Dr. Downie is author of numerous scholarly publications on the Stockholm Convention, the Montreal Protocol, the United Nations Environment Program, and other topics in global environmental politics. From 1994 to 1999, Dr. Downie served as Director of Environmental Policy Studies at the School of International and Public Affairs at Columbia University.

SETH DUNN is a research associate at the Worldwatch Institute, where he investigates energy and climate policy and strategy. He has contributed to five editions of the institute's annual *State of the World* report, including most recently "Moving the Climate Change Agenda Forward" (2002). He has also authored four WorldWatch papers, including "Micropower: The Next Electrical Era" (2000), "Hydrogen Futures: Toward a Sustainable Energy System" (2001), and "Reading the Weathervane: Climate Policy from Rio to Johannesburg" (2002). His contributions to *World Watch* magazine include "Iceland's Hydrogen Experiment" (2000) and "King Coal's Weakening Grip on Power" (1999). He holds a B.A. in history and studies in the environment from Yale University.

YUMIKO KURA is a research associate in the World Resource Institute's Information Program. Her recent work focuses on coastal ecosystems, water resources, and global fisheries. She coauthored WRI's 2001 *Pilot Analysis of Global Ecosystems: Coastal Ecosystems,* which analyzes quantitative and qualitative information on the condition of the world's coastal ecosystems. Before joining WRI, she worked for Conservation International, World Bank, and World Wildlife Fund as a consultant. She is originally from Japan and has a master's degree in environmental science and policy from Clark University, Worcester, Massachusetts.

CARMEN REVENGA is a senior associate with the Information Program at the World Resources Institute. Her current work focuses on water resources, global fisheries, and species conservation. She specializes in environmental indicators that measure the condition of ecosystems at the global and regional level, and is also part of WRI's Global Forest Watch team, coordinating forest monitoring activities with Global Forest Watch partners in Chile. Ms. Revenga is lead author of the WRI report *Pilot Analysis of Global Ecosystems: Freshwater Systems* (2000) and a contributing author to the WRI's *Pilot Analysis of Global Ecosystems: Coastal Ecosystems* (2001). These two reports assess the condition of freshwater and coastal ecosystems as well as their capacity to continue to provide goods and services on which humans depend. Ms. Revenga is also the lead author of *Watersheds of the World: Ecological Value and Vulnerability* (1998), which is the first analysis of a wide range of global data at the watershed level. Before joining WRI in 1997, she worked as an environmental scientist with Science and Policy

Associates, Inc., an environmental consulting firm in Washington, D.C. Her work covered topics in sustainable forestry and climate change.

ROBIN WHITE is a senior associate with the World Resources Institute, an environmental think tank based in Washington, D.C. Her focus at WRI has been on the development of environmental indicators and statistics for use in the *World Resources Report* and in global ecosystems analysis. She was the lead author of the WRI report *Pilot Analysis of Global Ecosystems: Grassland Ecosystems* (2000), which analyzes quantitative information on the condition of the world's grasslands. Her current work focuses on developing an ecosystem goods and services approach to the analysis of the world's drylands. A recent publication regarding this work is WRI's Information Policy Brief, *An Ecosystem Approach to Drylands: Building Support for New Development Policies*. Ms. White completed her Ph.D. in geography at the University of Wisconsin, Madison, with a minor in wildlife ecology. Before joining WRI in 1996, she was a policy analyst with the U.S. Congress, Office of Technology Assessment.

Contributors

WILLIAM BENTLEY is Chair in the Faculty of Forest and Natural Resources Management in the College of Environmental Science and Forestry at the State University of New York, Syracuse. Dr. Bentley is a specialist in forest policy and management and has worked in several Asian countries. His overseas work focuses on social forestry, agroforestry, sustainable forestry, and policy issues like property rights and common property resources. Bentley was a program officer for the Ford Foundation in India from 1983 to 1985 and a senior program officer for Winrock International from 1985 to 1994, serving as director of Winrock's Development Studies Center. He was an adjunct faculty member at Yale from 1990 to 1997, and a senior Fulbright fellow helping establish a center of excellence in agroforestry for New Zealand over the 1991–1995 period. His forestry degrees are from the University of California and the University of Michigan.

SETH DUNN is a research associate at the Worldwatch Institute, where he investigates energy and climate policy and strategy. He has contributed to five editions of the institute's annual *State of the World* report, including most recently "Moving the Climate Change Agenda Forward" (2002). He has also authored four WorldWatch papers, including "Micropower: The Next Electrical Era" (2000), "Hydrogen Futures: Toward a Sustainable Energy System" (2001), and "Reading the Weathervane: Climate Policy from Rio to Johannesburg" (2002). His contributions to *World Watch* magazine include "Iceland's Hydrogen Experiment" (2000) and "King Coal's Weakening Grip on Power" (1999). He holds a B.A. in history and studies in the environment from Yale University.

Population and Land Use

Asia is the fastest-growing region of the world in terms of population growth. Of the world's total population of more than 6 billion people, the United Nations estimated that in mid-2002, approximately 3.5 billion lived in Asia. Two Asian countries—China and India—hold more than one-third of the global population themselves, with each nation accounting for more than 1 billion people (UN Economic and Social Commission for Asia and the Pacific 2002). (See Table 1.1)

China, India, and numerous other developing countries on the Asian continent have experienced considerable economic growth over the past half-century—and especially over the last three decades. Increased agricultural productivity, robust industrial development, and rapid diversification of the economy into nonfarming areas have all been hallmarks of Asia's recent history. These trends have helped push the continent to a near tripling of per capita gross domestic product since 1970 and enabled millions of Asians to emerge from poverty (Asian Development Bank 2001; Pinstrup-Anderson and Cohen 2000).

But Asia is also carrying increasing signs of "demographic fatigue" in its quest to provide for the social, educational, medical, and economic needs and wants of its exploding population (Brown et al. 1998). Environmental degradation has been one of the most visible manifestations of this evolving struggle. This degradation has taken numerous forms, including large-scale and haphazard conversion of forests, wetlands, and other habitat areas for agricultural and industrial use and human settlement; increasing emission of pollutants into the air; the creation of respiratory hazards in urban areas; and acid rain damage in forests and lakes; and intensive forms of agriculture that rely on unsustainable levels of irrigation or ecologically damaging volumes

Table 1.1 World's Largest Countries in 2002 and 2050 (Projected)

| | 2002 | | | 2050 (Projected) | |
Rank	Country	Population (millions)	Rank	Country	Population (millions)
1	China	1,281	1	India	1,628
2	India	1,050	2	China	1,394
3	United States	287	3	United States	413
4	Indonesia	217	4	Pakistan	332
5	Brazil	174	5	Indonesia	316
6	Russia	144	6	Nigeria	304
7	Pakistan	144	7	Brazil	247
8	Bangladesh	134	8	Bangladesh	205
9	Nigeria	130	9	Congo, Dem. Rep. of	182
10	Japan	127	10	Ethiopia	173
11	Mexico	102	11	Mexico	151
12	Germany	82	12	Philippines	146
13	Philippines	80	13	Vietnam	117
14	Vietnam	80	14	Egypt	115
15	Egypt	71	15	Russia	102

SOURCE: Population Reference Bureau. "2002 World Population Data Sheet of the Population Reference Bureau: Demographic Data and Estimates for the Countries and Regions of the World." http://www.prb.org/pdf/WorldPopulationDS02_Eng.pdf.

of pesticides and fertilizers. All of these problems will have to be effectively addressed if the nations of Asia hope to maintain their recent progress in improving the lives of their peoples.

Poverty Levels Reduced across Asia despite Growing Populations

In mid-2002, the United Nations estimated the total population of Asia (excluding the 144 million residents of the Russian Federation) at 3.45 billion. This total included 1.5 billion people in East and Northeast Asia (consisting of China—including Hong Kong and Macao—North and South Korea, Japan, and Mongolia); 538 million people in Southeast Asia (Brunei Darussalam, Cambodia, Indonesia, Lao People's Democratic Republic, Malaysia, Myanmar (Burma), Philippines, Singapore, Thailand, and Vietnam); 1.55 billion people in South and Southwest Asia (Afghanistan, Bangladesh, Bhutan, India, Iran, Maldives, Nepal, Pakistan, Sri Lanka, and Turkey); and 219 million people in North and Central Asia (Armenia, Azerbaijan, Georgia, Kazakhstan, Kyrgyzstan, Tajikistan, Turkmenistan, and Uzbekistan). In terms of individual countries, China is the global leader in total population, with 1.3 billion Chinese spread across its vast valleys and steppes in mid-2002. But India is close behind, with an estimated 1.05 billion people. Other Asian countries with large numbers of people include Indonesia (217 million), Pakistan (316 million), Bangladesh (134 million), and Japan (127 million) (Population Reference Bureau 2002).

On a regionwide basis, annual population growth rates are highest in South and Southwest Asia at 1.7 percent, followed by Southeast Asia (1.4 percent) and East and Northeast Asia (0.8 percent). North and Central Asia, on the other hand, have actually experienced a modest population decline (minus 0.2 percent annually) as their various states grapple with fundamental socio-economic changes associated with the dissolution of the Soviet Union (ibid.). (See Table 1.2 for a country-by-country population breakdown with projections to 2025.)

Asia still contains a higher number of people living in poverty than any other region of the world. At the close of the twentieth century, it housed about 900 million poor people, about 68 percent of the world total. Of those poor people, 500 million are in South Asia, 300 million in East Asia, and 100 million in Southeast Asia and the Pacific (World Bank 1998). Indeed, many urban and rural areas of Asia remain beset by grinding poverty, with basic amenities—potable water, sanitation, shelter and fuel for heating, health care, nutritional food—either absent or in short supply. But although the Asian Development Bank observes that "the absolute numbers of people living in poverty in Asia today are unacceptable," it also notes that the continent has made remarkable progress in addressing poverty: "In 1970, 60 percent of all Asians lived in poverty. That figure has been cut by almost half, with about one-third of all Asians living in poverty in 2000. Also, countries such as Bangladesh, the People's Republic of China, and India have moved from periodic famines to almost self-sufficiency in food production" (Asian Development Bank 2001). Indeed, gains in East Asia and the Pacific and South Asia are primarily responsible for a 6 percent drop in the global poverty rate (from 29 percent to 23 percent) between 1990 and 1999 (World Bank 2002).

Meeting the Challenges of Population Growth

Asia's improving living standards have been attributed not only to increased economic growth and opportunity but also to the proliferation of policies that promote social development and family planning. These programs, which have been credited with stabilizing population levels in Sri Lanka and elsewhere, include increased educational opportunities for girls, expansion of economic opportunities for women, and growing investment in nutrition and health programs (Sadik 1997). But progress in these areas has not been uniform

Table 1.2 Population Trends across Asia

	Population (thousands)			Average Annual Population Change (percent)		Percentage of Population in Specific Age Groups Year 2000 (a)			Total Fertility Rate (average number of children per woman)	
	1950	2000 (a)	2025 (a)	1975–80	1995–00 (a)	<15	15–65	>65	1975–80	1995–00 (a)
World	2,521,495	6,055,049	7,823,703	1.7	1.3	30	63	7	3.9	2.7
Asia (Excl. Middle East)	1,333,740	3,420,234	4,307,665	X	X	48	47	5	X	X
Armenia	1,354	3,520	3,946	1.8	(0.3)	25	67	9	2.5	1.7
Azerbaijan	2,896	7,734	9,403	1.6	0.4	29	64	7	3.6	2.0
Bangladesh	41,783	129,155	178,751	2.8	1.7	35	62	3	6.7	3.1
Bhutan	734	2,124	3,904	2.3	2.8	43	53	4	5.9	5.5
Cambodia	4,346	11,168	16,526	(1.8)	2.2	41	56	3	4.1	4.6
China	554,760	1,277,558	1,480,412	1.5	0.9	58	37	5	3.3	1.8
Georgia	3,527	4,968	5,178	0.7	(1.1)	22	65	13	2.4	1.9
India	357,561	1,013,662	1,330,449	2.1	1.6	33	62	5	4.8	3.1
Indonesia	79,538	212,107	273,442	2.1	1.4	31	65	5	4.7	2.6
Japan	83,625	126,714	121,150	0.9	0.2	55	34	12	1.8	1.4
Kazakhstan	6,703	16,223	17,698	1.1	(0.3)	28	65	7	3.1	2.3
Korea, Dem. People's Republic	9,488	24,039	29,388	1.6	1.6	60	36	4	3.3	2.1
Korea, Rep	20,357	46,844	52,533	1.6	0.8	57	37	5	2.9	1.7
Kyrgyzstan	1,740	4,699	6,096	1.9	0.6	35	59	6	4.1	3.2
Lao People's Dem Rep	1,755	5,433	9,653	1.2	2.6	44	53	3	6.7	5.8
Malaysia	6,110	22,244	30,968	2.3	2.0	34	62	4	4.2	3.2
Mongolia	761	2,662	3,709	2.8	1.6	61	36	3	6.6	2.6
Myanmar	17,832	45,611	58,120	2.1	1.2	28	67	5	5.3	2.4
Nepal	7,862	23,930	38,010	2.5	2.4	41	55	4	6.2	4.5
Pakistan	39,513	156,483	263,000	2.6	2.8	42	55	3	7.0	5.0

Table 1.2 Population Trends across Asia (*continued*)

	Population (thousands)			Average Annual Population Change (percent)		Percentage of Population in Specific Age Groups Year 2000 (a)			Total Fertility Rate (average number of children per woman)	
	1950	2000 (a)	2025 (a)	1975–80	1995–00 (a)	<15	15–65	>65	1975–80	1995–00 (a)
World	2,521,495	6,055,049	7,823,703	1.7	1.3	30	63	7	3.9	2.7
Asia (Excl. Middle East)	1,333,740	3,420,234	4,307,665	X	X	48	47	5	X	X
Philippines	20,988	75,967	108,251	2.3	2.1	37	60	4	5.0	3.6
Singapore	1,022	3,567	4,168	1.3	1.4	22	71	7	1.9	1.7
Sri Lanka	7,678	18,827	23,547	1.7	1.0	26	67	7	3.8	2.1
Tajikistan	1,532	6,188	8,857	2.8	1.5	40	55	5	5.9	4.2
Thailand	20,010	61,399	72,717	2.4	0.9	25	69	6	4.3	1.7
Turkmenistan	1,211	4,459	6,287	2.5	1.8	38	58	4	5.3	3.6
Uzbekistan	6,314	24,318	33,355	2.6	1.6	37	58	5	5.1	3.4
Viet Nam	29,954	79,832	108,037	2.2	1.6	33	61	5	5.6	2.6

SOURCE: United Nations Population Division. http://www.wri.org/wr-00-01/pdf/hd1n_2000.pdf

NOTES: Negative values are shown in parentheses. "0" is either zero or less than one-half the unit of measure. "(0)" indicates a value less than zero and greater than negative one-half.

a. Data include projections based on 1990 base year population data.

Women dig through garbage for usable items in Ho Chi Minh City, Vietnam. PETER TURNLEY/CORBIS

across the continent, and Asia's developing nations also face a host of other pressing challenges associated with population growth.

Food Security

Asia has labored mightily to meet the food demands of its growing population. For instance, it has dramatically increased its total area of cropland, from about 210 million hectares in 1900 to about 453 million hectares by 1994. This expansion was achieved primarily by clearing forestlands; an estimated 42 million hectares of Asian forestland were sacrificed for agriculture from 1980 to 1995 alone (UN Environment Programme 1999). It also expanded its cultivation of high-yielding varieties of rice and wheat and increased its use of fertilizers, pesticides, and herbicides. Another tool brought to bear to address Asia's food needs has been irrigation, arguably the biggest factor of all in the region's increased food production.

Worldwide, the amount of irrigated land has tripled since 1950 to cover 270 million hectares, and irrigated fields currently account for more than one-third of global harvests. Much of this irrigation activity has been centered in Asia, where it has enabled some farmers to harvest two or three crops annually. China, India, Indonesia, South Korea, Pakistan, and Sri Lanka all irrigate more than 30 percent of their total cropland (UN Food and Agriculture Organization 1999).

These efforts to squeeze greater volumes of crops out of the agricultural sector have paid handsome dividends in the past half-century. Grain yields in China nearly quadrupled between 1952 and 1996, and between 1980 and 1990 food production in Southeast Asia grew faster than anywhere else in the world (UN Conference on Trade and Development 1994). But as in other regions of the world, irrigation-dependent Asian countries are being confronted with increasing evidence that their diversions of water from rivers and underground aquifers into fields are not sustainable over the long term, especially given forecasts of even greater water demand in the future (UN Food and Agriculture Organization 1999).

Moreover, unsustainable freshwater withdrawal is just one food security issue that concerns analysts. Another is the appalling contamination of waterways from agricultural, industrial, and municipal sources. In some regions, emissions of pollutants into rivers and bays have been so overwhelming that they have obliterated freshwater ecosystems (many of which contain fisheries that are staples in the diets of Asian communities) and rendered the waterways useless as sources of potable water. Concerns have also been raised about diminishing rates of yield growth. In the 1990s, for example, gains in rice productivity fell to less than 2 percent after regularly posting 3 percent gains during the 1970s (Conway 1997). Finally, soil erosion, nutrient depletion, and other forms of land degradation associated with unsustainable agricultural practices have ruined significant quantities of arable land. Between 1957 and 1990, for example, China lost arable land equal to all the cropland in France, Germany, Denmark, and the Netherlands combined as a direct result of land degradation (UN Economic and Social Commission for Asia and the Pacific 1995).

These trends have led some to conclude that Asia's historical and continuing misuse of its land and water resources will eventually render it unable to feed large segments of its population. According to some scenarios, subsequent increased importation of grain and other foods by China, India, and other nations with large populations could create a deadly ripple effect in world food markets, increasing rates of malnutrition and starvation in some areas of Asia, Africa, and other poverty-stricken regions of the world (Brown, *Who Will Feed China?* 1994). Another viewpoint, however, holds that technological innovations such as genetically modified crops will enable Asia and other regions to meet growing food needs, and that increased demand for food could have the salutary effect of reviving declining agricultural sectors in the developed world (UN Food and Agriculture Organization 1996). "Low till" farming also has been touted as an efficient and (comparatively) environmentally benign mode of agriculture that could relieve some pressure on finite arable land resources. Under low till regimens, farmers sow wheat in rice straw left standing from a previous harvest rather than in soil that has been re-peatedly plowed over. The roots of the rice straw provide channels for wheat roots to grow, habitat for beneficial insects to prey on invasive insects, and a natural fertilizer of organic matter for the wheat crop. This method has gained favor in some areas of Asia, including Bangladesh, India, Nepal, and Pakistan. Usable by farmers with little equipment or land, the practice has reportedly increased harvest yields while simultaneously reducing reliance on irrigation and herbicides ("Plow Less, Grow More" 2001).

Consumerism

The twin forces of economic expansion and population growth have produced swelling levels of energy consumption and increased demand for material goods in many regions of Asia. In some instances, surging income levels have triggered veritable explosions in per capita consumption of resources at the local, regional, and international level. In Hong Kong, for instance, a 30 percent rise in population was accompanied by 300 percent increases in gross domestic product (GDP) and waste generation. In Brunei, high rates of population growth and growing affluence have combined to place heavy pressure on fragile coastal ecosystems, where construction and other development has concen-trated (Yencken et al. 2000). Moreover, high-consumption lifestyles are end-lessly promoted by advertising-drenched electronic media that have infiltrated even the remotest corners of the continent. "Asians have become full-fledged members of the energy-intensive, mass-consumption, mass-refuse society," concluded one analysis. "On one hand, the spread of this lifestyle is a manifesta-tion of the growing middle class, which is itself a product of higher incomes, but another cause is the early appearance of the consumer loan in Asian countries. It is a fact that the increase in goods like automobiles and electric appliances outstrips the rise in income" (Japan Environmental Council 2000).

Of course, some consumption patterns in Asia are more a barometer of in-dustrial, urban, and infrastructure development than individual disposable income. For example, developing countries in Asia have emerged in recent years as the hottest market for the international cement industry. In 1996 the top three countries for per capita use of cement were South Korea, Taiwan, and Malaysia. Each used more than twice as much cement per capita as the United States and four times as much as typical, established industrial nations with well-developed infrastructures, such as the United Kingdom (Harrison and Pearce 1999; World Wildlife Fund 1999).

Finally, some high levels of natural resource consumption have been attrib-uted to the lingering impact of old political systems on individual and commu-nity attitudes. In Central Asia, for example, communities are still recovering from a "Soviet system of central planning" that "[undermined] individual incentives and responsibilities in the household economy" (Asian Development Bank 1998). According to this perspective, the absence of personal responsibility and choice produced major environmental repercussions because it provided no economic incentives for people to conserve water or energy resources (ibid.).

Green Space in Singapore: Real or Perceived?

One of the most notable environmental success stories in Asia has been Singapore, a city that has effectively incorporated environmental considerations into most operational aspects since gaining independence from Britain in 1965. Located on the southern tip of Southeast Asia's Malay Peninsula, this affluent city-state has established strict controls on air and water pollution. It has also acted decisively in removing slums, squatter settlements, and other environmentally damaging landscapes and replacing them with public housing, all with the ultimate goal of creating and maintaining a "clean and green" city.

This "garden city" concept, devised at independence, has been adhered to without swerving for the past four decades. Indeed, authorities have addressed all manner of threats to the environmental integrity of the island during that time, imposing hygiene regulations on markets and food centers, abolishing polluting activities such as pig and duck farming, and nourishing the long-polluted Singapore River back to a measure of its former ecological health (Yencken et al. 2000).

Singapore's green-oriented management philosophy has received praise from environmental groups and proponents of sustainable development. But despite its laudable history in the realm of urban environmentalism, the city-state has been faulted for perceived indifference to the maintenance of natural ecosystems. Charges that Singapore is more concerned with cosmetic appearances than true conservation of fragile habitat often center on its poor record in the area of mangrove forest preservation. These forests once girded much of Singapore's coastline, but over the years significant portions have been removed in favor of commercial development.

Sources:

Lee, William K. M. 2001. "The Poor in Singapore: Issues and Options." *Journal of Contemporary Asia* 31(1).

Yencken, David, John Fien, and Helen Sykes, eds. 2000. *Environment, Education, and Society in the Asia-Pacific: Local Traditions and Global Discourses.* London: Routledge.

Urbanization and Migration

Urbanization is on the upswing across Asia. In fact, the nations of Asia are at the forefront of the worldwide surge in urbanization, though other developing regions, particularly Latin America, are also key contributors. In 1995, 34 percent of all Asians (1.067 billion individuals) lived in urban areas scattered across the great continent. This figure does not match the urban percentages in North America and Europe, but it constitutes a jump of more than 10 percentage points from the 1975 urban population total. Much of that growth occurred in the 1990s. From 1990 to 1995, for example, Asia's urban population grew at an average annual rate of 3.2 percent (by contrast, Asia's rural populations registered only 0.8 percent growth during the same period) (UN Population Division 1998). Overall, the urban population in the Asia-Pacific region increased by 560 million people (or 260 percent) between 1970 and 2000, and between 2000 and 2030 it is expected to increase by another 1.45 billion people (or 250 percent). Every day, in fact, the urban population in Asia increases by 140,000 people (UN Economic and Social Commission for Asia and the Pacific 2001).

This explosion in urbanization has been powered by overall population growth and rising rates of rural-to-urban migration. The latter trend can be traced to the increasing mechanization of agriculture, which has diminished demand for labor in rural areas, and the quest, common to all nations and peoples, to achieve a higher standard of living and quality of life for self and family. But while the cities of Asia deliver on their promise of economic and social betterment for some migrants, "the wealth produced in cities does not necessarily translate into prosperity for all. Increasing urbanization has the potential for either improving human life or increasing misery. The cities can provide opportunities or frustrate their attainment; promote health or cause disease; empower people to realize their needs and desires or impose on them a simple struggle for basic survival" (Sadik 1997).

The rapid pace of urbanization has also had a significant influence on the environment across Asia. Negative ecological developments directly linked to the galloping growth of cities include conversion of forests, wetlands, and other natural habitats rich in flora and fauna to agricultural, business, and settlement use; overexploitation of groundwater; stunning increases in the volume of solid municipal and industrial waste; and heavy volumes of air and water pollution, which have been blamed for a host of respiratory and waterborne diseases and—in the case of airborne emissions—have been cited as an important factor in global warming. Urban areas of Vietnam and neighboring Cambodia provide a fairly representative sampling of the environmental havoc wrought by many of Asia's developing cities. In Phnom Penh, sprawling squatter settlements besiege many canals and flood protection levees. This occupation has further polluted already oversubscribed local water supplies and degraded waterway banks at the same time that demand for fuelwood and land for agricultural and commercial activity has led to significant deforestation of the surrounding watershed. This deforestation has further exacerbated the city's vulnerability to flooding and taken a heavy toll on local biodiversity. In Hanoi and Ho Chi Minh City, meanwhile, infrastructure for treating and discharging domestic and industrial liquid waste is practically nonexistent. By some estimates, industrial wastewater discharges from Ho Chi Minh City alone—which includes effluents from oil refining, chemical, and food processing operations—account for 20 to 30 percent of the total flow in Vietnam's river systems (Asian Development Bank 2001).

Asian cities are also saddled with some of the most notorious traffic congestion in the entire world. This problem, the end result of population growth and soaring rates of motor vehicle ownership, has done enormous harm to the environment as well. Impacts include localized air pollution that compromises the health of residents; global and regional air pollution that affects global climate and regional ecosystems; fragmentation of important wildlife breeding, feeding, and migratory routes; escalating consumption of nonrenewable resources (especially oil); noise pollution; and environmental repercussions associated with oil extraction and transport.

Moreover, major Asian cities are increasingly choosing car-oriented land use patterns as they expand. In Malaysia's Kuala Lumpur, for example, unrestrained road building and construction of numerous low-density real estate developments designed for private vehicle access threaten to neutralize the benefits of new mass transit investment. These choices have a tremendous and long-lasting impact on urban transport and land use because they dictate the distribution and densities of population and jobs. For example, very low urban densities and dispersed locations of employment and services make it difficult to fund and maintain effective public transportation. Moreover, they often contribute to increased private vehicle ownership and expansion of motorway systems. Conversely, high population densities are linked to heavy concentrations of jobs and services, which in turn enable smaller public transport systems to be more profitable (Barter 1997).

Not surprisingly, Asia's rapid urbanization has boosted the number of large cities within its boundaries and pushed those cities to historically unprecedented sizes. At the dawn of the nineteenth century, London and Peking (now Beijing) were the only cities in the world with 1 million or more inhabitants. By 1990 there were 293 such cities, including 34 metropolitan areas boasting

Expanding Populations Threaten Regional Biodiversity

Habitat conversion and degradation and associated biodiversity loss are among the myriad environmental drawbacks of rapid population growth in Asia. In the mountainous Deqin region of southwest China, for example, fragmentation, conversion, and degradation of vital wildlife habitats are a serious problem, despite the establishment of the Baimaxueshan Nature Reserve and new legal protections for the Yunnan snub-nosed monkey and other endangered species. Most habitat loss in the region has been blamed on population pressure and limited economic opportunity, which in turn have fueled a variety of ecologically destructive practices, including unsustainable levels of agricultural expansion, fuelwood collection, logging, overgrazing, and illegal hunting. Thus far, regional and national authorities responsible for policy development and implementation in such areas as population, land tenure, timber pricing, fiscal devolution, poverty alleviation, regional development, and nature reserve management have done little to alleviate the conditions that contribute to biodiversity loss in Deqin (Wood et al. 2000).

Many of these same dynamics are in play in numerous other regions of Asia as well. Southeast India's Chilika Lake, for example, is an internationally famous bird habitat. But population pressure in the form of chemical contamination from watershed-based industries, agricultural intensification of the Chilika basin, and the spread of prawn-culture ponds have increased pollution and eutrophication of the lake. Weed growth associated with eutrophication has been particularly severe, claiming more than 14 square kilometers of the lake annually since 1973. These factors are blamed for a marked decline in the quantity and variety of fish in Chilika Lake, fish upon which area birds rely for sustenance. Deforestation in the Chilika basin and hunting of 15,000 to 20,000 birds annually is putting further pressure on stressed bird populations (ibid.).

The degradation of this valuable bird sanctuary has had economic repercussions for nearby human communities as well. Ecotourism used to bring considerable economic activity to the region, but that source of revenue has dwindled away in another manifestation of the lake's decline. This, in turn, has forced the impoverished people around the lake to engage in unsustainable fishing practices for their very survival.

Sources:

BirdLife International. 2001. *Threatened Birds of Asia: The BirdLife International Red Data Book.* Cambridge, UK: BirdLife International.

Bryant, Dirk, D. Nielson, and L. Tangley. 1997. *The Last Frontier Forests: Ecosystems and Economies on the Edge,* Washington, DC: World Resources Institute.

Wood, Alexander, Pamela Stedman-Edwards, and Johanna Mang, eds. *The Root Causes of Biodiversity Loss.* 2000. London: Earthscan.

World Wildlife Fund. 1999. Living Planet Report 1999. WWF.

more than 5 million residents. Of those 34 cities, which collectively accounted for about 15 percent of the world's urban population, more than half—18— were located in Asia. Moreover, Asia was home to 7 of the world's 12 so-called mega-cities—those with 10 million or more inhabitants—in 1990, including the largest, Tokyo (Hardoy et al. 2001). By the close of the 1990s, meanwhile, the Asia-Pacific region claimed 160 of the world's 369 cities with more than 750,000 residents. North America, by comparison, had only 64 (UN Population Division 2001).

According to the United Nations, the region of the continent that currently has the highest percentage of its total population in urban areas is North and Central Asia, at 67 percent (this percentage includes Russia— discussed in the *Europe* volume of this series—where 78 percent of the population is urban). The region is also posting a modest annual growth rate in its urban population (0.4 percent), even though its overall population has actually declined in recent years. Next is Southeast Asia, where 40 percent of the population is urban. But the annual growth rate of urban population in Southeast Asia has been about 3 percent in recent years, leading analysts to forecast majority-urban status for the region in several years. Approximately 39 percent of the population in East and Northeast Asia is urban, but rates of growth are robust there as well (1.9 percent annually). Moreover, some of the countries in this region have the highest percentage of urban populations anywhere on the continent, including Singapore and Hong Kong (100 percent), South Korea (83 percent), and Japan (79 percent). Finally, only one-third of the population of South and Southwest Asia could be found in urban centers at the close of the twentieth century, despite the existence of major cities like Mumbai, Delhi, and Calcutta (in India), and Dhaka (in Bangladesh). But urban populations are expanding at a dizzying rate there as well, growing by 3 percent every year (UN Economic and Social Commission for Asia and the Pacific 2002; UN Population Division 2001).

Many of the people flocking to Asia's swelling urban centers are motivated more by desperation than by optimism. A great deal of Asian migration from rural community to labyrinthine city is prompted by warfare, usually within national boundaries. The UN Commissioner for Refugees has estimated the total number of Asians displaced by violence at up to 7 million (Harrison and Pearce 1999). Others are fleeing appalling environmental conditions, from rivers that have been ruined by generations of pollution to croplands that are withering after years of intensive farming. For example, it has been estimated that almost 40 percent of the regional population (more than 1.3 billion people) live in rural areas prone to drought and desertification.

Moreover, these conditions prevail across large swaths of high-population nations like China (with almost 180 million degraded hectares), India (110 million hectares), and Pakistan (62 million hectares) (UN Environment Programme 1997).

But most migrants are flocking to cities for economic reasons. In China, for instance, higher crop yields and rising population on a dwindling arable land mass have created an estimated 100 million surplus laborers. Some of these people have remained in the countryside pursuing subsistence lifestyles. But China also has a floating population of 80 million rural people that have relocated to cities in search of work, and in some cities these "temporary residents" compose a significant segment of the overall population. In Shanghai, for example, an estimated 3.3 million of the city's 13.6 million people at the end of the 1990s were migrants (Irwin 1999).

This influx of labor has been a cornerstone of China's—and Asia's—tremendous economic growth, and many people hailing from rural areas find that they have greater access to clean water and basic sanitation than they did in their former lives. But large numbers of migrants live in squalid and crowded conditions in which epidemics of tuberculosis, diarrhea, and other communicable diseases sweep through on a regular basis. In Colombo, Sri Lanka, for example, half of the population lived in slums and squatter settlements in the mid-1990s. In Karachi, Pakistan, a city of 10 million that is adding another half-million every year, 40 percent of the population lives in squatter colonies and one in five babies dies before its first birthday (Harrison and Pearce 1999). And in Indonesia, only 35 percent of the country's burgeoning urban populace have access to safe drinking water (Association of South-East Asian Nations 1997).

Most migrants from rural areas settle on the fringe of cities, where quality of life ranges from good to abominable. Authorities at the national, regional, and local levels are cognizant of the poor living conditions that often prevail in these areas, but in most cases, existing social services and infrastructure are already under enormous strain. Moreover, these slums and settlements are swelling in size every year, sometimes by hundreds of thousands of people. This makes the task of providing quality education, medical care, and living conditions for all city dwellers a truly herculean one, especially since governments have extremely limited funds at their disposal. For that reason, it is widely forecasted that Asia's major urban centers will experience additional expansion into previously undisturbed land areas; increases in traffic congestion, water, and air pollution; progressively severe shortages of potable water; and increasingly urgent infrastructure repair and development costs in the coming years.

Land Management

The human populations of Asia are growing so rapidly that they are converting and encroaching upon vital forest and wetland habitat for a wide array of creatures, from Asian elephants to birds. For example, the conservation group BirdLife International believes that some 300 Asian bird species face extinction because of habitat loss and degradation caused by logging and agriculture, and that fully one-quarter of the continent's identified avian species face varying degrees of survival threat (BirdLife International 2001). In addition, "unplanned and uncontrolled city expansion…destroys natural landscapes in or close to cities that should be preserved as parks, nature reserves, historic sites, or simply as areas of open space for recreation and children's play. The need to preserve or develop such areas might seem less urgent than, say, land for housing. But once an area is built up, it is almost impossible (and very expensive) to remedy a lack of open space. In addition, the richer groups suffer much less. Their residential areas usually have plenty of open space. Their homes often have gardens. They are much more mobile and so can travel more easily out of the city" (Hardoy et al. 2001).

In addition, many Asian cities are consuming some of the continent's most productive farmland, since many cities originated in highly fertile areas. For example, the urban area of Delhi (including New Delhi) has grown more than thirteenfold since 1900, washing over surrounding agricultural areas and absorbing more than 100 villages in the process (Betinck 2000). Analysts note, however, that agricultural declines associated with land conversion can be blunted by maximizing the ecological value of densely populated landscapes. Some forms of "agroecology," which seeks to maximize biological production while moving away from chemical supplements, and traditional farming systems have been immensely productive even when operating on relatively small plots. For example, the "home gardens" that dot the Indonesian island of Java may support up to ninety species of plants, including crops of coffee, mango, guava, and tomato, underneath a forestlike canopy (Harrison and Pearce 1999).

The combination of urbanization and inadequate (or nonexistent) land use and development plans is felt in myriad other ways as well. For example, the presence of sprawling squatter settlements and traffic chaos are directly related to land management shortcomings. In fact, these problems, which endure to one degree or another in all Asian urban centers, are closely intertwined. "Appropriate land for housing exists, sometimes in relatively central locations, [but] it is not accessible to vast sections because of factors such as land speculation and lack of public investment in infrastructure and transport facilities"

(UN Economic and Social Commission for Asia and the Pacific 2001). In many cities, overcrowding, traffic congestion, and environmental problems are also aggravated by overlapping and contradictory land laws and control mechanisms, spotty monitoring and enforcement of building regulations, and rampant land speculation (ibid.).

In recognition of the numerous and acute land management problems that many Asian nations are facing, momentum for major revision of current policies and practices is growing across the continent. "It is already evident that land-use management within the region must be dramatically improved if the negative impacts of land-use changes and conflicts are to be reduced to allow for an environmentally sustainable development process" (Hardoy et al. 2001). For such revisions to have their desired effect, however, they will have to target issues such as planning, zoning, property taxation, and infrastructure provision. They will also have to take the measure of imposing obstacles to land use reform. The chief impediments include ineffective coordination of land use policies among various government agencies, inadequate incentives to steer land-use changes away from environmentally sensitive areas, and "the absence of a clear political will to implement existing policies and regulations" (Douglass 1989).

Regional Population and Land Use Trends

East Asia

About 1.5 billion people live in East Asia, including approximately 1.26 billion in China, the planet's most populous nation. This region has enjoyed sustained economic growth for most of the past half-century, fueled in part by growing populations. Migrant workers from rural regions were particularly pivotal factors in this explosive development, helping to turn nations such as China, Japan, and South Korea into major economic powers. But the combination of economic expansion and population growth has also placed enormous pressure on the regional environment, triggering alarming downturns in water and air quality and widespread conversion of natural areas to human use. In Japan, for instance, development activity around inland and coastal waters has degraded roughly 30 percent of the lakeshores and 56 percent of marine coastlines (Japan Environment Agency 1998). As a rule, environmental conditions are worse in the region's developing countries.

The rate of population growth is particularly evident in East Asian cities, many of which are expanding at a dizzying pace. In Japan, where a quarter of the population lives in one city (Tokyo), the percentage of Japanese living in urban areas grew from 50 percent in 1950 to 79 percent by the close of the century (World Bank 1998; UN Economic and Social Commission for Asia and the Pacific 2002). In the Republic of Korea, urbanization has proceeded even more quickly than in Japan. Whereas one out of five South Koreans lived in urban areas in 1950, four out of five did so by 1990 (Japan Environmental Council 2000). And China's urban population rose from 192 million to 377 million just between 1980 and 1996 (World Bank 1998). Smaller states like Mongolia have also seen major demographic shifts from rural to urban settings over the past few decades.

Japan is the region's most affluent society, blessed with advanced medical care, high nutrition, and a superior educational system (adult literacy is nearly 100 percent). China has enormous reserves of natural resources and human capital, however, and it appears poised to take its place as a global titan. One potential obstacle to this ascension is the country's huge population and the enormous investments necessary to provide for them. But China has long recognized that the stability of the state could be imperiled if the population burden becomes too great for its social, agricultural, political, and economic infrastructure. Indeed, population control has long been one of the cornerstones of China's national policies. Over the past half-century, the Chinese government has consistently advocated one-child families, promoted the use of birth control, and encouraged late marriages. It has also maintained a variety of public health and family planning programs. These efforts have been credited for a significant drop in China's fertility rate, from 6.1 between 1965 and 1970 to 2.47 between 1985 and 1990 (Harrison and Pearce 1999). This concern has also prompted Chinese authorities to try to slow the pace of rural-to-urban migration. Finally, a number of major Chinese cities, including Dalian, Zhubai and Xiamen, Zhangjiagang, Shenzhen, and Weihai, are giving priority to urban environmental planning, pollution prevention, and other issues associated with rapid urbanization (State Environmental Protection Administration of China 1997).

Southeast Asia

Approximately 540 million people live in Southeast Asia, a region that features some of the most densely populated countries in the world (Asian Development Bank 2001). In recent decades, this corner of Asia has experienced significant economic growth, but it remains riddled with environmental and social problems in both rural and urban areas. As always, closer examination of these problems reveals multiple linkages. In places such as Thailand, Indonesia, and the Philippines, for example, high levels of poverty in rural farming communities and rising rates of land conversion from agricultural use to industrial use have convinced many rural people to migrate to the cities. Most cities are groaning under this unplanned population surge, which has degraded environmental conditions. Traffic congestion; air, water, and land pollution; and sewage and trash disposal problems are serious issues in most cities. In metropolitan Manila, for example, all four major river systems have been rendered biologically dead from pollution (Yencken et al. 2000).

Indeed, urbanization has emerged as perhaps the single greatest influence on Southeast Asia's economic, social, and environmental fortunes. Even nations like Thailand and Indonesia, where the majority of the people are still living in rural settings, feature Bangkok (Thailand) and Jakarta (Indonesia), metropolitan agglomerations of breathtaking size, feverish economic activity, and rampant—and escalating—levels of overcrowding (Japan Environmental Council 2000). Unfortunately, states in the region have had great difficulty meeting the soaring social and infrastructure costs associated with this rapid urbanization. A particularly severe example of this problem can be found in Cambodia, which has seen its urban centers decline markedly over the past several decades. "Since the country's political life more or less stabilized, private investment in home improvement and construction has easily outstripped investment in public infrastructure. Cambodia continues to live off inherited urban assets that are quickly deteriorating (if some of these are not already disintegrated), putting at risk both the health of people in the urban areas and discouraging foreign investment from a lack of support infrastructure. . . .Over 80 percent of existing sewage and stormwater drains in Cambodia's urban centers are no longer functioning" (Asian Development Bank 2001a).

Central Asia

Population densities in Central Asia are very low in comparison with the rest of the continent. Kazakhstan, for example, is the ninth largest country in the world, equal in terms of land area to all of Western Europe. But much of the country consists of lightly inhabited deserts and semiarid steppes, making it one of the more sparsely populated regions of the world (Asian Development Bank 1998).

Moreover, population levels across the region have been affected by the severe economic and social dislocation that followed the dissolution of the Soviet Union. All Central Asian countries suffered declines in gross domestic product to one extent or another during the 1990s, forcing authorities to dramatically curtail social welfare programs. Surging unemployment, declining income, and reduced access to social services protection have subsequently marked all communities, especially those located in isolated industrial centers and rural agricultural areas. Demographic groups such as pensioners, children, unemployed youth, and women have borne a disproportionate share of the social welfare cuts as well (ibid.). Not surprisingly, these developments prompted many struggling families to migrate elsewhere in search of better lives, and economic hardship is believed to be a key reason why the populations of both Kazakhstan and Georgia have actually declined since independence (UN Population Division, 1998).

The other significant influence on Central Asian population trends in the post-Soviet era has been anti-Russian sentiment. "After the break-up of the Soviet Union, much of the anger that had built up against the colonisers was released. Russians, some of whom had lived in Central Asia for generations, were made thoroughly unwelcome, indeed told to go home. Many did, rather than face the official discrimination that now gave them the status of second-class citizens. Between 1989 and 1998, the number of Russians fell throughout Central Asia: in Kazakhstan, from 37 percent to 31 percent of the population; in Kyrgyzstan, from 21 percent to 14.6 percent; in Tajikistan, from 7.6 percent to 6 percent; in Turkmenistan, from 9.5 percent to 7 percent; and in Uzbekistan, from 8.3 percent to 6.5 percent. The hostility to the Russians passed as quickly as the euphoria that had come with independence. Nevertheless, with most of Central Asia afflicted by hyperinflation and other economic woes, the Russians were in no mood to stay. At the peak of emigration in 1994, 283,000 Russians left Kazakhstan" ("Central Asia" 1999).

South Asia

More than 1.5 billion people live in South Asia, which has population densities that are among the highest in the world. Two out of three people in the region can be found in India, which in 2001 became the second nation in the world to surpass the 1 billion mark in population (China was the first). But while India currently has almost 300 million fewer people than China, it adds 18 million people annually (roughly equivalent to Australia's total population) and its fertility rate is now considerably higher than that of China. These trends have prompted widespread forecasts that India will overtake China as the world's most populous nation sometime in the middle of the twenty-first century.

Indeed, populations are rising quickly throughout much of South Asia, driven by sharply reduced death rates and a much slower reduction in birth rates. "This rate of growth continues to challenge and constrain the ability of governments to improve the quality of life, with the result that South Asia has the bulk of the world's poor in its midst as well as the highest concentration of need for reproductive health and family planning information and services" (Sadik 1997).

Aerial view of Udaipur, India. DAVID ZIMMERMAN/CORBIS

On the whole, those nations that have allocated significant resources for basic health services—including family planning—and education have fared better in curbing population growth than those that have embraced economic expansion as the only pathway toward population stability and sustainable development. For example, Bangladesh, Sri Lanka, and Kerala state in India have all used increased investment in family planning and health programs to make striking gains in population stability in recent years. In impoverished Bangladesh, for instance, high rates of fertility were long regarded as an immutable fact because of perceived linkages between poverty and population growth. But when Bangladesh dramatically improved public access to family planning, it reduced its fertility rate from 6.44 between 1980 and 1985 to 3.1 just fifteen years later. In Sri Lanka—which has completed the transition to replacement level fertility (that is, approximately two children per woman)—and the Indian state of Kerala, meanwhile, fertility decline has been attributed not only to the institution of strong family planning programs but also to high levels of female literacy and generous overall investment in education and health (Harrison and Pearce 1999; Sadik 1996).

Conversely, states and regions of South Asia that have made few or no advances in social progress continue to register high fertility levels. In both Pakistan and Nepal, for example, women were having between five and six children on average during the mid-1990s. The persistence of high fertility in both of those countries has been attributed to inadequate reproductive health and family planning information and services, the low status of women, and low levels of female education (Sadik 1997).

Of course, population trends in India cast the longest shadow over the region. The country has made some modest gains in slowing its growth in recent years. India's 2001 census, for example, indicated that the average annual rate of population growth fell from 2.1 percent in the 1980s to 1.9 percent in the 1990s. At the same time, literacy rates rose to 65 percent from 52 percent in a single ten-year period, providing further evidence that education can be an important asset in population stabilization efforts. Social and economic improvements have been most significant in the southern states of Tamil Nadu, Karnataka, and Andhra Pradesh, where economic reforms and social service programs have been most energetically implemented.

But India's annual population growth rate still hovers around 2 percent, a pace that could boost the country's total population above 1.8 billion by 2060. This escalation will place even greater pressure on the nation's overwhelmed social service network. Indeed, India is already "virtually synonymous with poverty in the Western mind. . . . More than half of the world's poorest people live in India, mostly in the rural north and east. Calcutta, the epicenter of this ocean of grief, has long been a universal metaphor for absolute poverty" (Cohen 2000). Other Indian cities, too, are struggling to accommodate the tidal wave of migrants fleeing played-out farmlands. It is estimated that about 30 percent of urban Indians live in slums located close to factories and other industrial complexes. This trend toward urbanization and industrialization has produced pollution-choked cities and towns that extend concrete tendrils deep into areas that were once undisturbed habitat (Yencken et al. 2000).

India's anticipated rate of population growth will also put additional pressure on its rural natural resources, which suffered considerable degradation during the twentieth century. Rampant deforestation and widespread erosion have turned nearly one-third of India's total land area into unproductive wasteland. By some estimates, approximately 100 million hectares of India's total arable land area of 160 million hectares have suffered some level of degradation from human activity (ibid.). Moreover, the International Water Management Institute (IWMI) has estimated that Indian withdrawals of underground water are double the rate of aquifer recharge (Brown et al. 1998). Falling water tables raise the specter of widespread shortages of water for both drinking and irrigation, a sobering possibility inasmuch as more than half of India's vital grain crop is harvested from irrigated land. IWMI estimates that aquifer depletion could eventually reduce India's grain harvest by

25 percent. If that comes to pass, millions of Indians would face the prospect of starvation without significant international aid (ibid.). Finally, India's problem with dwindling usable land is further compounded by its enormous cattle population (406 million head), the largest in the world. This livestock is currently supported on pasture land, but pasture constitutes less than 4 percent of India's total land area, and overgrazing is a growing problem (Yencken et al. 2000).

All in all, South Asia's challenges in the twenty-first century—rapid urbanization, high levels of poverty, social inequities, ecological degradation, unsustainable freshwater use, food security uncertainties—are many and great. Effectively addressing these needs—which are expected to become more acute as the region's population continues to expand—will require the regional governments, bilateral and multilateral agencies, nongovernmental organizations, the private sector, and civil society to form cooperative partnerships dedicated to instituting real changes in population and land management planning (Sadik 1997).

Sources:

Asian Development Bank. 2001. *Agricultural Biotechnology, Poverty Reduction, and Food Security.* Manila: ADB.

———. 2001a. *Asian Development Outlook 2001.* Manila: ADB.

———. 1998. *Central Asian Environments in Transition.* 1998. Manila: ADB.

———. 2001b. *Environments in Transition: Cambodia, Lao PDR, Thailand, Viet Nam.* Manila: ADB.

Association of South-East Asian Nations. 1997. *First ASEAN State of the Environment Report.* Jakarta: ASEAN.

Barter, Paul. 1997. "Urban Transport in Kuala Lumpur/Klang Valley in a Global and Regional Perspective." In *State of the Environment in Malaysia.* Penang, Malaysia: Consumers' Association of Penang.

Betinck, Johan V. 2000. "Unruly Urbanization on Delhi's Fringe: Changing Patterns of Land Use and Livelihood." *Netherlands Geographical Studies* 270.

BirdLife International. 2001. *Threatened Birds of Asia: The BirdLife International Red Data Book.* Cambridge, UK: BirdLife International.

Brown, Lester. 1994. *Who Will Feed China? Wake-Up Call for a Small Planet.* Washington, DC: Worldwatch Institute, 1994.

Brown, Lester, Gary Gardner, and Brian Halweil. 1998. *Beyond Malthus: Sixteen Dimensions of the Population Problem.* Washington, DC: Worldwatch Institute.

"Central Asia." 1999. *Economist* 24 (April 3).

Cohen, Stephen P. 2000. "India Rising." *Wilson Quarterly* 24 (Summer).

Conway, G. 1997. *The Doubly Green Revolution: Food for All in the Twenty-First Century.* London: Penguin.

Douglass, Mike. 1989. "The Environmental Sustainability of Development." *Third World Planning Review* 11(2).

Hardoy, Jorge E., Diana Mitlin, and David Satterthwaite. 2001. *Environmental Problems in an Urbanizing World: Finding Solutions for Cities in Africa, Asia, and Latin America.* London: Earthscan.

Harrison, Paul, and Fred Pearce. 1999. *AAAS Atlas of Population and Environment.* Berkeley: University of California Press.

International Food Policy Research Institute. 1997. *The World Food Situation: Recent Developments, Emerging Issues, and Long-Term Prospects.* Washington, DC: IFPRI.

Irwin, James. 1999. "Shanghai's Migrant Millions." *UNESCO Courier* 52 (June).

Japan Environment Agency. 1998. *White Paper on the Environment.* Tokyo: Japan Environment Agency.

Japan Environmental Council. 2000. *The State of the Environment in Asia 1999–2000.* Tokyo: Springer.

McGranahan, Gordon, and Frank Murray, eds. 1999. *Health and Air Pollution in Rapidly Developing Countries.* Stockholm: Stockholm Environmental Institute.

Pinstrup-Anderson, Per, and Marc J. Cohen. 2000. "Modern Biotechnology for Food and Agriculture: Risks and Opportunities for the Poor." In G. J. Persley and M. M. Lantin, eds., *Agricultural Biotechnology and the Poor.* Washington, DC: Consultative Group on International Agricultural Research.

"Plow Less, Grow More." 2001. *Environment* 43 (December).

Population Reference Bureau. 1996. "2001 World Population Data Sheet." (http://www.prb. org).

Sadik, Nafis. *The State of the World Population 1996, Changing Places: Population, Development and the Urban Future.* 1996. New York: UNFPA.

———. 1997. "Women, Population, and Sustainable Development in South Asia." *Journal of International Affairs* 31 (Summer).

Satterthwaite, David, ed. 1999. *The Earthscan Reader in Sustainable Cities.* London: Earthscan.

Sperling, Daniel, and Deborah Salon. 2002. *Transportation in Developing Countries: An Overview of Greenhouse Gas Strategies.* Arlington, VA: Pew Center.

State Environmental Protection Administration of China. 1997. *Report on the State of the Environment in China 1997.* Beijing: State Environmental Protection Administration.

UN Conference on Trade and Development. 1994. *UNCTAD Commodity Year Book.* New York: UNCTAD.

UN Economic and Social Commission for Asia and the Pacific. 2001. *Municipal Land Management in Asia: A Comparative Study.* New York: UNESCAP.

———. 2002. "Population and Development Indicators for Asia and the Pacific, 2002." (http://www.unescap.org/pop/data_sheet/2002).

UN Economic and Social Commission for Asia and the Pacific, and Asian Development Bank. 1995. *State of the Environment in Asia and the Pacific 1995.* New York: UNESCAP and ADB.

UN Environment Programme. 1999. *Global Environment Outlook 2000.* London: Earthscan.

———. *World Atlas of Desertification.* 1997. New York: Arnold and Wiley.

UN Food and Agriculture Organization. 1996. *Food for All.* Rome: FAO.

———. *Irrigation in Asia in Figures.* 1999. Rome: FAO.

UN International Conference on Population and Development. 1995. *Programme of Action.* New York: UN.

UN Population Division. 1998. *Annual Populations 1950–2050: The 1998 Revision.* New York: UN.

———. 1998. *Demographic Indicators 1950–2050: The 1998 Revision.* New York: UN.

———. 2001. *World Urbanization Prospects: The 1999 Revision.* New York: UN.

UN Populations Fund. 1996. "Sri Lanka Focuses on Reproductive Health in Post-ICPD Era." ICPD News. New York: UNFPA, February.

Wood, Alexander, Pamela Stedman-Edwards, and Johanna Mang, eds. 2000. *The Root Causes of Biodiversity Loss.* London: Earthscan.

World Bank. 1997. *China 2020: Development Challenges in the New Century.* Washington, DC: World Bank.

———. 1997. *Clear Water, Blue Skies.* Washington, DC: World Bank.

———. 1997. *Environment Matters: Towards Environmentally and Socially Sustainable Development.* Washington, DC: World Bank.

———. 1998. *World Development Indicators 1998.* Washington, DC: World Bank.

———. 2002. *World Development Indicators 2002.* Washington, DC: World Bank.

World Resources Institute. 2000. *World Resources 2000–2001, People and Ecosystems: The Fraying Web of Life.* Washington, DC: World Resources Institute.

World Wildlife Fund. 1999. *Living Planet Report 1999.* WWF.

Yencken, David, John Fien, and Helen Sykes, eds. 2000. *Environment, Education, and Society in the Asia-Pacific: Local Traditions and Global Discourses.* London: Routledge.

Biodiversity

Blessed with a rich variety of creatures and plant life, the Asian continent is one of the world's biodiversity strongholds. But Asian biodiversity—the number of species occupying an ecosystem, country, continent, or other defined region (including the planet)—has suffered enormously in the last half-century from an onslaught of destructive human activities that have obliterated or degraded huge swaths of natural habitat, from lowland forests to coastal estuaries. This grim trend is due to the fact that many of Asia's most biodiversity-rich nations also hold rapidly expanding human populations that are understandably thirsty for socioeconomic advancement. Asian governments have sought to accommodate the needs and wants of their growing populations—and realize their own ambitions—by expanding the size of their cities, harvesting their forests, minerals, and other forms of "ecological capital," and clearing land for agricultural use. In most instances, these habitat-altering activities have been undertaken without consideration for their impact on regional flora and fauna. As a result, some species of Asian flora and fauna have already been driven to extinction, and another 5,000 species of Asian mammals, birds, reptiles, amphibians, fishes, invertebrates, and plants are believed to be threatened (World Conservation Union 2000).

Chief Threats to
Asian Flora and Fauna

Asia's current wealth of biodiversity, as well as its very high number of endemic species—those species found nowhere else in the world—is attributable in part to climate. Historically, the tropical conditions that prevail across much of the continent have provided a most hospitable environment for the development of Asia's startling array of creatures and vegetation. The other reason for Asia's remarkable concentration of biological wealth, and in particular its high rates of endemism, is topography. The region has become segmented into unique ecoregions over countless millennia by an assortment of barriers, including rugged mountain ranges, huge and powerful rivers, "islands" of rain forest embedded in vast stretches of dry forests, and true islands separated by deep ocean trenches. These features isolated populations of plants and animals, which subsequently evolved in unique and exciting ways. Finally, the region's stunning wealth of biodiversity and endemic species was further augmented by periodic drops in sea level. These events exposed land bridges that allowed species to migrate into new areas, where they subsequently evolved in accordance with their environment, and to breed with other species, sparking the creation of countless additional species and subspecies (Wikramanayake 2002).

Today, however, this bounty of wildlife is at great risk from Asia's swelling human population. "It is an observable fact that biodiversity is maintained when nature remains intact over large areas. Large areas of unprotected natural habitat [in Asia] will, however, soon be a thing of the past. Pressures for increasingly intensive land use, fed by burgeoning human populations and unsustainable land-use practices, will see to this" (Terborgh and Van Schaik 1997). Indeed, the rapid increase in the number of people in China, India, and other nations has placed great pressure on forests, grasslands, wetlands, rivers, bays, and other vital natural habitats. As these areas are lost, degraded, or fragmented by human exploitation and activity, species have fewer and fewer places to which they can flee. Asia's forests, once seemingly limitless, have endured particularly harsh treatment. Of the more than 16 million square kilometers of original forest that once covered Asia and Oceania, only a little over 1 million square kilometers remain intact in tracts large enough to maintain all of their biodiversity, including viable populations of leopards, tigers, and other creatures that require lots of territory to roam. Most of these remnants are in Indonesia, Cambodia, and the remote mountain ranges of continental Asia (Bryant 1997).

But while land-use changes that result in habitat loss, degradation, and fragmentation are widely seen as "the most severe, overarching threats to [Asian] terrestrial biodiversity" (Wikramanayake 2002), other significant threats exist as well, such as wildlife exploitation for commercial purposes (both legal and illegal) and intrusions of invasive species. In fact, these factors constitute an even greater threat to biodiversity and ecosystem integrity than land conversion in some pockets of Asia.

Land Conversion and Fragmentation

The list of land conversion activities that are destroying and degrading biologically rich habitat is a long one. It encompasses infrastructure developments such as factories, roadways, irrigation systems and dams, power and energy projects, and ports and harbors; agricultural activities such as cultivation and grazing that clear land and render it unable to regenerate naturally; exploitation activities such as logging and mining, which in Asia are usually conducted without any regard for long-term environmental consequences; and expansion of cities and other settlements into previously intact natural areas. All of these activities can wreak havoc on biodiversity in a host of ways. Some pollute soil and water, others shatter breeding and migration patterns, and still others remove trees, plants, and predator/prey species that are essential elements of vibrant and healthy ecosystems. And when one species vanishes from a region as a result of these changes, the fortunes of other species are inevitably impacted by that absence as well. In India, for example, subsistence hunting undertaken by settlers can produce reductions of more than 90 percent in the population of deer and other ungulate prey upon which tigers depend. This in turn produces declines in regional tiger populations and densities, and necessitates dietary shifts among those tigers that remain, all of which trigger a cascade of other impacts that resonate all the way down the ecosystem food chain (Madhusadan and Karanth 2000).

Of all the ecologically destructive land conversion activities currently in full swing in Asia, commercial logging is perhaps the single greatest threat to biodiversity, for it directly impacts the tropical and mountain forests that host the greatest concentrations and varieties of the continent's flora and fauna. For the past half-century, Asia has been logging its forests on an epic scale, taking particularly deadly aim at biologically rich lowland forests. This deforestation has not only eliminated vast swaths of habitat outright but also has left behind extensive road networks that have produced extensive soil erosion, choked rivers and streams with silt and debris, and fragmented the territories of tigers, leopards, and other wide-ranging species. Most significantly, the existence of these roads often leads to the establishment of new human settlements. The arrival of these settlements subsequently sets another cycle of degradation in motion, as logged-over land is permanently converted for agricultural use, mining and other extraction activities take root, remnant forests are raided for fuelwood, and commercial and subsistence hunters use the community as a base from which to infiltrate deeper into the wilderness (Wikramanayake 2002).

At the close of the twentieth century, it was estimated that more than one-third of the tropical and subtropical moist forest ecoregions of Asia and Oceania had been reduced to a highly fragmented state, with forest areas in the Philippines, Southeast Asia, and the Indian subcontinent in particularly bad shape. Indeed, from Cambodia to Kalimantan (the Indonesian section of

The Convention on International Trade in Endangered Species (CITES)

International trade—both legal and illegal—has been mentioned alongside destruction and fragmentation of habitat as one of the most significant threats to endangered species of plants and animals. Legal trade in wildlife and related products was estimated at $10 billion per year worldwide at the end of the twentieth century ("CITES at a Glance" 2001), with illegal trade adding another $5 billion to $8 billion to that total (Sain-Ley-Berry 2001). This trade ranges from wild plants used as food or in medicines to animals captured in the wild and sold for research, as pets, or as parts used in food, clothing, or medicine.

Recognizing the threat that trade poses to endangered species, the international community has developed several efforts at controlling it. The best known of these efforts is the Convention on International Trade in Endangered Species of Wild Fauna and Flora, or CITES, an international treaty that has been signed by 154 countries. CITES was originally drafted as a result of a 1963 meeting of the IUCN (World Conservation Union). It was signed ten years later by 80 participating countries (known as parties to the treaty), and it took effect in 1975.

The main goal of CITES is "to ensure that international trade in specimens of wild animals and plants does not threaten their survival" ("What Is CITES?" 2001). Toward this end, participating countries agree to regulate trade in some 30,000 species—including 25,000 plants and 5,000 animals—to which trade poses a threat. The treaty regulates trade in species through a system of import and export permits. Countries that violate the treaty are subject to trade sanctions. Although CITES is legally binding for its member states, each country must develop its own domestic legislation to implement the rules.

CITES divides protected species into three groups, or appendices, that are subject to different levels of restriction on trade. Appendix I includes more than 800 species that are already threatened with extinction. The treaty bans trade in these species by member countries except under rare circumstances. Appendix II includes 29,000 species "in which trade must be controlled in order to avoid utilization incompatible with their survival" (ibid.). The treaty places strict limits upon trade in these species in order to prevent them from becoming endangered. Finally, Appendix III contains species that are protected in at least one member country that desires assistance from other CITES members in controlling trade. The species protected under CITES include several entire groups—such as primates, cetaceans, cacti, and orchids—as well as subspecies and geographically distinct populations. They range from charismatic megafauna, such as bears and whales, to lesser-known plants and animals such as leeches, aloes, and corals.

CITES is widely considered to be a successful conservation tool. In fact, no species that receives protection under CITES has become extinct as a result of trade since the treaty took effect in 1975. The treaty does have some acknowledged shortcomings, however, which may need to be addressed as the world economy becomes increasingly global. For example, there have been problems with enforcement in several countries, as well as problems in regulating the behavior of nonparticipating nations (which include many former Soviet republics, Eastern European nations, and Arab countries). Another shortcoming of the treaty frequently mentioned by critics involves the "reservations" granted to participants at the time of signing. These reservations allow the countries to engage in international trade of specific species without violating CITES. As of 2001, ninety-seven of the species listed in Appendix I were subject to reservations in one or more countries (Wagener 2001). Finally, some member countries

have successfully lobbied to prevent new species from being listed in CITES despite scientific evidence that the species were threatened by international trade.

Despite the positive impact of CITES and similar efforts at controlling international trade in endangered species, some experts claim that the only way to protect species over the long term is to reduce demand. They suggest educating people about the need for conservation, launching campaigns to discourage the purchase of endangered species, and developing alternatives to plants and animal parts that are used as medicinal ingredients.

Sources:

"CITES at a Glance." Traffic web site, 2001, http://www.traffic.org/factfile/factfile_cites.html.

Sain-Ley-Berry, C. "New Campaign Launched to Fight Illegal Wildlife Trade." *Earth Times,* 2001, http://earthtimes.org/aug/europenewcampaignlaunchedaug21.00.htm.

Wagener, Amy. "Endangered Species: Traded to Death." *EarthTrends,* August 2001. World Resources Institute web site, http://earthtrends.wri.org/conditions_trends/feature_select_action.cfm?theme=7.

"What Is CITES?" Convention on International Trade in Endangered Species web site, 2001, http://www.cites.org/eng/disc/what_is.shtml.

Borneo), vast swaths of the earth's most species-rich rain forests are being sacrificed to make way for oil palm plantations, rice fields, expanding settlements, and commercial developments (Bryant 1997; Wikramanayake 2002). Several tree species prized for their timber—such as the ironwood and ebony trees of the Indonesian islands of Sumatra and Sulawesi, respectively—have been exploited so systematically that they are almost extinct in the wild (Terborgh 1992).

The total extent of habitat loss remains unquantifiable in some parts of Asia because of meager research and monitoring data. However, it has been estimated that as much as two-thirds of Asia's total wildlife habitat had already been destroyed by the early 1990s, and by most accounts, conversion of natural areas for human use in Indonesia and other biodiversity treasurehouses has, if anything, accelerated since that time (Braatz 1992; UN Environment Programme 1999).

In recognition of Asia's rapid depletion of its forests and other vital types of habitats, conservationists have urged individual countries to incorporate environmental sustainability considerations into all policy areas. They have also called for significant expansion of protected areas programs. But additions to Asia's protected area systems have been slow in arriving, and in many countries, endangered and threatened species remain squarely in the path of the twin juggernauts of population growth and land development. Moreover, many of the parks and other protected areas currently in place are bedeviled by illegal logging, poaching, and other activities destructive to regional biodiversity. "All too often, impoverished governments are unable or unwilling to implement the enabling legislative acts, and the parks quickly turn into 'paper parks,' unprotected by any formal apparatus" (Terborgh and Van Schaik 1997).

Alien species

Alien species—also referred to as exotic, invasive, or non-native species—are animals and plants that are introduced into areas beyond their native range by human activity. Sometimes these introductions are made in conjunction with natural resource management plans. On many other occasions, however, alien species are introduced accidentally, such as during the transport of trade goods from one region to another. Whatever the means of introduction, alien species often have significant repercussions for delicately balanced regional ecosystems. Negative consequences associated with invasive species include dilution of the genetic purity of native flora and fauna, outright replacement of native species, introduction of diseases (including maladies that affect humans), and disruption of the regional food chain (when, for example, exotic species consume prey upon which native predators rely).

In Asia, the full impact of non-native species on local, regional, and continental ecosystems is unknown because of the paucity of research on the subject. Anecdotal evidence suggests, however, that the potential threat of exotic species is not fully appreciated. In Southeast Asia, for example, fishery managers have introduced numerous non-native fish species in attempts to boost fish production, but in some cases, they have forsaken all but the most cursory research on likely ecosystem changes prior to introduction. In fact, "the effects of these introductions on native species usually are grossly ignored or overlooked by fisheries and development agencies and their foreign sponsors and advisors; too often they perceive the importance of the fish fauna in terms of landed kilograms rather than number of species. Recommendations to introduce exotic fish species in waterbodies of protected areas still proliferate, which in a biodiversity conservation context is nonsense" (Wikramanayake 2002). Other exotic species have been introduced via the aquarium and pet trade, in potted plants, and in shipments of crops and other cargo (Mittermeier et al. 1999).

Overharvesting and the Asian Wildlife Trade

Hunting for wildlife is rampant in many regions of Asia, though it takes a host of forms. Some hunters stalk deer, wild pig, and other creatures for food, and in countries that harbor large populations of impoverished people, species loss from subsistence hunting can be significant. But commercial hunting constitutes an even greater threat to Asian biodiversity. These practitioners specifically target rare and charismatic species, either for capture and sale to international markets that traffic in exotic pets, or to harvest body parts that are prized for their beauty (such as the ivory tusks of Asian elephants and the hides of black caimans), taste (the meat of freshwater turtles and manatees), or alleged medicinal properties (the bones and other body parts of the tiger and Asian bear) (Terbourgh and Van Schaik 1997; Mills and Jackson 1994).

In many cases, hunting of these creatures for sale as exotic pets or for harvesting of body parts is blatantly illegal. But illicit trade in creatures and body parts nonetheless thrives in many regions of Asia, especially now that higher income levels have given more people the ability to acquire expensive medicines and foods laced with powdered tiger bone, rhinoceros horn, Asian bear gallbladder, and other such ingredients. Among the most notorious transgressors of international prohibitions on trade in products harvested from endangered species are China, Japan, South Korea, Taiwan, and Singapore (Wagener 2001).

The Decline of the Tiger in Asia

Indian security forces seized three tiger skins and fifty leopard skins from a poacher on the outskirts of Delhi. BAGLA PALLAVA/CORBIS SYGMA

Tigers once roamed across a huge swath of Asia, from the icebound realms of the Russian Far East to the steamy jungles of Indochina. But the number of wild tigers in Asia declined by 95 percent over the course of the twentieth century, from an estimated 100,000 tigers in 1900 to an estimated 5,000 in 2000. The number of subspecies of the great predators also declined from eight to five during that period. In the face of continuing habitat destruction and fragmentation, poaching, and conflict with humans along the borders of protected areas, some experts predict that tigers may become extinct in the wild within twenty-five years (Scarlott 2000).

Still, large-scale conservation efforts have demonstrated some success in maintaining tiger populations. In India, for example, the number of Bengal tigers dropped to around 1,700 in the early 1970s as a result of habitat destruction and widespread killing of the animals as "pests." The Indian government responded by launching Project Tiger in 1973. That initiative— which had a stated goal of ensuring a viable population of tigers in the wild and preserving natural areas for future generations—banned tiger hunting throughout the country, created a network of tiger preserves, and relocated entire villages outside the boundaries of protected areas. Project Tiger appeared to be a significant conservation success story until the late 1980s, when independent studies showed that tigers were not as numerous as the Indian government claimed. In fact, the studies revealed that tigers were being killed by poachers at an average rate of one per day in order to supply body parts to the black market in China, where they are used in traditional medicine (ibid.).

Today, India supports a total population of between 2,000 and 3,750 tigers, which live mainly in sixty-six protected areas (twenty-three of which were created as part of the Project Tiger network). The largest single population—consisting of between 400 and 500 tigers—can be found in the Sundarban mangrove forests, which stretch over 6,000 square kilometers along the coasts of India and Bangladesh ("Tigers in the Wild"). Bengal tigers can also be found in several other countries on the Indian subcontinent, including Bangladesh, Bhutan, China, India, Nepal, and Myanmar. China was once home to several subspecies of tigers, including Siberian tigers in northeastern China and rare South China tigers in southern China, as well as Bengal and Indochinese tigers along the border regions. Experts estimate that fewer than 100 tigers remain in China today, however, because of poaching and dwindling habitat (ibid.).

Some experts suggest that establishing protected areas is only a first step in ensuring the survival of the species. Like other large carnivores, tigers range widely in search of prey and often face threats along the borders of their habitat, such as poisoning by farmers worried about their livestock, exposure to disease from domestic animals, and collisions with vehicles. In addition, forest fragmentation poses a greater problem for tigers than for some other predators because they dislike crossing open areas. As a result, deforestation and the proliferation of roads in tiger habitat create barriers to dispersal and separate tigers into small, unsustainable population segments. Finally, tigers depend on the availability of large ungulates as prey. When these species decline through overhunting or other human activities, tiger populations decline as well (Seidensticker 2002).

"For a tiger, survival means land— large tracts of pristine forest where prey can flourish," wrote one expert. But "forests that should, by law, surround and support the tiger reserves are being rapidly destroyed by the demands of industry and the needs of local people. Ranthambhore [Tiger Reserve], like a great many of India's protected areas, is becoming an island, surrounded by hostile territory….The forests that encircled the park have been ripped apart by quarries, mines, agricultural fields, and road projects financed by the Asian Development Bank" (Sahgal and Scarlott 2001).

During the 1990s, the World Bank came under criticism by conservationists for its role in the decline of tiger populations. The World Bank funded numerous infrastructure development projects throughout India and the Indian subcontinent— including dams, mines, roads, and tourism and forestry projects—that critics claim have accelerated the destruction and fragmentation of tiger habitat. For example, the World Bank financed the construction of 495 coal mines in Hazaribagh National Park in central India, which critics claimed would block important migration corridors for tigers and elephants. Another example involves the construction of Kotku Dam in the Indian state of Bihar, which opponents claimed would submerge important forests in the Palamau tiger preserve. Finally, World Bank–sponsored forestry projects in Andhra Pradesh have converted native forests that provided habitat for tigers to monocultures of eucalyptus, teak, bamboo, and other lucrative tree species (Scarlott 2000).

The Indian government has also come under criticism for sponsoring development projects that could be detrimental to tigers. "There are more than 100 private industry or government projects and proposals, at various stages of approval and development, that will directly or indirectly threaten tiger habitat in India," one expert noted. "A nuclear plant near the Sundarbans Tiger Reserve and an international steamer channel right through it; iron ore mining in Kudremukh National Park; bauxite mining in the Radhanagari Sanctuary; the Turial hydroelectric project in the Dampa Tiger Reserve; highways through some of the finest tiger forests. The list goes on....A new

kind of conservation approach is needed. More than love, sympathy, or even money, the tiger needs space: large, contiguous areas of habitat, linked by viable, verdant corridors. This strategy will require a radical change in policy, a willingness among politicians to serve interests larger than those of the developers they currently embrace" (Sahgal and Scarlott 2001). One promising possibility in this regard is the Terai Arc Wildlife Corridor, an effort to restore degraded forest areas and use them to link eleven separate nature reserves in Nepal and India into a single, contiguous wilderness area (Wikramanayake et al. 2002).

Sources:

Sahgal, Bittu, and Jennifer Scarlott. 2001. "Stranded." *Amicus Journal* 23, no. 2 (summer).

Scarlott, Jennifer. 2000. "Killing Them Softly." *E: The Environmental Magazine* 11, no. 1 (January–February).

Seidensticker, John. 2002. "Tigers: Top Carnivores and Controlling Processes in Asian Forests." In Eric Wikramanayake, Eric Dinerstein, and Colby J. Loucks, eds., *Terrestrial Ecoregions of the Indo-Pacific: A Conservation Assessment.* Washington, DC: Island.

"Tigers in the Wild." World Wildlife Fund web site, http://www.panda.org/ resources/publications/species/tiger9 9/glance_india_china_russia.html.

The intensity of wildlife exploitation varies across the Asian continent. In India and other countries of South Asia, wildlife exploitation is relatively light. The wildlife trade's minor presence there has been attributed both to the region's historical and cultural acceptance of wildlife protection principles and its distance from China and Japan, the continent's main consumers of wildlife products (Wikramanayake 2002). But in other sectors of Asia, large numbers of hunters employ a variety of methods, ranging from the crude to the ruthlessly efficient, to capture or slay valuable creatures. "A diverse arsenal consisting of small snares baited with seeds to trap pheasants and jungle fowl, log-fall traps that crush small deer and mongooses, pitfall traps set for elephants, explosive-laden bait to blow up tigers, and home-made crossbows and automatic rifles in the hands of hunters spares no animal, big or small" (ibid.). Even rare Asian plants reputed to carry medicinal qualities have fallen victim to the continent's burgeoning appetite for traditional "nature-based" medicines.

The wildlife trade is at its most feverish in Southeast Asia. This region still holds tigers, rhinos, and other prized creatures—albeit in dwindling numbers—and it is situated fairly close to the Chinese and Japanese markets. As a result, the numbers of animals such as freshwater turtles—valued both as food and as a source of ingredients used in traditional medicines—have declined precipitously. Of ninety species of Asian freshwater turtles and tortoises, 74 percent are considered threatened and more than half are endangered (including eighteen listed as critically endangered), according to a 2000 joint study of the World Wildlife Fund, the Wildlife Conservation Society, and IUCN/The World Conservation Union.

Even within Indochina, however, levels of hunting pressure vary. In Vietnam, hunting has eviscerated forest ecosystems by removing top predators and larger deer and other ungulates. As a result, otherwise undisturbed Vietnamese forests are now largely devoid of wildlife, a phenomenon known as the "empty forest syndrome" (Redford 1992). In the Malaysian state of Sarawak, meanwhile, the wild meat trade in 1996 was conservatively estimated at 1,000 tons per year, with the bulk of that total composed mainly of bearded pigs, barking deer, and other large ungulates that are vital not only to the survival of large carnivores like leopards and tigers but also to the fortunes of plants that depend on those creatures for seed dispersal (Wildlife Conservation Society 1996). Elsewhere, tribespeople in southern Laos have derived 30 to 60 percent of their annual income from the sale of wildlife and other forest products in some recent years. To the south, however, in Cambodia, hunting pressure has thus far been relatively modest, sparing regional ecosystems and enabling some large wildlife species to maintain stable populations (Bennett and Robinson 2002).

In areas where illegal commerce in animal products is high, the impact on endangered species can be crushing. Indeed, in the last two decades, illegal trade in animal parts has emerged as the single greatest threat to some of Asia's most seriously endangered and highly valued species, including tigers, rhinoceros, and Asian bears (Wagener 2001). Similarly, heavy levels of hunting for subsistence have disrupted some regional ecosystems beyond repair, especially in countries where population densities are highest. "Ominous distortions of predator-prey and plant-herbivore interactions are already a fact in superficially pristine primary forests all over the tropics, as natural ecosystems are perturbed by systematic overhunting of large birds and mammals. Among the most heavily affected functional groups are top predators, large herbivores, seed predators, and seed dispersers. . . .[T]he fundamental alterations of ecosystem function that accompany the loss of species that mediate such important biological processes can be expected to result in cascades of secondary extinctions, as the absence of key species causes interaction webs to collapse" (Terbourgh and Van Schaik 1997).

Reducing the impact of overhunting and the wildlife trade on Asian species is likely to be a difficult and arduous process. Poaching for banned or endangered species and black market trading in wildlife products are so financially lucrative that they have attracted the attention of professional criminal organizations. Moreover, the money that can be pocketed from poaching or trading in endangered species is enormously tempting to impoverished men and women seeking to lift their families out of grim socioeconomic straits. In addition, Asia's rapid economic development has expanded the number of people who are able to afford traditional oriental medicines and other wildlife products. Finally, in many Asian countries, sentences for poachers or people who traffic in illegal animals or animal parts are so modest that they have no practical effect as a deterrent (Terbourgh and Van Schaik 1997; Bennett and Robinson 2002). Conservationists say that Asia needs to follow the example of China, which dramatically curtailed exploitation of its rare panda when it imposed life sentences on poachers and smugglers of the creature (Wagener 2001; Motavalli and Bogo 1999).

"The problem [of the illegal wildlife trade in Asia] is multifaceted and diffuse, both geographically and socially, and solutions must be sensitive to this complexity," acknowledged one analysis. "Management must include targeted trade bans, with proper legal, administrative, and logistical mechanisms for enforcing them and education programs at all levels of society. Commercial trade must be regulated, and valuation of wildlife products must incorporate ecological and social values. Proper land-use planning is essential, with a mosaic that includes strictly protected areas where hunting is prohibited both in law and in practice" (Bennett and Robinson 2002). Perhaps most important, "conservationists seem poised, at last, to sufficiently address the stubborn social, economic, and political reasons that tigers and other commercially valuable species of wild animals and plants are worth more dead than alive to the very people who could ensure their survival" (Mills 2002). To that end, conservation groups, scientists, and other interested parties have urged Asian governments to provide rural communities with economic incentives to protect endangered species and preserve essential habitat. Anecdotal evidence suggests that such programs can have a pronounced impact on rural attitudes toward area wildlife. In Nepal's Royal Chitwan National Park, for example, resident tigers, rhinoceros, and bears have benefited enormously from a program that provides nearby villagers with direct economic benefits for protecting the park's natural resources from poaching and development (Dinerstein 1999).

Regional Biodiversity Trends

Large areas of Asia remain unsurveyed even at the dawn of the twenty-first century, so the full extent and condition of the continent's biodiversity remains unknown. As gaps in scientific knowledge gradually fill in, however, it is clear that numerous species have yet to be formally recognized. In 1996, for example, Laos was reported to have 219 species of freshwater fish. Subsequent surveys of freshwater habitat over the following two years, however, revealed another 261 species that had previously escaped notice (Kottelat 2000b). Conversely, the full extent of species endangerment and loss is also only apparent in countries where systematic surveys have taken place.

Based on the best available knowledge, however, the World Conservation Union has counted 774 threatened species of flora and fauna in East Asia alone, with China (385 threatened species) and Japan (159) posting the highest totals. The number of threatened species is far greater in South and Southeast Asia. According to the World Conservation Union's *2000 IUCN Red List of Threatened Species*, 2000, these regions house 3,855 threatened species, including mammals, reptiles, amphibians, birds, fishes, invertebrates, and plants. Malaysia leads all countries of the region in threatened species, with 805, but Indonesia (763 threatened species), India (459), the Philippines (387), Sri Lanka (333), and Vietnam (229) all have staggering numbers as well. Among Central Asian nations covered in this volume, another 320 species have been classified as threatened, with Kazakhstan and Pakistan each housing 47 species (World Conservation Union 2000).

In terms of threatened mammal species, the Asian countries with the highest totals are Indonesia (140), India (86), China (76), and the Philippines (50).

The countries with the highest number of threatened bird species are Indonesia (113), China (73), India (70), and the Philippines (67). Countries with the most threatened reptile species are China (31), Indonesia (28), India (25), and Vietnam (24), while countries with high numbers of threatened fish species include Indonesia (67), China (33), the Philippines (28), and Thailand (19). Malaysia is home to the highest number of threatened plants in Asia, with 681; other nations with large numbers of imperiled plant species include Indonesia (384), Sri Lanka (280), India (244), the Philippines (193), and China (167) (ibid.).

These grim statistics illustrate that biodiversity is endangered all across the Asian continent. But the outlook for species preservation varies within each region, with prospects for successful wildlife conservation shaped by such variables as political and socioeconomic trends, cultural values, and current levels of ecosystem integrity.

China

A wide range of terrestrial ecosystems are found in the East Asia subregion, most of which occur in China alone. Indeed, China holds approximately 600 distinct types of terrestrial ecosystems, including a wide range of forests, scrublands, steppes, meadows, savannas, deserts, and alpine tundra (China Department of Nature Conservation 1999). Within these ecosystems are more than 30,000 species of advanced plants (10 percent of the world total) and over 6,300 kinds of vertebrates (14 percent of the world total), totals that make China the third richest nation in the world in terms of biodiversity (State Environmental Protection Administration 1996). The Hengduan Mountain region of south-central China contains a particularly impressive array of plants, vertebrates, and insects. The region features extremes of climate and topography, with many isolated peaks that have been called "islands in the sky" (Mittermeier et al. 1999). These features have contributed to tremendous diversity of species and high levels of endemism. For example, of the 196 known species of pheasant in the world, 52 occur in China, and 27 of those live in the Hengduan Mountains (ibid.).

South-central China also features 230 species of rhododendrons, many of which are endemic and quite rare. In addition, the region is home to snow leopards and such unusual ungulates as the forest musk deer, the takin antelope, and the Bailey's goral (a species of goat). But the best-known resident of south-central China is the giant panda, which has become an internationally recognized symbol of wildlife conservation (ibid.). Pandas once roamed over wide areas in China, but climatic changes and habitat destruction reduced their range significantly. The Chinese government has taken a number of steps to increase panda numbers, including captive-breeding programs and habitat protection initiatives. In fact, most of the panda's remaining range—including the Wolong and Huanglongsi areas—has been designated as nature preserves. These efforts have also benefited other threatened species. "Given that panda reserves cover moderate to large areas of natural habitat and are the best patrolled and protected areas in China, numerous other species are also effectively protected, making the giant panda a flagship species in the broadest sense of the term" (ibid.).

The primary factor reducing China's biodiversity is habitat destruction, particularly the loss of temperate forests to commercial logging, fuelwood collection—which actually exceeds the logging harvest by volume in some areas—and the expansion of agriculture (Wood et al. 2001). Experts predict that the remaining forests will face increasing demands in the future, as reforestation projects have thus far not kept pace with forest losses (MacKinnon et al. 1996). One factor that may help to mitigate deforestation, however, is the China National Forest Conservation Action Programme. Established in 1998, the programme has the potential to be a valuable tool in creating new nature preserves to protect old-growth forests, strengthening the management of existing preserves, and reducing or developing alternatives to commercial logging (Wood et al. 2001).

South Asia

In South Asia, biodiversity conservation is an integral element of the region's religious, cultural, and social traditions (Mittermeier et al. 1999). But the regional population's historically high regard for nature's creatures is being sorely tested by rates of economic expansion and population growth that are putting heavy pressure on fragile and dwindling habitat. In Pakistan, for example, seven of the eight mangrove species that were found there a half-century ago are now extinct or endangered, their numbers withering under a barrage of land conversions, water pollution, and upstream irrigation projects that have diminished freshwater flows upon which coastal mangroves depend (Wood et al. 2001). Even relatively remote territories have become vulnerable to disturbances from humans. For example, the Himalayan mountains of South-Central Asia are one of the most productive ecoregions for alpine plants in the entire world, but these same alpine meadows are being fundamentally transformed by large herds of domestic livestock and the commercial harvest of plants for traditional medicines (Wikramanayake et al. 2002).

South Asia is also home to some of the world's most extensive montane (mountain) and lowland forest ecosystems. Stellar examples of the former forest systems include the eastern Himalayas of Nepal, Bhutan, and India, and the Ghats range of western India and Sri Lanka, while India's Sundarbans—the largest contiguous mangrove forest in the world—is a standout example of biologically rich lowland forest (Spalding et al. 1997). The variety of creatures that roam and grow beneath the canopy of these forests is remarkable, ranging from approximately 3,400 distinct species of flowering plants in Sri Lanka to the Asian elephant and the loris, a nocturnal primate of squirrel-like dimensions (Mittermeier et al. 1999).

The outlook for these and numerous other species in the region is predicated in large part on India. India is by far the largest country in the region, and it has the highest level of biodiversity in South Asia. But it is expected to become the most heavily populated country in the world by the mid-twenty-first century, and heavy population densities and high rates of poverty have created an environment in which land and resource exploitation for short-term profit has been the rule rather than the exception. As a result, enormous swaths of important wildlife habitat have been lost or degraded. Indeed, by the late 1980s it was estimated that India had lost more than 80 percent of its original forest cover, and by the late 1990s less than 11 percent of India's total land area was covered by natural forest, with proliferating monocultural forest plantations accounting for another 11 percent (UN Food and Agriculture Organization 2001). Observers fear that current logging practices in India could ultimately result in the loss of all natural forests that are not within officially protected areas. Obviously, if such a scenario comes to pass, the damage to the country's remaining forest-dependent animals, reptiles, birds, plants, and other species would be catastrophic (Mittermeier et al.1999).

Southeast Asia

The nations of Southeast Asia harbor many of the continent's most exotic animals, from the orangutans of the Indonesian island of Sumatra to the Javan rhinoceros—a species now reduced to fewer than fifty individuals scattered across the island of Java and the Southeast Asian coastline—to the Asian bonytongue or golden arowana, the most highly prized aquarium fish in the world, to the Tam-Dao salamander of Vietnam. In addition, this region of estuaries, humid jungles, and windswept ridges is home to countless strange and wondrous plants, including one species of the flower *rafflesia*, which ranks as the largest flower in the world (ibid.). Moreover, among the multitudes of plants, reptiles, mammals, and birds that grace this region are a high number of endemic species found nowhere else in the world. The 7,000 islands that constitute the nation of the Philippines, for example, hold the fifth highest number of endemic mammals and birds in the entire world (ibid.), and the central islands of Indonesia—sometimes known as Wallacea—house nearly

250 endemic bird species, more than 35 percent of the regional bird species (Coates and Bishop 1997).

But as in other areas of the continent, many of these species are under imminent threat from burgeoning human populations that are consuming greater quantities of limited natural resources with each passing year. Deforestation is a particularly dire threat to the well-being of numerous species. In many areas of the Southeast Asian mainland (defined as Myanmar, Laos, Thailand, Cambodia, and Vietnam), low-lying forests have nearly vanished, and shifting cultivation and logging activities have caused widespread erosion within montane forest areas. Heavy demand for fuelwood for heating and cooking is also a serious problem near some rural communities (UN Food and Agriculture Organization 2001).

Island nations in this region have also invaded and converted large expanses of land that once provided pristine habitat for creatures great and small. In the Philippines, for example, forests once covered virtually the entire country. But commercial logging and shifting cultivation have reduced total forest cover to only 20 percent of the total land area, and numerous watersheds have suffered serious abuse in the form of erosion, pollution, and other by-products of unsustainable land use (Department of Environment and Natural Resources 1997).

This epidemic of habitat loss, degradation, and fragmentation has diminished overall wildlife numbers across much of the archipelago and pushed numerous species to the precipice of extinction. For example, the Philippine eagle, the second largest eagle in the world, once flew over most of the large islands of the country. But this raptor is now believed to be extinct on all but Luzon, Mindanao, and Samar, where the only large tracts of forest remain. The dwarf water buffalo of Mindoro Island, meanwhile, has largely vanquished, reduced to 100 to 200 individuals by rampant deforestation and hunting. And the freshwater crocodile, the most endangered of all global crocodile species, has been virtually extirpated by overhunting and conversion of land to agriculture and aquaculture (Mittermeir et al. 1999).

All told, the situation in the Philippines has deteriorated so badly that rates of biodiversity loss among endemic species have reportedly reached as high as 60 percent (Wood et al. 2001), and biologists are concerned that "the loss of only a little more forest habitat may bring about the first major extinction spasm of the twenty-first century. With one of the densest and most rapidly-expanding human populations in Asia, the country's need for economic and social reform that will alleviate the causes of poverty is even more closely tied to biodiversity conservation than is usually the case. . . .Given the massive scale of destruction of natural habitat in the Philippines, it might reasonably be said that the greatest threat to biodiversity is maintenance of the *status quo*—simply continuing to do things as they have been done during the last several decades" (Mittermeier et al. 1999).

On the other side of the South China Sea from the Philippines is Indonesia, which ranks with Brazil as one of the top two "megadiversity" countries on the planet (ibid.). Indeed, the Indonesian archipelago occupies a singular place in any discussion of Asian biodiversity, for it hosts 11 percent of the world's total plant species, 10 percent of its mammal species, and fully 16 percent of its bird species, even though it has only 1.3 percent of the earth's total land surface (Barber et al. 2002). But deforestation and other land use practices that are destructive to biodiversity have, if anything, been practiced on an even more rapacious scale here than in the Philippines or the Southeast Asian mainland. Today the country's brilliant array of wildlife is under imminent threat from unbridled avarice in the form of unchecked commercial logging and government corruption. Together, these two factors are combining to sweep away Asia's largest remaining contiguous areas of tropical forest at a breathtaking pace.

In 1950, Indonesia's total forest cover was estimated at approximately 162 million hectares. By 2000 that total had dropped to 98 million hectares, with the most valuable natural forests—the lowland forests of larger islands such as Sulawesi, Sumatra, and Kalimantan (the Indonesian section of Borneo)—almost entirely gone. Much of this damage has been done over the last two decades. In the 1980s the country began losing about 1 million hectares of forest to legal and illegal logging operations each year. The following decade, rising political instability, corruption, and lawlessness fueled even greater rates of deforestation. By the late 1990s, Indonesia was losing nearly 2 million hectares of forest every year—including stands of timber located in national parks—and illegally harvested wood accounted for as much as 65 percent of the country's timber supply by 2000 (Barber et al. 2002). And in 2002 the Indonesian government admitted that over the previous five years, the country had lost 5,000 hectares (12,300 acres) of forest to illegal logging a day. "Neither the presence, at least on paper, of a permanent forest estate nor national and international concern and donor assistance [have] had much effect in preventing this rapid increase in forest loss," acknowledged one study (Wikramanayake et al. 2002).

This frightening and unprecedented rate of forest habitat loss has been further exacerbated by enormously destructive forest fires that swept across Indonesia in 1997 and 1998 (and, to a lesser degree, in 2000). Those fires, blamed in part on tinderbox conditions created by the El Niño weather phenomenon, are viewed in some quarters as a disquieting indication of possible disasters to come. Indeed, some analysts forecast that future El Niño events could be even more destructive unless Indonesian loggers stop leaving large quantities of "slash"—woody debris that serves as potent fuel for wildfires—in logged-over areas.

In recent years, the Indonesian government has belatedly shown some recognition that it needs to reduce pressure on the forest resources that remain the primary incubator for its rich bounty of flora and fauna. In 2002, for example, Indonesia announced a permanent ban on log exports as part of an effort to preserve its remaining tropical forests. But observers believe that much more dramatic steps will need to be taken in the near future to save Indonesia's forests and associated biodiversity. "Unless radical and far-reaching steps are taken to enforce existing laws, regulations and policies and new policies are established for sound forest management, some of the most species-rich forests on earth will disappear" (ibid.).

In Thailand, meanwhile, myopic government policies have also had a dele-terious impact on biodiversity. For example, Thailand's Wild Animals Preservation and Protection Act, its primary law providing legal protection to birds and mammals, includes a provision that allows any person to possess up to two individuals of most species. This exception, say critics, "renders the provisions outlawing the capture, purchase, or sale of wild animals almost meaningless" (Graham and Round 1994). As in other Asian nations, however, deforestation is the single greatest threat to biodiversity in Thailand. From the early 1960s to the early 1990s, land clearing for timber sales and agricultural expansion reduced the country's total forest cover by about half, to about 26 percent of its total land area (Gray and Graham 1994). Moreover, conserva-tionists note that official forest cover statistics include both commercial tree plantations and degraded fallow agricultural land; if those sectors are removed from the equation, the actual area of intact natural forest in Thailand is estimated to be no more than 15 percent of its total land area (Mittermeier et al. 1999).

With most easily accessible and valuable timber stands gone, logging in Thailand has declined markedly. But Southeast Asian loggers have not closed shop; instead, they have simply moved their activities to Vietnam, Cambodia, and Myanmar, "where timber is extracted as rapidly and extensively as tech-nology and infrastructure permit" (ibid.).

Preserving Asian Biodiversity

Given the myriad pressures on Asia's dwindling wildlife habitat, and the re-gion's poor overall record on nature conservation, the future of many of the

In Thailand, domesticated elephants are used for a variety of commercial purposes. STONE LES/CORBIS SYGMA

continent's flora and fauna appears uncertain, to put it charitably. Indeed, a 2002 study of the Indo-Pacific region carried out by researchers affiliated with the Conservation Science Program of the World Wildlife Fund concluded that the region's belated efforts to preserve biodiversity and associated natural habitat could result in three dramatically different outcomes. The first scenario is one of utter failure, in which Asia presides over "wholesale destruction of the remaining intact forests and grasslands of the region and attendant widespread extinctions. In this scenario, large-scale commercial logging and its aftermath will hasten the conversion of all remaining lowland forests to oil palm and other monoculture crops. Only archipelagos of inaccessible montane forests will remain, only the most irreplaceable habitats will be stoutly defended, and only the most unproductive lands will be spared from encroachment." Researchers also offer a second scenario, in which some wilderness forests are saved, but efforts to curb the wildlife trade falter, leaving ecosystems permanently crippled. "Many of the ecoregions in the Indochina bioregion currently reflect this scenario," warns the study. The most optimistic scenario forecasts an Asia characterized by bold and effective biodiversity conservation mechanisms, visionary political and social leadership, and heightened awareness of environmental sustainability ideals. In this model of

Figure 2.1 World Trade Comparisons, 1986 and 1997

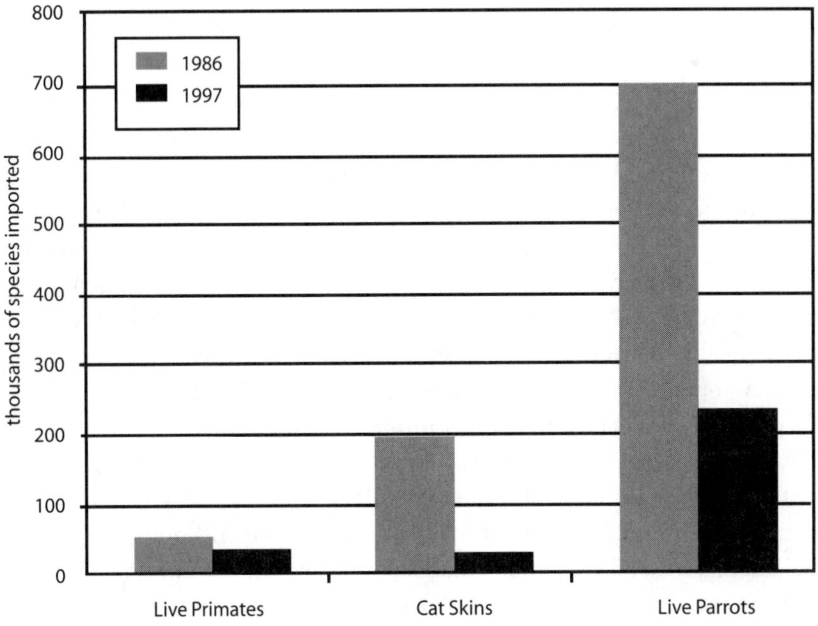

SOURCE: World Resources Institute

the future, Asian countries currently charging to the precipice of ecological crisis embrace the ideology of Bhutan, a tiny kingdom nestled in the foothills of the southern Himalayas that has "pledged to proceed with economic development cautiously, primarily in deference to the consequences of environmental degradation and biodiversity loss" (Wikramanayake et al. 2002).

To bring this hopeful vision of the future to fruition, the nations of Asia must take immediate and decisive action to protect threatened species and their habitats. Expansion of protected areas programs is one priority, with special emphasis on identification and protection of areas featuring high levels of diversity or endemism (Soulé and Terborgh 1999). Protected reserve programs should also focus on creating large, intact wilderness areas in which top carnivores can thrive. Indeed, erecting and defending protected areas that can support tigers and leopards has become a top conservation priority among international experts (ibid.). This increased interest in protecting snow leopards, Bengal tigers, and their brethren stems from a rising recognition that "critically endangered populations of top carnivores are indicators of ecosystems in decline. As we set our conservation sights on recovery, top carnivores can be the stars in our ongoing efforts to restore and maintain biodiversity. But the star power of top carnivores, their flagship and umbrella role, is more than symbolic. Without top carnivores our efforts to stem the loss of biodiversity will ultimately fail" (Seidensticker 2002).

Asian countries that are serious about protecting biodiversity in forest, wetland, marine, freshwater, and agricultural ecosystems will also have to introduce nature conservation considerations into all other policy-making areas; institute effective regulatory, management, and enforcement policies to protect habitat and species; provide economic incentives and educational programs for citizenry to embrace wildlife conservation; and dramatically increase investment in monitoring and evaluation of biodiversity levels and species health. "Governments that seriously embrace the concept of sustainable development must begin a process of comprehensive science-based land-use planning and back it up with appropriate legislation and enforcement," concluded one expert. "Not to do so is tantamount to abandoning the future. Sustainable development absolutely requires, among other conditions, the halting and eventual reversal of the land-use cascade. Although technically challenging, soil and vegetation rehabilitation can restore some level of utility to much of the vast acreage of abandoned land around the world. Still the best solution will be to protect rain forests before they are damaged or destroyed" (Terbourgh and Van Schaik 1997).

Sources:

Barber, Charles Victor, et al. 2002. *The State of the Forest: Indonesia.* Washington, DC: Global Forest Watch, World Resources Institute, and Forest Watch Indonesia.

Bennett, Elizabeth L., and John G. Robinson. 2002. "Into the Frying Pan and onto the Apothecary Shelves: The Fate of Tropical Forest Wildlife in Asia?" In Eric Wikramanayake, Eric Dinerstein, Colby J. Loucks et al., eds., *Terrestrial Ecoregions of the Indo-Pacific: A Conservation Assessment.* Washington, DC: Island.

Birdlife International. 2000. *Threatened Birds of the World.* Barcelona and Cambridge, UK: Lynx Edicions and BirdLife International.

Braatz, S. 1992. *Conserving Biological Diversity: A Strategy for Protected Areas in the Asia-Pacific Region.* Washington, DC: World Bank.

Bryant, Dirk. 1997. *The Last Frontier Forests: Ecosystems and Economies on the Edge.* Washington, DC: World Resources Institute.

China Department of Nature Conservation. 1999. *A Country Study: The Richness and Uniqueness of China's Biodiversity.* Beijing: China Department of Nature Conservation.

Coates, B. J., and K. D. Bishop. 1997. *A Guide to the Birds of Wallacea: Sulawesi, the Moluccas and Lesser Sunda Islands, Indonesia.* Alderley, Queensland: Dove.

Collar, N. J., M. J. Crosby, and A. J. Stattersfield. 1994. *Birds to Watch 2: The World List of Threatened Birds.* Cambridge, UK: BirdLife International.

Cracroft, Joel, and Francesca T. Grifo. 1999. *The Living Planet in Crisis: Biodiversity Science and Policy.* New York: Columbia University Press.

Department of Environment and Natural Resources (Philippines) and UN Environment Programme. 1997. *Philippine Biodiversity: An Assessment and Plan of Action.* Makati City, Philippines: DENR and UNEP.

Dinerstein, E., et al. 1999. "Tigers as Neighbours." In J. Seidensticker, S. Christie, and P. Jackson, eds., *Riding the Tiger: Tiger Conservation in Human Dominated Landscapes.* Cambridge: Cambridge University Press.

Graham, Mark, and Philip Round. 1994. *Thailand's Vanishing Flora and Fauna.* Bangkok: Finance One.

Gray, D., C. Piprell, and M. Graham. 1994. *National Parks of Thailand.* Bangkok: Industrial Finance Corp.

Kottelat, M. 2000a. *Ecoregions and Fish Diversity in the Indochinese Area.* Washington, DC: World Wildlife Fund.

———. 2000b. *Fishes of Laos.* Colombo, Sri Lanka: Wildlife Heritage Trust, 2000.

Mackay, Richard. 2002. *Atlas of Endangered Species: Threatened Plants and Animals of the World.* London: Earthscan.

MacKinnon, J., et al. 1996. *A Biodiversity Review of China.* Hong Kong: WWF International.

Madhusadan, M. D., and K. U. Karanth. 2000. "Hunting for an Answer." In J. G. Robinson and E. L. Bennett, eds., *Hunting for Sustainability in Tropical Forests.* New York: Columbia University Press.

Mills, Judy. 2002. "Taking the Bounty off Wildlife in Asia." In Eric Wikramanayake et al., eds., *Terrestrial Ecoregions of the Indo-Pacific: A Conservation Assessment.* Washington, DC: Island.

Mills, J. A., and P. Jackson. 1994. *Killed for a Cure: A Review of the World-Wide Trade in Tiger Bone.* Cambridge, UK: TRAFFIC International.

Mittermeier, Russell A., Patricio Robles Gil, and Cristina Goettsch Mittermeier. 1998. *Megadiversity: Earth's Biologically Wealthiest Nations.* Mexico City: CEMEX.

Mittermeier, Russell A., Norman Myers, and Cristina Goettsch Mittermeier. 1999. *Hotspots: Earth's Biologically Richest and Most Endangered Terrestrial Ecoregions.* Mexico City: CEMEX, Conservation International.

Motavalli, Jim, and Jennifer Bogo. 1999. "The Last of Their Kind." *E: The Environmental Magazine* (May–June).

Novacek, Michael J., ed. 2001. *The Biodiversity Crisis: Losing what Counts.* New York: New Press.

Oldfield, S., et al. 1998. *The World List of Threatened Trees.* Cambridge, UK: World Conservation.

Redford, Kent H. 1992. "The Empty Forest." *Bioscience* 10, no. 42.

Rifai, M. A. 1994. "A Discourse on Biodiversity Utilization in Indonesia." *Tropical Biodiversity* 2, no. 2.

Saghal, Bittu, and Jennifer Scarlott. 2001. "Stranded." *Amicus Journal* 23, no. 22.

Seidensticker, John. 2002. "Tigers: Top Carnivores and Controlling Processes in Asian Forests." In Eric Wikramanayake et al., eds., *Terrestrial Ecoregions of the Indo-Pacific: A Conservation Assessment.* Washington, DC: Island.

Soulé, M. E., and John Terborgh. 1999. *Continental Conservation: Scientific Foundations of Regional Reserve Networks.* Washington, DC: Island.

Spalding, M. D., F. Blasco, and C. D. Field, eds. 1997. *World Mangrove Atlas.* Okinawa, Japan: International Society for Mangrove Ecosystems.

State Environmental Protection Administration of China. 1996. *Report on the State of the Environment in China.* Beijing: SEPA.

Terborgh, John. 1992. *Diversity and the Tropical Rain Forest.* New York: Freeman.

Terborgh, John, and Carel P. Van Schaik. 1997. "Minimizing Species Loss: The Imperative of Protection." In Randall Kramer, Carl van Schaik, and Julie Johnson, eds., *Last Stand: Protected Areas and the Defense of Tropical Biodiversity.* New York: Oxford University Press.

UN Environment Programme. 1999. *Global Environment Outlook 2000.* London: Earthscan.

UN Food and Agriculture Organization. 2001. *State of the World's Forests 2001.* Rome: FAO.

Wagener, Amy. 2001. "Endangered Species: Traded to Death." *EarthTrends,* World Resources Institute, http://earthtrends/wri/org/conditions_trends/feature_select-action.cfm?theme=7 (accessed August 2001).

Wikramanayake, Eric, et al. 2002. *Terrestrial Ecoregions of the Indo-Pacific: A Conservation Assessment.* Washington, DC: Island.

Wildlife Conservation Society and Sarawak Forest Department. 1996. *A Master Plan for Wildlife in Sarawak.* Kuching, Sarawak: WCS/SFD.

Wilson, E. O. 1993. *The Diversity of Life.* New York: W. W. Norton.

Wood, Alexander, Pamela Stedman-Edwards, and Johanna Mang. 2001. *The Root Causes of Biodiversity Loss.* London: Earthscan.

World Conservation Union. 1996. *1996 IUCN Red List of Threatened Animals.* Gland, Switzerland: IUCN.

———. 2000. *2000 IUCN Red List of Threatened Species.* Gland, Switzerland: IUCN.

World Resources Institute. 2000. *World Resources 2000–2001: People and Ecosystems, the Fraying Web of Life.* Washington, DC: UN Environment Programme.

3

Parks, Preserves, and Protected Areas

The sprawling continent of Asia houses some of the planet's most biologically rich ecosystems, filled with unique and spectacular plants and animals. Conservation of this biodiversity is a global priority, and during the last
half-century, one of the principal means by which Asian countries have
sought to meet this goal has been through the institution of protected area
networks. Today, these national parks, wildlife sanctuaries, and nature reserves protect many of the regions' most fragile and valuable natural areas.

However, conservation groups, international donor agencies, wildlife biologists, and natural resource agencies both within and outside Asia are nearly
unanimous in their conviction that Asia's current protected area system is
woefully inadequate for the long-term protection of vital habitat and associated flora and fauna. The ecological integrity of many of the parks, reserves,
and sanctuaries that are already in existence is under severe threat from a host
of human activities, including logging, mining, farming, commercial development, and the establishment of new settlements. These problems bedevil protected area networks around the world to one degree or another, but in Asia
they are mightily exacerbated by high levels of population growth and population density, significant areas of chronic poverty, and rapid economic development that has escalated extractive pressure on dwindling natural resources.
Moreover, many of Asia's most ecologically valuable areas enjoy no protection
whatsoever. This shortcoming has prompted widespread calls for significant
expansion of park and reserve systems, but responsiveness to these entreaties
has been spotty, in part because of institutional and social apathy but also because of the extremely limited financial resources available to many countries.

Defining Protected Areas

Protected areas are defined by the World Commission on Protected Areas (WCPA) of the World Conservation Union (IUCN: International Union for the Conservation of Nature and Natural Resources) as "an area of land and/or sea especially dedicated to the protection and maintenance of biological diversity, and of natural and associated cultural resources, and managed through legal or other effective means." In practice, protected areas are managed for a wide range of purposes that include scientific research, wilderness protection, preservation of species and ecosystems, maintenance of environmental services, protection of specific natural and cultural features, tourism and recreation, education, sustainable exploitation of natural resources, and maintenance of cultural and traditional attributes. The classification systems used by individual countries vary in accordance with objectives and levels of protection, and title designations are different from country to country as well. For example, strictly protected areas accessed primarily for scientific research are called "nature conservation areas" in Japan, "strict natural reserves" in Sri Lanka, and "strict nature reserves" in Bhutan (Green and Paine 1997).

The World Conservation Union classifies each formally designated protected area in one of six management categories. Category I and Ia parks and reserves are protected areas managed primarily for science or wilderness protection. Category II areas are national parks managed for both ecosystem protection and human recreation. Other management classifications are available for natural monuments and landmarks (Category III), species and habitat protection areas that are subject to tree felling and other active forms of management (Category IV), protected landscapes and seascapes with dual conservation/recreation management mandates (Category V), and "managed resource protection areas" (Category VI), which seek to balance biodiversity protection with extractive activities such as logging. Data on all but the smallest of the aforementioned parks and reserves are collected by the WCPA and used to create the *United Nations List of Protected Areas,* the definitive listing of protected areas around the globe (World Commission on Protected Areas, wcpa.iucn.org; see Table 3.1 for a detailed WCPA summary of country-by-country protected area data as of 1997).

Asia's Protected Area
Networks, Past and Present

Asia's first protected area was Cambodia's Angkor Wat National Park, which was formally created in 1925. Other early national parks designated in Asia included Mount Arayat and Mount Roosevelt in the Philippines (1933), Corbett

Angkor Wat in Cambodia. COREL

National Park in India (1938), Rhuhuna and Wilpattu national parks in Sri Lanka (1938), and Taman Negara in Malaysia (1939). China, the largest country on the continent in both land area and human population, did not designate its first protected area until 1956, when it created tiny (11 square kilometers) Zhaoging Dinghushan Natural Reserve in Guangdon Province.

Designation of protected areas in Asia accelerated in the 1950s and 1960s, when international organizations such as the UN Food and Agriculture Organization (FAO) and conservation groups such as the IUCN and World Wide Fund for Nature (WWF)—known in North America as the World Wildlife Fund—actively sponsored conservation projects in Nepal, India, Indonesia, Burma (now Myanmar), and other places (Mishra et al. 1997; Child 1984). One of the most heavily publicized conservation efforts of this era was India's Project Tiger, which established an extensive system of wildlife reserves to preserve vanishing habitat for the charismatic carnivores.

During the 1970s and 1980s, Asian conservation organizations lent their muscle to the habitat preservation cause as well, creating additional momentum for the establishment of new reserves, sanctuaries, and parks. By the early 1990s, the results of this sustained conservation drive were plain to see. Across tropical Asia, the total amount of protected land had been doubled from 442,000 square kilometers (170,000 square miles) in 1960 to more than

Table 3.1 State of Asia's Protected Areas by IUCN Category

Country	Total Land Area (Sq.km)	Ia/Ib Parks No.	Area (Sq. km)	% of Land Area	II Parks No.	Area (Sq. km)	% of Land Area	III Parks No.	Area (Sq. km)	% of Land Area	IV Parks No.	Area (Sq. km)	% of Land Area	V Parks No.	Area (Sq. km)	% Land Area	VI Parks No.	Area (Sq. km)	% of Land Area	Total Parks No.	Area (Sq. km)	% of Land Area
South-East Asia																						
Brunei Darussalam	5,765	24	715	12.40	1	488	8.46							6	9	0.16				31	1,212	21.02
Cambodia	181,000				7	7,362	4.07				8	13,850	7.65	5	7,420	4.10	3	4,039	2.23	23	32,671	18.05
Indonesia	1,919,445	154	25,869	1.35	36	126,887	6.61	15	52	0.00	47	35,959	1.87	79	3,772	0.20	738	152,589	7.95	1,069	345,118	17.98
Lao People's Democratic Republic	236,725																17	27,563	11.64	17	27,563	11.64
Malaysia	332,965	113	1,107	0.33	17	8,153	2.45	1			12	5,798	1.74	1	10	0.00	1	206	0.06	145	15,274	4.59
Myanmar	678,030				1	1,605	0.24							2	130	0.02				3	1,735	0.26
Philippines	300,000	2	149	0.05	5	4,481	1.49				1	893	0.30	11	9,017	3.01				19	14,540	4.85
Singapore	616										1	27	4.38	4	2	0.32				5	29	4.71
Thailand	514,000				74	39,473	7.68				37	27,275	5.31	1	131	0.03				158	70,771	13.77
Viet Nam	329,565				9	2,024	0.61	46	3,892	0.76	45	7,927	2.41							54	9,951	3.02
South Asia																						
Bangladesh	144,000										7	833	0.58	3	147	0.10				10	980	0.68
Bhutan	46,620	1	644	1.38	4	6,923	14.85				4	2,411	5.17							9	9,978	21.40
India	3,166,830	3	1,969	0.06	67	32,514	1.03	1			421	108,451	3.42	1	186	0.01				493	143,120	4.52
Maldives	298																					
Nepal	141,415				8	10,174	7.19				4	941	0.67				2	1,590	1.12	14	12,705	8.98
Pakistan	803,940				6	8,821	1.10				70	27,216	3.39	5	1,229	0.15	2	181	0.02	83	37,447	4.66
Sri Lanka	65,610	29	784	1.19	23	4,562	6.95				58	3,348	5.10							110	8,694	13.25

(continues)

Table 3.1 State of Asia's Protected Areas by IUCN Category (*continued*)

Country	Total Land Area (Sq.km)	Ia/Ib Parks No.	Area (Sq. km)	% of Land Area	II Parks No.	Area (Sq. km)	% of Land Area	III Parks No.	Area (Sq. km)	% of Land Area	IV Parks No.	Area (Sq. km)	% of Land Area	V Parks No.	Area (Sq. km)	% of Land Area	VI Parks No.	Area (Sq. km)	% of Land Area	Total Parks No.	Area (Sq. km)	% of Land Area
East Asia																						
China	9,597,000	37	486,282	5.07	20	8,156	0.08	44	1,297	0.01	205	56,369	0.59	101	46,291	0.48	403	84,012	0.88	810	682,407	7.11
China – Hong Kong	1,062										18	28	2.64	25	433	40.77				43	461	43.41
Japan	369,700	15	272	0.07	15	12,959	3.51				53	4,837	1.31	13	7,522	2.03				96	25,590	6.92
Korea, Democratic People's Republic of	122,310				9	1,501	1.23	12	107	0.09	10	1,550	1.27							31	3,158	2.58
Korea, Republic of	98,445										10	365	0.37	20	6,473	6.58				30	6,838	6.95
Portugal – Macao	17																					
Mongolia	1,565,000	11	102,218	6.53	6	48,596	3.11	17	9,978	0.64	1	499	0.03							35	161,291	10.31
Taiwan	36,960	18	632	1.71	6	3,222	8.72				9	82	0.22							33	3,963	10.65
Central Asia																						
Afghanistan	652,225				1	410	0.06				6	1,776	0.27							7	2,186	0.34
Armenia	29,800	4	634	2.13	1	1,500	5.03													5	2,134	7.16
Azerbaijan	86,600	14	1,920	2.22							20	2,856	3.30							34	4,776	5.52
Georgia	69,700	16	1,688	2.42	2	265	0.38													18	1,963	2.80
Iran, Islamic Repub.	1,648,000				7	10,753	0.65	5	63	0.00	27	30,518	1.85	39	41,697	2.53				78	83,031	5.04
Kazakhstan	2,717,300	8	8,837	0.33	3	3,840	0.14				62	60,696	2.23							73	73,373	2.70
Kyrgyzstan	198,500	6	2,474	1.25	5	521	0.26				67	3,944	1.99							78	6,939	3.50
Tajikistan	143,100	3	857	0.60	2	15	0.01				14	4,998	3.49							19	5,870	4.10
Turkmenistan	488,100	8	8,190	1.68							13	11,560	2.37							23	19,773	4.05
Uzbekistan	447,400	9	2,197	0.49	2	5,987	1.34	2	23	0.00										11	8,184	1.83

SOURCE: Greene, Michael J. B., and James Paine. 1997. *State of the World's Protected Areas.* Cambridge, UK: World Conservation Monitoring Centre.

880,000 square kilometers (340,000 square miles). Some countries, including Brunei, Bhutan, and Sri Lanka, had placed significant percentages of their land area under legal protection, including large areas of forest for watershed protection. Indonesia, for example, declared that it was setting aside more than 731,000 square kilometers (281,250 square miles) of forest reserves for that purpose alone (World Conservation Union 1991).

International recognition of Asian habitat and its high levels of species diversity and endemic animals and plants (those found nowhere else in the world) also increased during this period. In 2002 the continent boasted twenty-three Natural World Heritage sites of "outstanding universal value" as determined by the UN Educational, Scientific, and Cultural Organization (UNESCO), including five sites in India. Other countries appearing on the list include China (3 sites), Indonesia (3 sites), Japan (2), Malaysia (2), Nepal (2), Philippines (2), Bangladesh (1), Sri Lanka (1), Thailand (1), and Vietnam (1).

But while a notable expansion of Asia's protected area networks took place during the second half of the twentieth century, the growth in the number of hectares technically under protection has been deceptive. Some protected areas have remained mere "paper parks"—formally declared by governments as reserves or sanctuaries, but given no financial, managerial, or other institutional resources to prevent them from being overrun by poachers, farmers, loggers, and other exploiters of the land and its flora and fauna. In addition, some countries have cobbled together protected area networks that provide lots of protection to remote montane (mountain) forests that feature light human presence or modest numbers of endangered or endemic species, but that safeguard few species-rich lowland forests and wetlands (MacKinnon and MacKinnon 1986).

In addition, analysts note that protected areas in Asia and elsewhere have become

increasingly subject to threats that even the best-managed areas cannot resist. These threats are well established, especially the multitudes of landless and destitute people—a problem that will grow for a long time to come (as many as one-third of developing country parks and reserves are already being overtaken by agricultural encroachment). The new threats also stem from more distant and diffuse problems, notably atmospheric pollution in the form of acid rain, ozone layer depletion, and global warming. These threats can be countered only by remedial measures that achieve much more than protection of specific wildlife environments. The measures include efforts to slow, halt, and reverse problems such as desertification, deforestation, overuse of water supplies, acid rain, and global warming. They also include population planning, poverty relief, and a host of other development activities. (Myers 1999)

Concerned biologists and conservationists grant that some of Asia's better-managed and better-funded protected areas have made significant progress in conserving important habitat and maintaining healthy populations of flora and fauna that are integral to fully functional ecosystems. But critics say that these successes are rare because most networks remain plagued by meager funding, marginal public and government support, and small, scattered reserves that make it impossible to preserve the full complement of the region's biodiversity (van Schaik and Kramer 1997).

Indeed, throughout much of tropical Asia, nature preserves and other protected areas are widely believed to be in a state of crisis. "A number of tropical parks have already been degraded almost beyond redemption; others face severe threats of many kinds with little capacity to resist. The final bulwark erected to shield tropical nature from extinction is collapsing" (van Schaik, Terborgh, and Dugelby 1997). Examples of ruinous degradation and exploitation abound. In the Philippines, fully two-thirds of the country's parks and preserves have been penetrated by human settlements (Mittermeier et al. 1998). In India, Kaziranga National Park and other fragile habitats are threatened by potential flooding along the Brahmaputra River, which has had much of its upper watershed denuded by large-scale commercial logging. In Indonesia, massive amounts of protected forests have been lost to wildfires exacerbated by illegal logging that leaves large quantities of bone-dry debris on the ground. In Thailand's Khao Sam Roi Yot National Park, large tracts of the country's largest remaining freshwater marshes have been converted to shrimp farms. Elsewhere in the country, in Doi Inthanon National Park, the number of people living in the park has increased so dramatically in recent years that 15 percent of the park's area has been cleared to grow opium poppies and other crops; pesticides have fouled area streams; and hunters have rendered the area almost devoid of large mammals (Mishra et al. 1997).

Of course, variations in the quality and size of protected area networks do exist across Asia, as the following summaries indicate:

East and Central Asia

East Asia's historical respect for nature and dedication to conservation ideals have been sorely tested in recent decades by rapid population growth and galloping economic development, both of which have heightened pressure to

Sri Lanka's Sinharaja Forest Reserve

The island nation of Sri Lanka maintains sixty-seven protected areas—including national parks, nature reserves, jungle corridors, and wildlife sanctuaries—covering 7,840 square kilometers, or 12 percent of its total land area. The majority of these areas (forty-three, covering 4,750 square kilometers) protect rain forest ecosystems. Sri Lanka's most biologically important protected area is the Sinharaja Forest Reserve, a 473-square-kilometer area in the southwestern part of the country that contains the last vestiges of original lowland rain forest vegetation on the island (Mittermeier et al., *Hotspots,* 1999).

For its size, which represents only 0.7 percent of Sri Lanka's total land area, the Sinharaja Forest Reserve holds a huge proportion of the island's endemic flora and fauna. For example, Sinharaja contains 215 species of trees—140 of which are endemic—and new species continue to be discovered. The forest also supports 270 species of vertebrates, 65 of which are endemic. Overall, this protected area holds 90 percent of Sri Lanka's endemic birds, 65 percent of its endemic trees, and 60 percent of its endemic mammals (ibid.).

The Sinharaja region's remarkable biodiversity was first recognized by Dutch explorers who mapped the island in the eighteenth century. Part of the region was set aside as a forest reserve as early as 1875. Yet a century later, the Sinharaja narrowly escaped destruction through logging. The region's timber potential was

convert or exploit undisturbed areas for human use. Not surprisingly, many species in the region—defined by the WCPA as China, Japan, Hong Kong, North and South Korea, Macau, Mongolia, and Taiwan—are now threatened or endangered.

The countries of the region have responded to these imminent threats to plant and animal communities and ecosystem health by expanding the protected areas systems that first took root in the 1930s and 1940s. Indeed, 60 percent of the protected areas currently in place in East Asia have been designated since 1982. This sustained flurry of activity extended formal protection to some coastal waters, primarily in Japan, China, and South Korea (World Commission on Protected Areas 2002a). More important, it provided a significant boost to the level of terrestrial protection in East Asia. By the close of the 1990s, East Asia had a total of 1,078 protected areas covering 883,681 square kilometers—7.4 percent of the total land area. The largest single component of the region's collective protected area system was eighty-one wilderness recognized during the 1960s, and selective felling began in 1970. However, the logging created widespread public protests led by scientists, clergy, and members of the Wildlife and Nature Protection Society of Sri Lanka. This environmental group conducted research and produced a report outlining the biological richness of the forest. The report spurred an even greater public outcry, which convinced the new government that took power in 1977 to halt the logging in Sinharaja.

In the following year, 8,800 hectares of land in the Sinharaja were declared an International Man and Biosphere Reserve. The region became a National Wilderness Area in 1988, and it was included on UNESCO's list of World Heritage Sites a year later. The Sinharaja Forest Reserve represents a conservation success story for Sri Lanka, as the region's biological importance is respected by the nation's government, its people, and the international community. Still, the Sinharaja continues to experience problems with the encroachment of surrounding villages, increased access through former logging roads, and collection of nontimber forest products. Several international agencies and environmental groups have provided Sri Lankan authorities with assistance in improving the management of this valuable area.

Source:

Mittermeier, Russell A., Norman Myers, and Cristina Goettsch Mittermeier. 1999. *Hotspots: Earth's Biologically Richest and Most Endangered Terrestrial Ecoregions.* Mexico City: CEMEX/ Conservation International.

---

areas and strict nature reserves, defined as Category I protected areas by the IUCN. These protected areas alone account for two-thirds of the total territory under protection and 5 percent of East Asia's total land area. Fifty-six national parks (Category II) account for 0.63 percent of East Asia's total land area, and seventy-three natural monuments and landmarks (Category III) extend protection to another 0.10 percent of the region's total land area (Green and Paine 1997).

The mean size of East Asia's 1,078 protected areas is 820 square kilometers, but that figure is skewed somewhat by several enormous protected areas in China. For example, China's protected area network of more than 640 distinct parks and reserves includes Qiang Tang Nature Reserve, which, at 247,120 square kilometers, is the fourth largest protected area on the planet. But despite such triumphs, China's response to threatened habitat in some regions has still been found wanting. For example, the Chinese government has extended protection to only 2.1 percent of the ecologically vital Hengduan Mountains region

Figure 3.1 Cumulative Growth in the Number and Extent of Protected Areas within East Asia

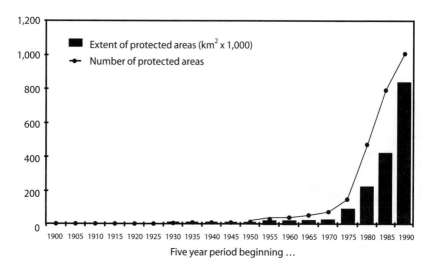

Five year period beginning …

SOURCE: Greene, Michael J. B., and James Paine. 1997. *State of the World's Protected Areas*. Cambridge, UK: World Conservation Monitering Centre. Available online at http://www.forest-trends.org/keytrends/pdf/wcmc%20state%20of%20protected%20areas.pdf

of south-central China. "Although some important areas are currently protected in this crucial hotspot, much more needs to be done. . . .The enormous watershed protection value of this region in and of itself provides more than adequate justification for protecting far more than 2.1 percent of the region's land area—especially since it is arguably one of the two or three most important major watershed regions on the planet" (Mittermeier et al. 1999).

Indeed, throughout much of East Asia, expansion of existing protected area networks is badly needed. "The total area protected is too small, omitting important plant and animal communities," summarized the World Commission on Protected Areas. "Remaining natural areas that are still unprotected face escalating pressures, which threaten the survival of plants and animals and the communities of which they are a part. The coverage and degree of protection for individual sites, as well as the public appreciation of protected areas, varies greatly. There are significant gaps, particularly in relation to the conservation of wetland and marine ecosystems, as well as arid ecosystems. . . .[T]here is an extremely high level of both domestic and international tourism to countries in the region. This inevitably focuses on protected areas and the volume of tourist use poses significant challenges to the integrity of such areas" (World Commission on Protected Areas 2002a).

Figure 3.2 Cumulative Growth in the Number and Extent of Protected Areas within South Asia

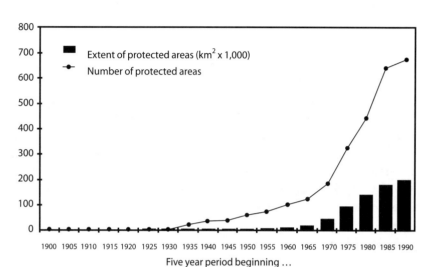

SOURCE: Greene, Michael J. B., and James Paine. 1997. *State of the World's Protected Areas.* Cambridge, UK: World Conservation Monitering Centre. Available online at http://www.forest-trends.org/keytrends/pdf/wcmc%20 state%20of%20protected%20areas.pdf

In Central Asia, meanwhile, levels of protection are also inadequate. A few nations have set aside large areas of land for habitat and biodiversity protection—such as Tajikistan, which safeguards more than 17 percent of its total land area—but most countries in the region have established protection over less than 5 percent of their lands (World Commission on Protected Areas 2002b). In addition, many of the areas under formal protection, including *zapovedniks* that provide the highest degree of nature protection, are struggling with acute shortages of funding and staff that make it impossible to conduct basic research and law enforcement.

South Asia

South Asia, composed of Bangladesh, Bhutan, India, Maldives, Nepal, Pakistan, and Sri Lanka, is another densely populated region that is laboring to protect its natural treasures, which range from spectacular landscapes such as the mountains of the Himalayas to the lush jungles of the Ganges and Bhramaputra river valleys. The flora and fauna that exist in this region are astonishing as well, from the Asian elephant to the tree-climbing crabs of Sri Lanka.

Currently, about 212,000 square kilometers of South Asia—4.8 percent of the region's total land area—are under formal protection. The percentage of protected area coverage varies greatly among countries, however. Bhutan, for example, has extended protection to more than 20 percent of its territory, and Sri Lanka has formally designated more than 20 percent of its biologically rich "Wet Zone" for conservation (Mittermeier et al. 1999). But Pakistan and India have shielded only 4 percent of their land areas from land conversion and other forms of exploitation, and the Maldives, an island nation situated in the Indian Ocean, had yet to designate any protected areas as of the late 1990s (Mishra et al. 1997).

All told, South Asia contained 719 protected areas at the close of the 1990s, with the vast majority of them (564) classified as Category IV sanctuaries and reserves subject to active management of habitat and species. This category of protected area shields 3.28 percent of South Asia's total land area. By contrast, only 33 wilderness areas and strict nature reserves (defined as Category I protected areas by the IUCN) have been established in the region, and they account for only 0.08 percent of the total land area (108 Category II national parks account for another 1.44 percent of South Asia's total land area). The mean size of South Asia's 719 protected areas is 296 square kilometers (Green and Paine 1997).

The chief areas of concern regarding South Asia's protected areas include commercial logging (both legal and illegal), mining, and development projects; degradation from fuelwood collection and grazing; poaching; and ecologically destructive forms of tourism, all of which can be exacerbated by weak management and enforcement provisions. In India, for example, secondary uses have heavily degraded some reserves. "The national park and sanctuary categories confer the highest legal status. Yet numerous activities occur that seem to go against the *spirit* of the Wild Life [Protection] Act of 1972, [India's main habitat conservation law]. For instance, livestock grazing is allowed in 66 percent of the conservation areas, human habitation in 46 percent, agriculture in 43 percent, and timber harvesting in 37 percent....Large chunks of the Sariska tiger reserve in India have been destroyed by large-scale mining operations sanctioned by the government....These activities, regardless of whether they are technically legal or not, threaten the biodiversity of India's parks" (van Schaik, Terborgh, and Dugelby 1997). Moreover, across South Asia many important areas of endemism and habitats containing threatened species remain wholly unprotected. This is especially true of marine areas, wetlands, and lowland forests that are under heavy pressure from rapidly growing urban and rural populations.

Nonetheless, the trends are not entirely grim. Observers note that tigers and other large mammals "are still holding on in many South Asian reserves, even in the face of intensive poaching pressure and degradation in some areas outside reserves. . . .From Sri Lanka to India to Nepal, reserves once set aside by maharajahs or by colonial rulers for their hunting exploits, which later became national parks, still maintain a visible if not vibrant megafauna" (Loucks and Dinerstein 2002). Moreover, significant expansions of existing networks are under active consideration by some regional governments. At the close of the 1990s, for instance, India proposed the creation of more than 290 new national parks and wildlife sanctuaries throughout the country. The average size of these reserves is modest (117 square kilometers), but they do signal increased recognition of the importance of formal habitat and species protection measures (Rodgers, Panwar, and Mathur 2000).

Southeast Asia

The countries listed under the Southeast Asia Region umbrella of the World Commission of Protected Areas are Brunei Darussalam, Cambodia, Indonesia, Laos, Malaysia, Myanmar, Philippines, Singapore, Thailand, and Vietnam. With few exceptions, the protected area networks erected by these nations are among the most troubled on the entire continent. Some countries are only in the early stages of establishing park and preserve systems, while others have instituted programs that are beleaguered by a host of pressures directly attributable to high levels of human population density and poverty, including

Figure 3.3 Cumulative Growth in the Number and Extent of Protected Areas within Southeast Asia

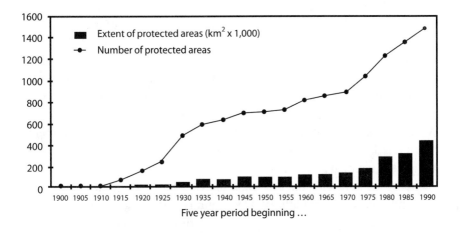

SOURCE: Greene, Michael J. B., and James Paine. 1997. *State of the World's Protected Areas.* Cambridge, UK: World Conservation Monitering Centre. Available online at http://www.forest-trends.org/keytrends/pdf/wcmc% 20state%20of%20protected%20areas.pdf

unsustainable levels of logging, agricultural encroachment, and wildlife hunting for food and trade on the black market. Indeed, this region is the epicenter of Asia's thriving animal wildlife trade, in which animals are sold as exotic pets (birds, primates) or harvested to cull ingredients used in traditional Oriental medicines (tigers, Asian black bears).

At first glance, the state of protected area networks in Southeast Asia does not appear so bleak. According to the World Commission on Protected Areas, the territory had 1,524 protected areas covering 11.5 percent of its total land area (518,864 square kilometers) in the late 1990s. The number of formally designated parks and reserves is far higher than in any other single region of the continent, and the percentage of land area ostensibly safeguarded is greater than in East Asia, Central Asia, or South Asia. But the mean size of protected areas in Southeast Asia is only 340 square kilometers, 41 percent of the mean size of those in East Asia. In addition, Southeast Asia contains only 293 wilderness areas and nature reserves that qualify as Category I protected areas, and those account for only 0.62 percent of Southeast Asia's total land area (Green and Paine 1997).

Another pernicious problem with Southeast Asia's protected area networks is that many of them do not focus on the region's most biologically rich or vital habitat. For instance, in the region known as Sundaland—consisting of Malaysia, Singapore, Brunei, and western Indonesia—120 protected areas cover about 90,000 square kilometers, but across the region, "the tendency is for the least threatened, least utilized, and least valuable habitats (such as upper montane forest) to be the best protected. Lowland forests on flat land or rolling hills where there is abundant water have generally been cleared for agriculture" (Mittermeier et al. 1999). Worst of all, many of the more than 1,500 protected areas in this region are just "paper parks"—formally designated by a government but given no meaningful resources to mount a defense against exploitation and degradation. "Unlike many other [conservation] hotspots, there is no great need in [Sundaland] for priority-setting exercises, for new policies or legislation, or for reform of the protected area system. Most of these are in place, although there is always room for improvement. What is lacking is implementation and much greater conviction, especially on the part of national governments, that biodiversity conservation is an investment in the future and both a national and global priority" (ibid.).

Conditions in a few Southeast Asian countries have engendered particular concern. One nation that has been a particularly poor steward of its abundant natural resources is the Philippines. Once rich in habitat that sustained a terrific variety of animal and plant species—including high levels of endemic species unique to that corner of the world—the Philippines has consumed about three-quarters of its original rain forest and pushed many species to the brink of extinction, despite the existence of protected area legislation dating back to the early 1930s. As recently as 1995, only 1.3 percent of the total land area of the Philippines was in protected areas, which is utterly inadequate to protect either its imperiled flora and fauna or its ecologically vital watersheds (ibid.).

In the early 1990s, a glint of hope appeared with the passage of the 1992 National Integrated Protected Areas System Act of 1992. The passage of this law provided for the expansion of the number of protected areas in the Philippines from 69 national parks, 8 game refuges and bird sanctuaries, and 16 wilderness areas to approximately 290 protected areas—including new parks in the northern Sierra Madra mountains of northeastern Luzon, the Kitanglad Range of Mindanao, and Sibuyan and Camiguin Islands. The law also provided for the protection of an additional 1.18 million hectares of fast-dwindling old-growth forest (Department of Environment and Natural Resources 1997; Mittermeier et al. 1999). But designating parks is only the first step in long-term conservation of the island nation's vanishing natural habitat. "When adequately conserved, protected areas are free from any actions that could destroy or completely eliminate the spectrum of habitat types that may be present within their respective boundaries. In reality, however, these protected areas receive inadequate protection partly due to lack of institutional support and resources, thus making them vulnerable or subject to all sorts of man-made problems or threats" (Department of Environment and Natural Resources 1997). Indeed, the illegal activities that continue to harry Philippine sanctuaries and parks—encroachment, occupancy, harvesting of fuelwood, hunting and trading of rare and endangered terrestrial and marine species, coral mining, logging, fishing by destructive methods (such as dynamite blasting and cyanide fishing), conversion of natural systems into agricultural or aquacultural areas, political intervention and bureaucracy, and inadequate management capacity and funding—are mind-boggling in their variety and destructive capacity (ibid.).

Indonesia is another country that has committed terrible damage to its natural resources over the years. "Forests once alive with birds and mammals are eerily silent," observed one analysis. "Why is this so? [Because] both the addition of new protected areas and strict protection of existing ones are features absent in the management of Indochina and Indonesia's wildlands. (Loucks and Dinerstein 2002). Indeed, Indonesia created few protected areas prior to 1970. Since then, habitat protection initiatives have fared somewhat better, with several protected areas created in the 1980s and two large reserves unveiled in the late 1990s (Gunung Lorentz on the island of Irian Jaya and Kayan Mentarang on Kalimantan, the Indonesian part of Borneo). But many recent additions exist in name only, and most protected areas that are not actively managed and protected—and some that are—have been torn apart by intensive levels of poaching and brazen logging of the country's last remnants of rain forest. In 1999, for example, a joint report issued by the Environmental Investigation Agency and the Indonesian environmental group Telepak Indonesia stated that virtual anarchy reigned in Tanjung Puting Park in Kalimantan and the Gunung Leuser Park in Sumatra, where loggers were harvesting "protected" forests at a feverish pace. Elsewhere, copper mining interests are pushing to expand into Lorentz National Park, one of Indonesia's last bastions of undisturbed mangroves and cloud and lowland forest (World Wide Fund for Nature and World Conservation Union 2001).

Other countries in Southeast Asia have also struggled to preserve vanishing habitat and species. Besieged by war, poverty, and high population growth, countries like Cambodia and Vietnam relegated creation of protected areas to the bottom of their priority lists. Those reserves and parks that were established were given little support. As a result, extensive logging, mining, agricultural and aquacultural encroachment, and harvesting of wildlife and medicinal plants in protected and unprotected regions alike became commonplace.

In some countries, however, encouraging signs of a new emphasis on habitat and species conservation are emerging. In 1993, Cambodia declared the creation of a new protected area system covering 18 percent of the country's total land area. Significantly, the network included meaningful protection for key sections of the Cardamom Mountains, a range that covers only 6 percent of the nation's land area but supports about half of the country's known resident birds, reptiles, and amphibians as well as many of its large mammals (Conservation International 2002). The same year, neighboring Laos, which previously had not maintained any protected areas, established seventeen protected areas covering nearly 24,700 square kilometers, approximately 10 percent of its total land area (Mishra et al. 1997).

In Thailand, meanwhile, the outlook for habitat and species protection is mixed. On the one hand, the government had, by the mid-1990s, extended formal protection to 18 percent of its land area originally covered by rain forest and 13 percent of its total land area. These reserves can be found throughout the country and include several large contiguous areas. In the mid-1990s at least nineteen Thai parks and wildlife sanctuaries exceeded 1,000 square kilometers in area, and six of them—including Khao Yai, Kaeng Krachan, and Huai Kha Khaeng—are more than 2,000 square kilometers in size. In addition, the neighboring Thung Yai Naresuan and Huai Kha Khaeng wildlife sanctuaries effectively constitute a single reserve of nearly 6,500 square kilometers, one of the largest protected areas in Asia (Graham and Round 1994).

But the country's network of protected areas also suffers from widespread illegal exploitation of wildlife, timber resources, and other natural resources (Wikramanayake et al. 2002), and high population densities and growing demand for resource exploitation make it unlikely that large additions to the existing network will be made in the future. "How good is the network? At the moment, it does in fact offer protection to the most significant remaining blocks of forest. But most of the nature reserves are poorly defended 'islands' of forest amid a sea of man-modified, intensively farmed, and unnatural landscape" (Graham and Round 1994).

The Quest to Improve
Asia's Protected Area Networks

Asia enters the twenty-first century engaged in a difficult struggle to balance its understandable ambitions to nourish economic development and provide for its expanding human populations with the need to preserve its natural heritage. And thus far, most area governments have given short shrift to habitat preservation in their pursuit of economic and social advancement. In Thailand, for example, government-sponsored developments ranging from hydroelectric dams to highways have been a perennial scourge to its system of parks and preserves.

> By law, national parks and wildlife sanctuaries are supposedly inviolate from development. Yet dams have already been constructed in many of them and more are planned—some in secret—at several other protected areas. These latter, such as Mae Wong, Khao Yai, and Pang Sida national parks as well as Khao Soi Dao Wildlife Sanctuary, include vital watersheds of the populous central plains and Bangkok. . . .In supporting their proposals, dam proponents claim that only a small proportion of any protected area is inundated. Yet this fails to take into account the fact that it is usually the most valuable single asset of the area, the lowland riverine habitat, which is lost in the construction of dams. . . .The impact of roads in opening up forests is also given scant attention as a setback for conservation. New roads have often led to a flood of illegal settlers entering the heart of an undisturbed forest in order to clear land for farming. Even when this is prevented, new roads increase the susceptibility of forests to fire; give easier access to poachers; and, as is well-documented, are an invitation to illegal loggers. (ibid.)

But Thailand, China, India, Indonesia, Japan, and the other nations of Asia are not without options in their quest to realize a future of environmentally sustainable prosperity. Expansion of existing park systems, carbon credits, conservation performance payments, local guardianship of natural habitats, and privately managed reserves have all been touted as potentially valuable tools in the continent's emerging efforts to establish effective and enduring protected area networks (Wikramanayake et al. 2002).

Certainly, one key to long-term ecosystem protection will be improved management of existing protected areas. Currently, as many as 95 percent of all tropical parks and reserves worldwide are thought to suffer from some degree of poaching (Groombridge 1992), and illegal logging, agricultural encroachment, and other forms of disturbance have long since reached epidemic proportions. "Whatever the form of unwanted human incursion, the general result is a decline in the ecological integrity of protected areas, whereupon their conservation value is reduced. Worse, these derogations of protected status seem to be increasing, largely in response to pressures from multitudes of impoverished peoples—a familiar factor in developing countries" (Myers 1999).

Another key to Asian aspirations of preserving its biological legacy for future generations is expansion of existing protected area networks. Indeed, many conservation biologists see this step as essential to conservation and "perhaps the only hope for the time being of maintaining source pools of species for future restoration efforts and for the survival of species sensitive to disturbance and with restricted distributions" (Wikramanayake et al. 2002). A related goal is for conservation groups and international aid agencies to reach consensus on the efficacy of Integrated Conservation and Development Projects (ICDPs), which seek to combine biodiversity conservation goals with socio-economic development opportunities for local communities. These programs proliferated during the 1980s and 1990s, but concerns have been raised about their environmental impact; it has been claimed that they divert attention away from efforts to establish new protected areas across the continent.

Whatever the ultimate verdict on ICDPs, conservationists need to better address the impact of protected area designations on local, indigenous communities and to incorporate their needs and wants into park and preserve management. In Southeast Asia, for example, the failure to effectively conserve biodiversity often stems from the exclusion of indigenous people from the planning and management of protected areas. "Local people often feel alienated from protected area programs—and, in many cases, have lost their land—largely because such efforts have been spearheaded by central or provincial governments. In many cases, villagers were forced to move to make way for a protected area and, in almost all cases, local residents were expected to curb their traditional uses of protected area resources. . . .Lacking significant involvement in the design and management of protected areas, local people often remain skeptical of the government's capacity to manage local resources on their behalf" (Mishra et al. 1997). It is believed that much of this resentment can be relieved through effective education programs that explain, for instance, how protected areas preserve the watersheds that support the irrigation systems upon which Asian farmers depend.

Still, biologists and conservationists caution that granting complete autonomy to local populaces in resource management is not always desirable, either. "Unfortunately, given growing population pressure, increased access to modern technology, increasing market orientation, and steady erosion of traditional cultures, there no longer are guarantees that biodiversity objectives will be any more likely to be achieved if resource control is placed [exclusively] in the hands of indigenous groups" (Kramer and Schaik 1997).

Some observers have cited ecotourism as another avenue by which conservation groups, biologists, and governments can enlist the willing support of local communities in ecosystem preservation. "A market transformation in the ecotourism industry could further strengthen the involvement of local citizens in protecting wildlife and their habitats," explained one study. "Only operators and concession holders that meet explicit criteria and return a certain percentage of their profits to local community development should be certified. A media campaign could be launched to educate ecotourists about the choices they can make that could have profound benefits for conservation" (Wikramanayake et al. 2002).

Another potential tool in the conservationists' arsenal is the "debt-for-nature" swap, in which rain forests or other vital ecosystems are given protected status in exchange for debt payments or waivers. In the Philippines and several other Asian countries, conservation groups such as the World Wide Fund for Nature have absorbed a portion of national debts in exchange for the institution of new conservation measures (Mishra et al. 1997).

Private management of habitat areas has also drawn increased interest in recent years. In fact, several countries have entrusted protected area management to private institutions or nongovernmental organizations in recent years. In Nepal, for instance, the nonprofit King Mahendra Trust operates the Annapurna Conservation Area, a 260,000-hectare haven for a wide array of flora and fauna. Far to the southeast, meanwhile, four nongovernmental organizations have signed management agreements with the Philippine government to operate Calauit Game Refuge, Iglit Baco National Park, Tubbataba Marine Park, and Bicol National Park (ibid.). And on the Indonesian island of Sumatra, the International Leuser Foundation has taken the reins of the internationally renowned Gunung Leuser National Park. Supported by the European Union (EU), this foundation has received a seven-year concession agreement to manage the 1.8-million-hectare "Leuser ecosystem," which includes not only the

Integrated Conservation and Development Projects

Tourists get an up-close view of a wild rhinoceros while riding an elephant at Chitwan National Park in Nepal. GALEN ROWELL/CORBIS

Integrated Conservation and Development Projects (ICDPs), also known as ecodevelopment projects, attempt to establish a link between conserving biodiversity in protected areas and creating new socioeconomic development opportunities for local communities. ICDPs first gained prominence in the mid-1970s. At that time, governments, environmental groups, and international aid agencies became increasingly cognizant of the problems inherent in establishing protected areas in the developing world, where the poverty of local people made it difficult to enforce the boundaries of parks and preserves. In many areas, the creation of a new protected area involved imposing significant restrictions on the activities of local people who had depended on the land for subsistence for generations. Understandably, local people tended to feel resentful toward such restrictions and ignored them whenever inadequate enforcement made it possible.

ICDPs attempt to address this problem by providing local people with alternative sources of income—such as ecotourism or agriculture—that promote sustainable use of the area's natural resources and create incentives for them to respect the boundaries of protected areas. One common ICDP strategy involves creating a "buffer zone" of compatible human use around protected areas. In exchange for gaining increased economic benefits from development projects in the buffer zone, the local people have to accept restrictions on access and exploitation of the core natural area. These restrictions might include rules about felling trees, hunting, gathering food, and protecting plants and animals.

Soon after their inception, ICDPs came to account for a major portion of international funding for maintaining forest biodiversity. Such projects were consistent with the development-oriented approach favored by many international aid agencies, and they garnered praise on humanitarian grounds for their emphasis on improving the living conditions of local people while also preserving biodiversity. In addition, the ICDP approach gained the support of many conservation organizations seeking ways to ease development pressure on protected areas around the world.

Beginning in the late 1980s, however, a number of problems became apparent in the implementation of ICDPs. Although the concept continued to hold appeal for many people, it gradually lost some support because of the disappointing results of numerous projects. One expert called ICDPs "experimental, complex, and generally very expensive undertakings," and noted that it was "unclear whether ICDPs, although motivated by humanitarian instincts, are the right vehicle to achieve either development or conservation" (Brandon 1997).

One common problem with ICDPs is that, regardless of the fact that they have alternative sources of income, local people often continue to pose a threat to the biodiversity of protected areas through hunting or collecting. In addition, some development projects actually create incentives for local people to expand buffer zones into protected areas. Another problem with the ICDP approach is that it addresses only local threats to biodiversity, when sometimes the most significant threats come from the outside. Furthermore, ICDPs require a long-term commitment of funding and resources in order to be successful. That tends to limit the effectiveness of such projects in protected areas that face immediate threats. Another problem is that authorities often lack the staff and budget to manage ICDPs successfully. Finally, some biologists claim that the emphasis on ICDPs has led to a steep decline in the number of new protected areas established in Asia since 1990.

Despite the host of concerns associated with ICDPs, however, the approach has yielded a few notable success stories, including Chitwan National Park in Nepal. The area surrounding Chitwan was the site of a series of development projects aimed at helping local communities reclaim pasturelands for forest. As a result of these projects, wildlife habitat increased and poaching pressure on the park decreased. In addition, the regenerated areas have been used as breeding grounds by tigers and rhinoceros, which has allowed the local communities to gain revenue through ecotourism. Although ICDPs played a role in protecting the biodiversity in Chitwan, some analysts claim that it was strict enforcement of the park's borders that ensured the presence of megafauna, which in turn made the tourism revenue possible.

Sources:

Brandon, Katrina. 1997. "Policy and Practical Considerations in Land-Use Strategies for Biodiversity Conservation." In Randall Kramer, Carel van Schaik, and Julie Johnson, eds., *Last Stand: Protected Areas and the Defense of Tropical Biodiversity.* New York: Oxford University Press.

"Conceptual Background." Biodiversity Conservation Network web site (http://www.bcnet.org/bsp/bcn/about/paradigm.htm).

Loucks, Colby, and Eric Dinerstein. 2002. "Protected Areas: Keystones to the Conservation of Asia's Natural Wealth." In Eric Wikramanayake, Eric Dinerstein, and Colby J. Loucks, eds., *Terrestrial Ecoregions of the Indo-Pacific: A Conservation Assessment.* Washington, DC: Island.

national park but also a huge buffer zone surrounding the park boundary. Under this arrangement, management costs are divided up between the EU and the Indonesian government's Restoration Fund. According to one conservation group, this arrangement has created the potential for perhaps "the best management ever for the beleaguered park, which had experienced decades of poor or no management and as a result had suffered all manner of encroachments" (Mittermeier et al. 1999).

Analysts also believe that the looming threat of climate change actually provides intriguing forest conservation opportunities for Asian nations. Intact forest areas act as "carbon sinks," holding carbon dioxide that would otherwise enter the atmosphere and contribute to global warming. International treaties that provide economic incentives for the maintenance of forest cover might be embraced by numerous countries in Asia and elsewhere. To ensure that carbon sink forests and their ecological processes are kept intact, however, strict regulations on road-building and other forms of development would have to be incorporated into any agreement (Wikramanayake et al. 2002).

Finally, conservation groups, wildlife biologists, and other interested constituencies have urged Asian governments to create wildlife corridors that connect protected areas that are currently isolated from one another. "Island-like nature reserves generally support fewer species than the original forest areas of which they are the remnants," explained one analysis. "Moreover, the farther apart these islands of protected forest are, the less likely it is that their populations of species will intermingle. Even such ostensibly mobile creatures as forest birds disperse only to a limited extent across open, cultivated, or de-forested expanses" (Graham and Round 1994).

One of the most ambitious efforts to connect isolated protected areas is taking place in India and Nepal. There, government agencies and interna-tional conservation groups are working together to link eleven individual re-serves that are home to dwindling populations of tigers, greater one-horned rhinoceros, and Asian elephants. These protected areas—Royal Bardia National Park, Royal Chitwin National Park, Koshi Tappu Wildlife Reserve, Parasa Wildlife Reserve and Royal Sukla Phanta Wildlife Reserve in Nepal, and Sohelwa Wildlife Sanctuary, Katarniaghat Wildlife Sanctuary, Dudhwa National Park, Kishanpur Wildlife Sanctuary, Valmiki Wildlife Sanctuary, and Corbett National Park in India—are already invaluable bastions of wilder-ness. But supporters of ecoregion-scale conservation schemes say that corri-dors of restored forest can be used to link these parks together into an unbroken "Terai Arc Wildlife Corridor," creating an immense network of habitat large enough for the long-term survival of tigers, elephants, and other wide-ranging mammals. Biologists and conservationists acknowledge that creation of the Terai Arc Wildlife Corridor faces daunting obstacles, including heavy human population densities, competition from acquisitive farming in-terests for control of undeveloped corridor areas, and limited governmental resources for corridor management and defense. But scientists hasten to add that "the long history of conservation activities in the Terai Arc, the strict pro-tection of core areas, and the encouraging success of local guardianship of buffer zones suggest that if we devote enough effort and resources to this proj-ect, we can safeguard one of the most spectacular wildlands on Earth. That this can be achieved in a place as impoverished and degraded as the Terai sug-gests that large landscapes in less populated and more prosperous areas in the Indo-Pacific are also possible" (Wikramanayake et al. 2002).

Sources:

Asian Bureau for Conservation and World Conservation Monitoring Centre. 1997. *Protected Areas Systems Review of the Indo-Malayan Realm.* Edited by J. MacKinnon. Canterbury, England: ABC and WCMC.

Barber, Charles Victor, et al. 2002. *The State of the Forest: Indonesia.* Washington, DC: Global Forest Watch, World Resources Institute, and Forest Watch Indonesia.

Braatz, S. 1992. *Conserving Biological Diversity: A Strategy for Protected Areas in the Asia-Pacific Region.* Washington, DC: World Bank.

Bryant, Dirk. 1997. *The Last Frontier Forests: Ecosystems and Economies on the Edge.* Washington, DC: World Resources Institute.

Child, Gil. 1984. "FAO and Protected Areas Management." In J. A. McNeely and Kenton Miller, eds., *National Parks, Conservation and Development: The Role of Protected Areas in Sustaining Society.* Washington, DC: Smithsonian Institution Press.

Collins, N. M., J. A. Sayer, and T. C. Whitmore. 1991. *The Conservation Atlas of Tropical Forests: Asia and the Pacific.* London: Macmillan.

Conservation International. 2002. "Cambodia," http//www.conservation.org/xp/CIWEB/regions/asia_pacific/cambodia (accessed July 2002).

Cracroft, Joel, and Francesca T. Grifo. 1999. *The Living Planet in Crisis: Biodiversity Science and Policy.* New York: Columbia University Press.

Department of Environment and Natural Resources (Philippines) and UN Environment Programme. 1997. *Philippine Biodiversity: An Assessment and Plan of Action.* Makati City, Philippines: DENR and UNEP.

A Global Overview of Forest Protected Areas on the World Heritage List. 1997. Gland, Switzerland: World Conservation Union-IUCN and World Conservation Monitoring Centre, September.

A Global Overview of Wetland and Marine Protected Areas on the World Heritage List. 1997. Gland, Switzerland: World Conservation Union-IUCN and World Conservation Monitoring Centre, September.

Graham, Mark, and Philip Round. 1994. *Thailand's Vanishing Flora and Fauna.* Bangkok: Finance One.

Gray, D., C. Piprell, and M. Graham. 1994. *National Parks of Thailand.* Bangkok: Industrial Finance Corp.

Green, Michael J. B. 1994. *Nature Reserves of the Himalayas.* Oxford: Oxford University Press.

Green, Michael J. B., and James Paine. 1997. "State of the World's Protected Areas at the End of the Twentieth Century." Paper presented at IUCN World Commission on Protected Areas Symposium, Albany, Australia, November.

Groombridge, B., ed. 1992. *Global Biodiversity: Status of the Earth's Living Resources.* London: Chapman and Hall.

Honey, Martha S. 1999. "Treading Lightly? Ecotourism's Impact on the Environment." *Environment* 41, no. 5 (June).

Kramer, Randall, and Carel P. von Schaik. 1997. "Preservation Paradigms and Tropical Rain Forests." In Randall Kramer, Carel P. van Schaik, and Julie Johnson, eds., *Last Stand: Protected Areas and the Defense of Tropical Biodiversity.* New York: Oxford University Press.

Kramer, Randall, Carel P. van Schaik, and Julie Johnson, eds. 1997. *Last Stand: Protected Areas and the Defense of Tropical Biodiversity.* New York: Oxford University Press.

Loucks, Colby, and Eric Dinerstein. 2002. "Protected Areas: Keystones to the Conservation of Asia's Natural Wealth." In Eric Wikramanayake et al., eds.,

Terrestrial Ecoregions of the Indo-Pacific: A Conservation Assessment. Washington, DC: Island.

Mackay, Richard. 2002. *Atlas of Endangered Species: Threatened Plants and Animals of the World.* London: Earthscan.

MacKinnon, J., and Kathy MacKinnon. 1986. *Review of the Protected Areas System in the Indo-Malayan Realm.* Gland, Switzerland: IUCN.

MacKinnon, J., et al. 1996. *A Biodiversity Review of China.* Hong Kong: WWF International.

Mishra, Hemanta R., Jeffrey A. McNeely, and J. W. Thorsell. 1997. "Tropical Asia Protects Its Natural Resources." *Forum for Applied Research and Public Policy* 12 (summer).

Mittermeier, Russell A., Patricio Robles Gil, and Cristina Goettsch Mittermeier. 1998. *Megadiversity: Earth's Biologically Wealthiest Nations.* Mexico City: CEMEX.

Mittermeier, Russell A., Norman Myers, and Cristina Goettsch Mittermeier. 1999. *Hotspots: Earth's Biologically Richest and Most Endangered Terrestrial Ecoregions.* Mexico City: CEMEX, Conservation International.

Myers, Norman. 1999. "Saving Biodiversity and Saving the Biosphere." In Joel Cracroft and Francesca T. Grifo, eds., *The Living Planet in Crisis: Biodiversity Science and Policy.* New York: Columbia University Press.

Rodgers, W. A., H. S. Panwar, and V. B. Mathur. 2000. *Wildlife Protected Area Network in India: A Review.* Dehra Dun: Wildlife Institute of India.

Soulé, Michael E., and John Terborgh. 1999. *Continental Conservation: Scientific Foundations of Regional Reserve Networks.* Washington, DC: Island.

State Environmental Protection Administration of China. 1996. *Report on the State of the Environment in China.* Beijing: SEPA.

Terborgh, John. 1992. *Diversity and the Tropical Rain Forest.* New York: Freeman.

UN Environment Programme. 2000. *Asia-Pacific Environment Outlook.* UNEP.

———. 1999. *Global Environment Outlook 2000.* London: Earthscan.

UN Food and Agriculture Organization. 2001. *State of the World's Forests 2001.* Rome: FAO.

Van Schaik, Carel P., and Randall Kramer. 1997. "Toward a New Protection Paradigm." In Randall Kramer, Carl van Schaik, and Julie Johnson, eds., *Last Stand: Protected Areas and the Defense of Tropical Biodiversity.* New York: Oxford University Press.

Van Schaik, Carel P., John Terborgh, and Barbara Dugelby. 1997. "The Silent Crisis: The State of Rain Forest Nature Preserves." In Randall Kramer, Carl van Schaik, and Julie Johnson, eds., *Last Stand: Protected Areas and the Defense of Tropical Biodiversity.* New York: Oxford University Press.

Wells, Michael, and Katrina Brandon. 1992. *People and Parks: Linking Protected Area Management with Local Communities.* Washington, DC: World Bank.

Wikramanayake, Eric, et al. 2002. *Terrestrial Ecoregions of the Indo-Pacific: A Conservation Assessment.* Washington, DC: Island.

Wood, Alexander, Pamela Stedman-Edwards, and Johanna Mang. 2001. *The Root Causes of Biodiversity Loss.* London: Earthscan.

World Commission on Protected Areas. 2002a. "East Asia," http://wcpa.iucn.org/region/ easia/easia.html (accessed July 2002).

———. 2002b. "North Eurasia," http://wcpa.iucn.org/region/neurasia/neurasia.html (accessed July 2002).

———. 2002c. "South Asia," http://wcpa.iucn.org/region/sasia/sasia.html (accessed July 2002).

———. 2002d. "Southeast Asia," http://wcpa.iucn.org/region/seasia/seasia.html (accessed July 2002).

World Conservation Union. 1997. *Action Plan for the Southeast Asia Region of the World Commission on Protected Areas.* Gland, Switzerland: IUCN.

———. 1991. *1992 Protected Areas of the World: A Review of National Systems.* Gland, Switzerland: IUCN.

———. 1998. *1997 United Nations List of Protected Areas.* Gland, Switzerland: IUCN.

———. 1996. *Regional Action Plan for Protected Areas in East Asia.* Gland, Switzerland: IUCN.

———. 1998. *Regional Action Plan for Protected Areas in South Asia.* Gland, Switzerland: IUCN.

World Resources Institute. 2000. *World Resources 2000–2001: People and Ecosystems: The Fraying Web of Life.* Washington, DC: UN Environment Programme.

World Wide Fund for Nature and World Conservation Union. 2001. *Metals from the Forest.* Gland, Switzerland: WWF and IUCN.

Forests
—WILLIAM BENTLEY

Asia is home to vast forests of stunning variety and biological richness, including tropical rain forests that hold some of the planet's greatest concentrations of endangered and endemic species. But this invaluable resource has suffered tremendous degradation in many areas of the continent, destroying some regional ecosystems and placing numerous others at significant risk. Analysts contend that pressure on forest resources from Asia's rapidly growing human populations and economic expansion must be curtailed to ensure the future vitality of forest ecosystems.

Deforestation in Asia

The continent of Asia (excluding the Middle East—also known as West Asia—which is covered in the Africa and the Middle East volume of this series) encompasses more than 2.386 billion hectares, or 5.89 billion acres (including the Middle East, the land area of Asia reaches 3.085 billion hectares, or 7.64 billion acres). Forests cover about 548 million hectares of Asia's total land area (Middle East included), about 18 percent of the continent's terrestrial total and 14 percent of the world forest total. Asia also holds about 21 percent of the world's tropical rain forests, primarily in Southeast Asia, as well as about one-third of the planet's subtropical mountain forests (UN Food and Agriculture Organization 2001).

UN surveys of Asian forests indicate that the continent lost 364,000 hectares of forest annually from 1990 to 2000, an annual decrease of 0.02 percent. The nations that showed the largest annual percentage declines were Nepal, with a yearly decrease of 78,000 hectares, or 1.8 percent; Pakistan, with an annual loss of 39,000 hectares, or 1.5 percent; Myanmar, with a yearly decrease of 517,000 hectares, or 1.4 percent; and the Philippines, with an annual loss of 89,000 hectares, or 1.4 percent. The steepest decline in land area covered by forest occurred in Indonesia, which lost 1.3 million hectares per year

A dirt road cuts into the remote West Kalimantan rain forest in Borneo to provide access for loggers.
WAYNE LAWLER; ECOSCENE/CORBIS

over the course of the decade. China showed the largest increase in forested land area, with a gain of 1.8 million hectares annually, primarily from its plantation operations (ibid.).

Forest loss in Asia is directly linked to rapid growth in its human communities. Asia contains more than 3.5 billion people, more than half the current world population. Two Asian countries—China and India—hold more than one-third of the global population, with each nation accounting for more than 1 billion people (UN Economic and Social Commission for Asia and the Pacific 2002). These human populations are pressing against the forest resource base throughout the region, and in many cases they are harvesting ecologically vital forests at wildly unsustainable rates.

Among the subregions of Asia, Southeast Asia continues to demonstrate the worst rate of deforestation, with the nations with the greatest forest wealth showing the highest rates of deforestation. The island nations of Southeast Asia (Malaysia, Indonesia, and the Philippines) are losing forest area at a particularly appalling rate, while continental Southeast Asian nations appear to have reduced some logging pressure through increased investment in plantations. In South Asia, India and Bangladesh have stopped the net loss of forest area with their plantation and protection programs, but Pakistan and Sri Lanka are still losing about 1.5 percent of their forest area every year, and Nepal is nearing 2 percent (UN Food and Agriculture Organization 2001).

The causes of deforestation in Asia are many. The most obvious is human population, which is high throughout most regions of Asia. Steadily expanding communities harvest timber, cut fuelwood and tree fodder, graze animals, and cause direct destruction with fire. The consequences of these activities are further exacerbated by meager reforestation efforts.

Population trends are further exacerbated by poverty and the uneven distribution of wealth and assets that characterizes rural and urban poverty (Bentley and Gowen 1994). Poor people cannot invest anything except their labor, and that is often directed toward short-term survival (Bentley et al. 1985). Concerns about rare and endangered species and ecosystem preservation often develop only after people achieve sufficient wealth to move beyond subsistence lifestyles. Some observers believe that when ownership of forests is transferred to local communities, they can be made very productive

China's Great Green Wall

China has experienced seasonal sandstorms for centuries. Each spring, winds from Siberia sweep southward across the Gobi Desert and pick up sand, which they deposit in northern China or carry out over the Pacific Ocean. These sandstorms have become increasingly troublesome in recent years because of deforestation of the arid lands in northern China. The conversion of land to agricultural use—as well as the degradation of that land through overgrazing, overcultivation, and poor irrigation practices—has removed the forest barriers that once blocked the wind and added to the volume of materials it carries. These factors have increased the intensity and frequency of the sandstorms, which are costly for Chinese citizens and for the environment.

Beijing, located 300 miles downwind of the Gobi Desert, receives nearly 1 million tons of windborne sand each year. The sand reduces visibility and affects transportation and human health in the Chinese capital. In addition, the sandstorms contribute to desertification: the desert, which currently covers 27 percent of China, is advancing at a rate of 950 square miles per year. Overall, the effects of sandstorms cost the Chinese economy about $6.5 billion per year ("Sandstorms and Deforestation Allow Desert Areas to Expand into China's Farmland," 2002).

In an attempt to mitigate the effects of these sandstorms, the Chinese government started the Great Green Wall project in 1978. This project involves planting a barrier of trees stretching 4,480 kilometers (2,800 miles) along the northwest rim of China. During the first phase of the program, which came to an end in 2001, the government planted hundreds of millions of trees (mostly Chinese elms) along the border. The second phase of the project will extend through 2050. Scientists hope that the Great Green Wall will halt the spread of the desert and help repair damage to the land. The Chinese government also announced an antidesertification program for Beijing, with a goal of doubling forest coverage around the city from 13.4 percent of total land area to 27 percent by 2005 ("China's Great Green Wall Taking Early Shape," 2001).

Although many environmentalists have praised China's afforestation efforts, some scientists worry that the Great Green Wall might actually create problems elsewhere. The dust from Gobi sandstorms—which can rise four miles above the ground—has historically traveled far out over the Pacific Ocean. These dust particles assist in the condensation of water vapor, which forms clouds. When the clouds release the particles in the form of rain, that rain supplies the ocean with nutrients that support the growth of phytoplankton. Some scientists suggest that studies are needed to uncover the long-term effects of dust reduction on these plants, which form the base of the marine food chain. Concerns have been raised that milder storms might reduce precipitation levels, which might in turn affect marine biology.

Sources:

"China's Great Green Wall." 2001. *BBC News Online,* March 3, http://news. bbc.co.uk/low/english/world/ monitoring/media_reports/newsid_ 1199000/.

"China's Great Green Wall Taking Early Shape." 2001. *Xinhua News Agency,* March 1.

"Sandstorms and Deforestation Allow Desert Areas to Expand into China's Farmland." 2002. *Panda Web,* March 25, http://pandas.si.edu/chinanews/ 032502sandstorms.htm.

in sustainable ways that demonstrate the potential of people enhance their own welfare while also caring for natural resources (ibid.). To achieve that goal, though, instituting economic incentives for adhering to sustainable models of forest stewardship is essential.

Indeed, indeterminate property rights can be critical to gaining an understanding of deforestation in Asia and the rest of the world (Bentley et al. 1987; Burch and Parker 1991). Asia, like Europe, experienced centuries of feudal relationships between local kings or lords and the rural peasants. Forests were generally reserved for royalty. Although commercial timber sometimes was important, hunting rights were more often the important forest resource. Poaching was the most critical form of theft. Throughout Asia, stories like the legend of Robin Hood are told of bandits who lived off the king's game. Today, most public forests in Asia are not well protected, and many of the concessionaire schemes used to allocate timber and grazing rights encourage overharvesting (Bentley and Gowen 1994).

But another traditional feature in Asia has been the local right to utilize forest areas for fuelwood, small building materials, fodder, and grazing (Bentley et al. 1987). Often elaborate social mechanisms developed to protect the forests from poaching and other forms of intrusion. These traditional tenurial rights and property rights provide lessons that are helpful in designing new social mechanisms. They underpin the faith given to local participation in forest management decisions and implementation. Adherents to this perspective assert that an emphasis on this sort of community-oriented management model can lead to reforestation, forest rehabilitation, afforestation, and other investment for the long-term benefit of both individuals and societies.

Major Ecological Regions of Asia

The forests of Asia are far from homogeneous. They range from rich tropical humid jungles to alpine conifers to desert shrubs. The plant and animal life in these forests is remarkable—species by species, as well as the total diversity within and across ecological zones. The same tropical nations that exhibit high rates of deforestation are also home to the most plant and animal species diversity. Not surprisingly, these same forests are where the most species are in danger of extinction.

All told, Asia contains four major ecological regions: tropical, which comprises 1,079 million hectares (2,580 million acres); subtropical, with 838 million hectares (2,011 million acres); temperate, 1,226 million hectares (2,942 million acres); and boreal, 17 million hectares (41 million acres). Asian forests are slightly more temperate than tropical, with almost another third falling within the subtropical ecological zone. Boreal forests make up only a small portion of Asia's total forest area (UN Food and Agriculture Organization 2001).

The tropical ecological zone is defined by closeness to the equator. It includes the tropical rain forest, which is commonly regarded as characteristic of this zone. There is no dry season in most equatorial lowlands—and only a short dry season elsewhere—while temperatures are always high. However, the tropical zone also includes several other subzones: moist forest, dry, shrub, desert, and mountain. Annual rainfall, rainfall patterns, and elevation are as critical as the angle of the tropic sun in defining the tropical zone.

The tropical rain forest includes the southwestern coasts of India and Sri Lanka, Myanmar and the eastern Himalayan foothills, the coastal lowlands of Southeast Asia, the Philippines, and most of the Malay Archipelago. Although not as concentrated as the rain forests of South America or central Africa, Asian tropical rain forests make up more than 20 percent of the world total. The 303 million hectares of rain forest are concentrated in Southeast Asia (271 million hectares), with the remaining 31 million hectares in South Asia.

In the wettest parts of the zone the vegetation type is dense moist evergreen forest. The dipterocarps (hardwood species that dominate lowland evergreen forests in Southeast Asia) are found only to the west of Wallace's Line, the approximate dividing line between Asian and Australian fauna in the Malay Archipelago. Teak and sal are among the best known of this group of tropical timbers. The mangrove forests of the Ganges Delta and western New Guinea are the most extensive in the world. Eastern Indonesia and the Himalayan foothills support semideciduous or moist deciduous forests. These include the valuable sal forests of Bangladesh. The Malay Archipelago supports the most complex rain forests. The rich flora on these islands includes more than half (220) of the world's flowering plant families and about one-quarter of the plant genera (2,400), 40 percent of which are endemic. This floral bounty includes 25,000 to 30,000 species of trees (ibid.).

Traditional Forestry and the Colonial Heritage

The forests of Asia have been a source of food and raw materials since the first human settlements. The history of Asian forests is much like that of European forests since empires formed. Forests traditionally were owned by kings or emperors and protected largely for hunting. Local peasants had rights to gather fuelwood or small building materials in most locales. The more isolated and often the poorer the circumstances, the more control local people had over the forest (Bentley and Gowen 1994).

Waves of invasions swept much of Asia, but the wave of European colonization had a higher impact. Europeans often began exercising power during periods of weakness in the local sovereign. The British gained control over India, for example, as the Mughal Empire crumbled. China fell under European domination during a period of weakness (Landes 1998).

Europe began to outstrip Asia in economic wealth, growth, and appetite for raw materials and markets in the 1700s. Forests were taking on commercial value for timber, especially lumber for export. As forests increased in value, the colonial rulers imported

The tropical moist deciduous forest includes lowlands of Sri Lanka; peninsular India away from the coast; the hilly basin of Burma; the Red River valley, lower foothills, and low plateaus on the western Annamitic Range in Vietnam; Laos and Cambodia; the plains and western foothills of the Philippines; the low, often swampy plains of southern New Guinea; and parts of Hainan Island and the Lezhou Peninsula in China. Annual rainfall generally ranges between 1,000 and 2,000 millimeters (mm), with a three- to six-month dry season. Temperatures are always high, with the lowest mean winter temperature of 20 degrees Celsius. The natural vegetation, meanwhile, is mostly deciduous or semideciduous forest. These include the teak forests of Thailand, Laos, Burma, and peninsular India. The sal forests in eastern India and the Ganges valley are of great economic value. Bamboo brakes are common in India and Burma.

The tropical dry forest covers the coastal plains along the Gulf of Bengal and the northeastern part of the Deccan Plateau in India and Sri Lanka. In Burma, it includes the basin around Mandalay. The zone occupies the wide, flat alluvial basin of the Chao Phraya River in Thailand as well as the Korat Plateau and the Mekong River valley. In Cambodia, tropical dry forest composes the whole low central plain built by the lower Mekong River and the

ideas on how to manage forest resources, most often from Germany. However, the enormous distances between the timber and export markets required different administrative arrangements. In India, an organizational system was developed to administer and manage forests across the subcontinent by Dietrich Brandis, a Prussian forester who was the first inspector general of forests. The system persists to the present day. Brandis's idea was adapted to U.S. conditions and remains the basic organizational structure of the U.S. Forest Service. With further adaptations, the idea moved to Canada, then to Australia and New Zealand. These experiments in turn influenced the structure of the Royal Commission of Forestry in the United Kingdom after World War I.

Sources:

Bentley, W. R., and M. M. Gowen, eds. 1994. *Forest Resources and Wood-Based Biomass Energy as Rural Development Assets.* Winrock/Oxford and IBH.

Landes, D. L. 1998. *The Wealth and Poverty of Nations: Why Some Are So Rich and Some So Poor.* New York: W. W. Norton.

Wikramanayake, Eric, et al. 2002. *Terrestrial Ecoregions of the Indo-Pacific: A Conservation Assessment.* Washington, DC: Island.

Tonle Sap. The Mekong delta in Vietnam is part of this zone. Narrow coastal stretches also occur in southern Papua New Guinea. Dry evergreen forest occurs on the eastern Coromandel Coast of India and in northern Sri Lanka. Dry deciduous dipterocarp forests and woodlands are common throughout Vietnam, Laos, Cambodia, and Thailand. Mixed deciduous woodlands are found in Thailand, Myanmar, the Lao People's Democratic Republic, and Vietnam. In India, woodlands are also common, but only a few dipterocarps occur, notably sal.

These areas are sheltered from the humid winds blowing from the oceans and only partially receive the southwest monsoon in summer. In winter they are influenced by the dry winds of the northeast monsoon. Rainfall ranges between 1,000 and 1,500 mm, with a dry season of five to eight months. Mean temperature of the coldest month is always above 15 degrees Celsius.

Tropical mountain systems include the eastern Himalayas; mountains stretching from Tibet to northern Indochina, the Malaysian Peninsula, and the Annamitic Range; the central mountain ranges of the islands of Indonesia and the Philippines; and relatively high peaks (over 2,000 meters) in India and Sri Lanka.

Most tropical mountains of Asia reaching at least 1,500 to 2,000 meters have a wet climate. The Himalayas have a subtropical northwestern part and a tropical wet southeastern part. Nepal is a transitional region between these two areas. In tropical mountains between 1,000 and 4,000 meters, the annual precipitation exceeds 1,000 mm and may be more than 2,000 mm. There are two rainy seasons, March to April and July to September.

The subtropical humid forest occurs in southeastern China below the Yangtze River, the southern tip of the Republic of Korea, and the southern half of Japan. There are two distinct small geographic units in the Near East, one in the Caucasus Mountains and the other in the foothills of the Talysh Mountains at the Caspian Sea. Winters are mild to warm and summers are hot and wet. Northerly cold fronts from Siberia heavily influence winter temperatures, while Pacific monsoons bring large amounts of precipitation to the region in the summer. Annual rainfall diminishes toward the west, away from the coast. The southern part of the zone in China includes one of the most important bamboo regions in the world. The island of Taiwan is under the strong influence of the maritime monsoon climate, with higher average temperatures and greater rainfall. The climate in Japan is greatly influenced by the monsoon. Generally speaking, the summers are very hot and the winters rather cold, with snow and frosts.

The subtropical dry forest zone is confined to the Near East. It makes up a narrow belt along the Mediterranean Sea and the low hills running parallel to the coast. The northern part of the Jordan-Arava Rift Valley is included. The zone has a typical Mediterranean climate with mild, humid winters and dry, moderately hot summers. Annual rainfall ranges from around 400 to 800 mm, decreasing from north to south. Various types of pine forest characterize the zone, with oak woodlands in the lower elevations.

The subtropical steppe can be found in western Asia, including the Near East, Afghanistan, and Pakistan. The climate is semiarid. Annual rainfall ranges from about 200 to 500 mm and falls during winter in the Near East. Eastern Afghanistan and Pakistan receive most of their rainfall from June to September. Winters are not severe, but summer heat creates a difficult environment for trees. Low shrubs and grasses are interspersed with sparse trees on the wetter sites. At higher and more humid elevations, a forest steppe can be found. Pakistan has a woody steppe vegetation of shrubs (acacias and oleander) and small trees.

Subtropical mountain systems form a nearly continuous west-east belt from the mountains and highlands of Turkey to the eastern reaches of the Himalayas in southern China. The climate of the Near Eastern mountain systems is extremely diverse, both in temperature and rainfall. Winter precipitation is predominant, ranging from 500 to 1,400 mm. The rainy season generally runs from September to May or June, while the rest of the summer is dry and hot. Along the Himalayas, rainfall increases from west to east, and the climatic regime changes gradually from Mediterranean to summer monsoon types. The rainfall decreases from the outer to the inner ranges. At the submontane and montane levels, rainfall ranges from less than 1,000 to 1,500 mm, with at least one or two dry months and possibly up to seven or eight. The mean temperature of the coldest month varies from around 15 degrees Celsius in the submontane zone to less than 10 degrees Celsius above 2,000 meters. Snow occurs above 3,000 meters, with frequent winter frost.

The subtropical mountain zone in northeastern China features well-stocked pine and spruce mixed forests on low mountains of 400 to 600 meters. Associated species include true firs, birch, oaks, maples, elms, and walnuts. Over the rest of the zone in China, however, there is little remaining forest. In contrast, the temperate forests of Japan are deciduous, summer-green, broad-leaved forests dominated by beech.

The temperate steppe consists of the vast steppes of Central Asia, including Inner Mongolia in China and central and eastern Mongolia. The zone has a long, cold winter and a short, warm summer. Annual average temperatures vary between 2 and 10 degrees Celsius, with mean temperatures ranging from −10 to −20 degrees Celsius in the coldest winter month and reaching 24 degrees Celsius in the warmest summer month. The growing season lasts 100 to 175 days. Annual rainfall ranges from 200 to 400 mm, locally up to 600 mm. The maximum rainfall occurs during the second half of summer, while spring is dry. The natural vegetation is primarily grass and shrub steppe, but pockets of woodland can be found. Tree species are pine, larch, and some firs. Poplars and birches are the common hardwoods.

The vast mountain systems of Central Asia, including the Tibetan Plateau in China and the Altai and Khangai mountain systems of Mongolia, make up the temperate mountain ecological zone. The mountains of Japan also form part of this zone. Mean annual temperatures and extreme winter temperatures follow an elevation gradient. Annual mean precipitation follows an east-west gradient from 800 mm on the eastern rim of the plateau to less than 50 mm in the west near the Pakistan-Afghanistan border.

The boreal coniferous forest is confined to the northern part of northeastern China. This zone can be found around Daxinganling (the Greater Xingan Range), a medium-altitude plateau. The zone has a rigorous climate with a long, cold winter. Mean annual temperature ranges between −1 and −6 degrees Celsius, with the mean minimum of the coldest month below −25 degrees Celsius and the extreme low below −45 degrees Celsius. Soils are either permafrost or frozen for most of the year. Relatively warm summers bring a monthly mean temperature of 15 degrees Celsius in the warmest months, with a growing season of about 90 days. Most of the annual mean precipitation of 500 mm falls during the summer season. Natural forests in this zone are simple stands of larch or pine with some birch and poplar.

Asia Forest Resources by Subregion

The forests of Asia fall into four major regions: Central Asia (Kazakhstan, Kyrgyzstan, Mongolia, Tajikistan, Turkmenistan, and Uzbekistan); South Asia (Bangladesh, Bhutan, India, Maldives, Nepal, Pakistan, and Sri Lanka); Southeast Asia (Brunei Darussalam, Cambodia, East Timor, Indonesia, Lao People's Democratic Republic, Malaysia, Myanmar, the Philippines, Singapore, Thailand, and Vietnam); and East Asia (China, Democratic People's Republic of Korea, Japan, and Republic of Korea). (A fifth region—West Asia or the Middle East—is discussed in the Africa and the Middle East volume of this series.) See Table 4.1 for detailed statistics on forest resources by subregion.

Details of each region reveal the diversity of forests and their ecological and social environments. Over all of Asia, the continent's 548 million hectares of forest represent less than 18 percent of the total land area. But some nations still retain much of their original forest or have augmented their forest totals with significant plantation operations. For example, Brunei Darussalam has almost 84 percent forest cover, Bhutan has 64 percent, and the Koreas have well over 50 percent. Much of Southeast Asia has been heavily logged, but extensive

Table 4.1 Asia: Forest Resources by Subregion

Subregion	Land area	Forest area 2000					Area change 1990–2000 (total forest)		Volume and above-ground biomass (total forest)	
		Natural forest	Forest plantation	Total forest						
	000 ha	000 ha	000 ha	000 ha	%	ha/ capita	000 ha/ year	%	m³/ha	t/ha
Central Asia	545 407	29 536	384	29 920	5.5	0.5	208	0.7	62	40
East Asia	992 309	146 254	55 765	202 019	20.4	0.1	1 805	0.9	62	62
South Asia	412 917	42 013	34 652	76 665	18.6	0.1	–98	–0.1	49	77
Southeast Asia	436 022	191 942	19 972	211 914	48.6	0.4	–2 329	–1.0	64	109
West Asia/ Middle East	698 091	22 202	5 073	27 275	3.9	0.1	48	0.2	101	87
Total Asia	3 084 746	431 946	115 847	547 793	17.8	0.2	–364	–0.1	63	82
Total World:	*13 063 900*	*3 682 722*	*186 733*	*3 869 455*	*29.6*	*0.6*	*–9 391*	*–0.2*	*100*	*109*

SOURCE: Food and Agriculture Organization of the United Nations

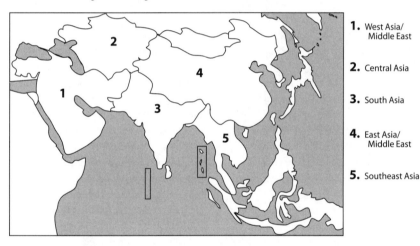

1. West Asia/ Middle East

2. Central Asia

3. South Asia

4. East Asia/ Middle East

5. Southeast Asia

plantation operations have given boosts in technical forest cover. Indeed, Asia leads the world in forest plantations, with more than 60 percent of the international total. The continent's total of almost 116 million hectares is increasing at a rate of more than 3 percent each year. China has over 45 million hectares of forest plantations, while India is approaching 33 million hectares. Several West Asian nations started out with no natural forests and created forest resources with plantations. The main tree species groups that are grown on plantations in Asia include pine, at 15.5 million hectares; other conifers, at 19.9 million hectares; eucalyptus, at 11 million hectares; rubber, at 9 million hectares; and other broad-leaved species, at 31.5 million hectares (ibid.).

Agroforestry and Social Forestry

Asia is the source of many old ideas that now are emerging as new social arrangements and land-use technologies. One of the most interesting is agroforestry. Agroforestry is the deliberate mixing of food crops with trees, generally close together, as in intercropping (Gordon and Bentley 1990). Sometimes the agroforestry mix is performed in cycles. The best known is swidden or "slash and burn" agriculture. Trees rehabilitate the soil after cropping, especially in terms of organic matter and nitrogen, and then these nutrients are released by cutting the trees and burning the slash. Proponents say that if the cycles are long enough, this can be a sound ecological method of managing tropical soils on a sustainable basis.

An even more important idea is social forestry or community forestry (Burch and Parker 1992). Community forestry describes arrangements under which local villages or groups own forest resources or jointly manage them with government forestry agencies. Formal and informal arrangements give villagers access and even ownership of the forest resources. The key to success is the guarantee of these rights, including enforcement should other private interests or government try to abridge them. When fully operative, these social arrangements allow for rehabilitation of degraded forest and grasslands, plantations to produce fuelwood and small building materials, and movement toward sustainable systems. Several experiments also have demonstrated equity improvement with distribution of new benefits toward the poorer members of a community.

Rehabilitation will be a major purpose of forestry activities for the first several decades of the twenty-first century. Ideally, replanting trees and perennial grasses, removing weed species, building soil and water conservation structures, and many other tasks will employ many people and provide enormous private and social benefits. The keys to making rehabilitation a reality are adequate financing, improved property rights, and enforcement that is fair to rich and poor alike.

Plantations are important for several reasons. Often located on highly disturbed sites, single- or mixed-species

The forest area per capita is not high in Asia, with an average of only 0.2 hectares per person (ibid.). Even where forests are common, high human populations generally mean low forest areas per capita. The notable exceptions are Bhutan, Brunei, Mongolia, and Laos, where forest area ranges from 1.4 hectares to 4.1 hectares per capita (ibid.).

A tour of the subregions and some specific national data bring the forest ecological zones together with the realities of preserving and improving plantations are sometimes the only way to rebuild organic material, stabilize slopes, and create a microclimate suitable for reintroduction of natural forest species. Moreover, some plantations have emerged as important sources of fuelwood that would otherwise be culled from remaining natural forests. In addition, plantations are more efficient and productive than natural forests in terms of timber volume generated. In recognition of this fact, some arrangements have developed in South and Southeast Asia wherein control of village plantations is given in exchange for protection of natural forests. This arrangement can produce more of what poor villagers need as well as environmental values, such as watershed protection and preservation of biodiversity.

Sources:
Burch, W. R., and J. K. Parker. 1992. *Social Science Applications in Asian Agroforestry.* New Delhi: Oxford and IBH.
Gordon, J. C., and W. R. Bentley. 1990. *Handbook on Agroforestry Research Management.* New Delhi: Oxford and IBH.

forests under severe population and economic stresses.

Central Asia

Forest and other wooded land accounts for just 5.5 percent of the total land area in Central Asia, which amounts to less than 1 percent of the world forest cover. Turkmenistan has the largest percentage of forest cover, while Tajikistan has the lowest percentage. Plantation areas are significant in Uzbekistan. Mongolia is the only country that shows a net loss of forest cover. The forests of Kyrgyzstan, Tajikistan, and Uzbekistan are not available for wood supply, mainly for economic reasons, although forests are important for environmental reasons, notably soil and water protection. On the other hand, Turkmenistan reported more than 90 percent of its forest area as available for wood supply (UNECE/FAO, 2000).

In all Central Asian countries, forests play an important role in soil and water protection and watershed management. Collection of nonwood forest products is important for the local population. The demand for forest products is met by imports, mainly from the Russian Federation. Mongolia has a relatively large land area under formal protection in a network of around forty-eight parks and reserves. Fires destroy significant areas of forest and steppe woodland each year. Saw-milling is the main forest industry in Mongolia.

Kazakhstan is a large, sparsely populated country. A significant part of the country is desert, but the northern regions, where the forests are located, are ecologically similar to southern Siberia. Kyrgyzstan is a mountainous country with a predominantly agricultural economy. The forests of Mongolia are located mainly in the northern part of the country along the Russian Federation border, forming a transition zone between the Siberian taiga forest and the central Asian steppes. The taiga forests are mainly larch and cedar, with Scotch pine and birches also relatively common. There are also significant areas of arid shrub land in the south.

South Asia

The forests of South Asia are famous for the many stories that they have inspired. The word "jungle" comes from the Hindi language, and Rudyard Kipling's *Jungle Stories* have helped form popular ideas about the humid tropical forest. Forests have long been an important part of local cultures in South Asia. The sacred groves of South India, for example, provide living insight into what the rest of the region looked like well before the Mughal invasions or the colonial period. Sandalwood is a wood of special importance, and under a Banyan tree on the Ghangetic plain is where Buddha found enlightenment.

The South Asia subregion spans seven countries (Bangladesh, Bhutan, India, Maldives, Nepal, Pakistan, and Sri Lanka). The land areas of these countries vary from 30,000 hectares (Maldives) to more than 297 million hectares (India). The total land area of South Asia is larger than all of Europe. The subregion supports about 22 percent of the global population, but it has only about 2 percent of the world's forests, spread over about 3 percent of its total land area (UN Food and Agriculture Organization 2001). Throughout this region, the capacity of remaining natural forests to meet soaring domestic timber and fuelwood demand is declining. As a result, harvests from private monocultural plantations and illegal logging in natural forests is soaring. Uncontrolled access and excessive use of forest resources in many places is leading to forest degradation, fragmentation, and deforestation on an ecologically devastating scale (Wikramanayake et al. 2002).

Poverty and population pressure are two primary causes of forest degradation in the subregion. Critical social goals are population control and higher rates of economic growth to provide additional employment and income. Over the past two decades, South Asian people have changed the way they perceive and value their forests. This is leading to new approaches to forest management and policy. Population growth and unsustainable models of economic development have been and continue to be critical factors in deforestation, but people and local institutions are also increasingly seen as part of the solution in promoting sustainable forests and ecosystems (Bentley et al. 1994b). This new perception, however, has not yet led to significant changes in the traditional use of forests. The collection of fuelwood is still a major factor in forest loss, because fuelwood is the main source of domestic energy. Domestic energy consumption in energy units per capita is modest by world standards, but when expressed in units per hectare of forest area it is quite high and not sustainable given the large rural population in South Asia (Bentley and Gowen 1994).

Forest health has also been influenced by South Asia's venerable traditions of active forest management. Many countries have more than 100 years of experience in raising forests (Champion and Seth 1968). This experience provides a base for plantation establishment and development. India has the largest area of plantations in the subregion for the production of industrial raw materials and fuelwood. The subregion has made a very large commitment to plantations for the size of its land area. With only about 3 percent of the world's land area, the region has 18.5 percent of the world's plantations. Similarly, with only about 13.4 percent of the total land area in Asia, the contribution of this subregion to the total plantation area is about 29.9 percent.

Strategic and commercial aspects motivated plantation activity in the subregion, starting with teak in 1840 in India, irrigated plantations of sheesham in Pakistan in 1866, teak plantations in Bangladesh in 1871, and similar plantations in Sri Lanka and Bhutan in 1947. The current level of private planting exceeds public planting. Plantations have changed the landscape picture across the subregion over the last two decades. The most preferred plantation species in India, Bangladesh, and Sri Lanka have been teak and eucalyptus, while in Pakistan and Nepal it has been sheesham. The yield results are higher than the world averages, but slightly below the Asian averages. Public programs focus on social conservation and environmental goals rather than commercial needs.

Overall, forest planning and management in South Asia continue to be guided by individual priorities. Countries in the subregion have increasingly recognized the importance of biodiversity contained in their natural forests and have set aside forests for conservation of biodiversity. The past decade has witnessed an increase in the involvement of the private sector, the empowerment and participation of stakeholders in local forest processes, and considerable investments in poverty alleviation and promotion of alternative sources of renewable energy. Several programs have also been initiated to increase the stock of trees outside the forest and forest plantations.

Southeast Asia

The forests of Southeast Asia are known around the world, both for their high levels of biodiversity and for the rapid pace at which they are being harvested by legal and illegal logging. Indeed, the subregion is a major player in the tropical timber trade. Timber from the dipterocarp forests and teak from Java, Myanmar, and Thailand are among the better known tropical timbers of the world. Plantation forestry is widely practiced here, with the teak plantations of Java and the rubber plantations of Malaysia serving as prime examples. But unsustainable harvesting of forests persists, and biologists note that most threatened species of flora and fauna are poorly served by monocultural plantations incapable of supporting well-rounded ecosystems.

The countries of the subregion vary widely in size, population, economic growth, and forest cover. Most countries have 50 percent or more forest cover. East Timor, the Philippines, Thailand, and Vietnam have forest cover ranging between 20 and 30 percent. Throughout the region, however, monocultural plantations account for a rising percentage of total forest cover. The total annual reduction of natural forest cover is greatest in Indonesia and Myanmar, where illegal logging is epidemic. The only country in the region that has actually boosted its total forest cover in recent years is Vietnam, a nation that significantly expanded its plantation operations during the 1990s.

The Southeast Asian subregion has been a major supplier of tropical wood since colonial times. Early logging was selective and restricted to accessible areas. Harvest levels were modest, and the environmental impact was low. After World War II, the technical advances that were made in wood preservation eliminated the advantage of natural wood durability. However, the market for general-purpose timbers increased. With mechanized harvesting, overharvesting of natural forest resources became commonplace. That, in turn, has led to an increased regional emphasis on plantation forestry. At the close of the twentieth century, Indonesia, Thailand, and Vietnam had the largest forest plantations. For example, the combined rubber plantation holdings of these three nations exceed 7 million hectares. These three nations also have a long tradition of raising teak in plantations, which cover more than 2.5 million hectares. More recently, acacias have been planted to supply fiber for pulp mills.

East Asia

The subregion of East Asia comprises China, the Democratic People's Republic of Korea, Japan, and the Republic of Korea. As in all other areas of Asia, unsustainable logging and degradation of forest habitat are serious problems in this sector. For example, South Korea and China are both industrializing rapidly and need forests for raw materials. But remaining forest areas also provide essential protection to watersheds that are integral for farming and water supplies. And since only about 20 percent of China's total land area is suitable for agriculture, protecting cropland is critical. As a result,

The panda is one of many species threatened by deforestation in Asia. COREL

rehabilitating deforested slopes in major watersheds like the Yangtze has emerged as a critical social and environmental goal.

Despite its relatively small size, Japan has widely varying climatic and topographic regions, which contribute to diverse forest vegetation. Coniferous forests or mixed coniferous and broadleaf forests are found in the boreal or alpine zones, with deciduous forests in the temperate zone, and evergreen broadleaf forests in the warm temperate or subtropical zones. Large natural forests exist only in the Hokkaido region, which has 59.5 percent of the total natural forests in Japan.

Across from the Japanese archipelago lies the Korean peninsula. Vegetation on the peninsula is associated with warm-temperate, temperate, and cold-temperate climates. In the north, the forest vegetation is primarily composed of conifers, which transition into mixed conifer and broadleaf forests in the center of the peninsula. Mixed conifer and broadleaf forests occur on the south, east, and west coasts. Warm-temperate vegetation is also found on the south coast and islands (Republic of Korea, Ministry of the Environment 2001).

The South Asia subregion had an annual increase of 1.8 million hectares of forest in the 1990s, mainly because of plantation programs in China. Small annual increases were reported in Japan, and small annual decreases were reported for the Republic of Korea. Forests cover about 60 percent of the land in all countries except China, which has a forest cover of about 18 percent.

Plantation operations are significant in China (27 percent of forest area), Japan (44 percent), and the Republic of Korea (21 percent). Forest volume and biomass per hectare is much higher in Japan than in the other countries, which may be explained by the former country's low levels of harvesting and extraction. China's low average forest volume and biomass are explained by the poor stocking of many of its forests and large areas of young plantations. Indeed, silvicultural activities in China center on plantation establishment and management. For example, extensive research and development has been carried out on high-yield plantation species. The most common plantation trees are pine, larch, eucalyptus, and poplar. Multipurpose species, such as paulownia, are also popular. Shelterbelt plantations are common in areas where wind erosion is a problem. In natural forests, rehabilitation and enhancement of secondary forest growth are research and operational targets to improve degraded lands.

Several forms of ownership are observed in China, Japan, and the Republic of Korea. In Japan, most forests are privately owned. Both China and the Republic of Korea have forests owned by cooperatives, but the cooperatives in Korea are more of an umbrella organization for private forest owners. In the Democratic People's Republic of Korea, all forests are owned by the government.

Building Sustainability into Asian Forest Management

Sustainability is an important issue throughout the world with regard to forests, agriculture, and other systems that are based on ecosystem dynamics (Miller et al. 1994). In one sense, it is a new issue that has emerged as nations and people become more knowledgeable about the limits of the earth because of natural systems. In another and perhaps more important sense, sustainability is a very old idea and social goal. The Western tradition of sustained yield in both agriculture and forestry came from a common feudal concern with soil productivity (Greeley 1953). If soil productivity declines—whether from soil erosion or nutrient depletion—yields cannot be maintained into the future.

The data and information regarding Asian forests can be read in two ways. One interpretation leads to a pessimistic view of the future. Despite rapid declines in birthrates, Asia's human population will continue to increase for the next several decades. Over half of the world's truly poor people live in eastern India and Bangladesh, and many people in the rest of Asia suffer in abject poverty. Governments face great difficulties as they face the need to change rapidly in response to the demands of their citizens. These are not social conditions that appear favorable to forest rehabilitation.

A more optimistic view starts with two observations. First, the Asian land-scape has many remarkable soils and local climates favorable to tree growth. Second, the continent has registered several encouraging reforestation efforts, such as rehabilitation of degraded lands in India and plantation programs in China. Moreover, increased international concern about the deteriorating state of Asian biodiversity is creating an environment in which formal protection of rain forests and other important habitat has emerged as a priority. It is hoped that expansion of protected area networks, combined with reform of property and tenure rights to forests, improved management of existing forest reserves, and increased investment in research and development, can slow rates of de-forestation and thus preserve the continent's myriad biological treasures.

Sources:

Appanah, S., and G. Weinland. 1990. "Will the Management Systems for Hill Dipterocarp Forests Stand Up?" *Journal of Tropical Forest Science*.

Bentley, W. R. 1991. "The Roles of Social Sciences in Research on Agroforestry and other Land-use Technologies." In W. R. Burch and J. K. Parker, eds., *Social Science Applications in Asian Agroforestry*. New Delhi: Oxford and IBH.

Bentley, W. R., et al. 1990. *Developing the Scientific Human Resources of the Indonesian Ministry of Forestry through Graduate Education*. A report by Winrock International to the Indonesian Ministry of Forestry.

Bentley, W. R., R. C. Chambers, and B. P. Ghildyal. 1985. "Agroforestry: A Complex System for Resource-poor Families." In P. K. Khosla and S. Puri, eds., *Agroforestry Systems, A New Challenge*. New Delhi: Nataraj.

Bentley, W. R., and M. M. Gowen, eds. 1994a. *Forest Resources and Wood-based Biomass Energy as Rural Development Assets*. New Delhi: Winrock/Oxford and IBH.

Bentley, W. R., C. R. Hatch, and J. C. Gordon. 1994b. "Forest Resources and Forest Policies as They Impact upon Agricultural Productivity and Environmental Quality." In *An Assessment of the Production Base for Agriculture: Environmental Quality, Natural Resources and Technologies for the 21st Century*. Morrilton, AR: Winrock International Institute of Agricultural Development.

Bentley, W. R., P. K. Khosla, and K. Seckler, eds. 1993. *Agroforestry in South Asia: Problems and Applied Research Perspectives*. New Delhi: Oxford and IBH.

Bentley, W. R., G. B. Singh, and N. Chatterjee. 1987. "Tenure and Agroforestry Potentials in India." In John Raintree, ed., *Land Trees and Tenure*. Nairobi: International Council on Agroforestry Research and Land Tenure Center.

Biodiversity Center of Japan. 1991. *Convention on Biological Diversity: The First National Report, 1991*, http://www.biodic.go.jp/english/biolaw/kunie/kunie_hon.html.

Brandis, Dietrich. 1984 [1897]. *Forestry in India: Origins and Early Developments*. New Delhi: Nataraj.

Burch, W. R., and J. K. Parker. 1991. *Social Science Applications in Asian Agroforestry.* New Delhi: Oxford and IBH.

Champion, H. G., and S. K. Seth. 1968. *A Revised Survey of the Forest Types of India.* Delhi: Government of India.

China Department of Nature Conservation. 1999. *A Country Study: The Richness and Uniqueness of China's Biodiversity.* China Environmental Sciences Press, State Environmental Protection Administration, 1999, http://www.zhb.gov.cn/english/biodiv/.

Ciriacy-Wantrup, S. V. 1952. *Resource Conservation.* Berkeley: University of California Division of Agriculture.

Gordon, J. C., and W. R. Bentley. 1990. *Handbook on Agroforestry Research Management.* New Delhi: Oxford and IBH.

Gowen, M. M., W. R. Bentley, and Eirik Stijfhoorn. 1994. "Tropical Forest Management and Wood-based Energy as Development Assets." In W. R. Bentley and M. M. Gowen, eds., *Forest Resources and Wood-based Biomass Energy as Rural Development Assets.* New Delhi: Winrock/Oxford and IBH.

Greeley, W. B. 1953. *Forest Policy.* New York: McGraw Hill.

Hardin, Garrett. 1977. *Managing the Commons.* New York: W. H. Freeman.

Korea Forest Research Institute. 1999. *Preliminary Report on the State of Plantation.* Republic of Korea, Forest Inventory Division.

Korea Forest Service. 2000. *Statistical Yearbook of Forestry 2000.* Seoul: Republic of Korea.

Landes, D. L. 1998. *The Wealth and Poverty of Nations: Why Some Are So Rich and Some So Poor.* New York: W. W. Norton.

Miller, Sandra, C. W. Shinn, and W. R. Bentley. 1994. *Rural Resource Managers: Problem Solving Tools for the Long Term.* Ames: Iowa State University Press.

Poore, D., and H. C. Thang. 2000. *Review of Progress towards the Year 2000 Objective.* Report presented at the 28th session of the International Tropical Timber Council, May 2000, Lima, Peru. Yokohama, Japan: ITTO.

Republic of Korea, Ministry of the Environment. 2001. *Korean Biodiversity Clearing-house Mechanism: Convention on Biological Diversity,* http://www.moenv.go.kr/.

Thailand Royal Forest Department. 2000. *Forestry Statistics of Thailand 1999.* Bangkok: Royal Forest Department.

UN Economic and Social Commission for Asia and the Pacific. 2002. "Population and Development Indicators for Asia and the Pacific, 2002," http://www.unescap.org/pop/data_sheet/2002.

UNECE/FAO. 2000. *Forest Resources of Europe, CIS, North America, Australia, Japan and New Zealand: Contribution to the Global Forest Resources Assessment 2000.* Timber and Forest Study Papers 17. New York and Geneva: United Nations Economic Commission for Europe/Food and Agriculture Organization, http://www.unece.org/trade/timber/fra/pdf/contents.htm.

UN Food and Agriculture Organization. 2001. *Global Forest Resources Assessment 2000: Main Report.* Rome: FAO, http://www.fao.org/forestry/fo/fra/main/index.jsp.

U.S. Library of Congress. *Country Studies,* http://lcweb2.loc.gov/frd/cs/.

Wikramanayake, Eric, Eric Dinerstein, Colbey J. Loucks et al. 2002. *Terrestrial Ecoregions of the Indo-Pacific: A Conservation Assessment.* Washington, DC: Island.

World Conservation Monitoring Centre. 1992. *Protected Areas of the World: A Review of National Systems.* Mongolian People's Republic, http://www.wcmc. org.uk/cgibin/pa_paisquery.p.

Agriculture

Implementation and maintenance of environmentally sustainable and efficient systems of agriculture are as imperative to Asia as to any other region of the world, for the continent's nutritional, economic, social, political, and environmental fortunes are inextricably intertwined with farming and food production. Asia contains two-thirds of the world's people—including China and India, the two most populous countries—but has only one-third of the globe's land area. Moreover, about 2 billion people—one-third of the global population—live in Asia's rural areas, where they depend on farming, forestry, and fishing for their livelihoods. In order to confront these inexorable numbers, Asia has devoted large swaths of its total land area to the essential task of providing food for its burgeoning human population. South Asia, for example, has 73 percent of its total land area under agriculture, and almost half of Southeast Asia's land area is under agricultural use (Wood et al. 2000).Unlike other areas of the world, most regions of Asia devote more land to crop cultivation than to pasture land (see Figure 5.1).

Asia has made remarkable productivity advances on these lands over the past four decades. These gains, built on a foundation of higher-yielding crop strains, expanded use of irrigation, intensified agrochemical applications, and institutional reforms, have enabled the continent's developing nations to cut rates of chronic malnourishment, boost average per capita calorie intake, and improve the economic circumstances of millions of Asian families. These gains have been realized despite continued robust population growth that has put added pressure on agricultural resources (Asia added another billion people during the last two decades of the twentieth century alone) (Asian Development Bank 2000b).

This so-called Green Revolution enabled Asia to evade the epidemics of malnutrition and famine that some analysts had predicted. Still, malnourishment and poverty did not wholly evaporate from the continent. Some of

Figure 5.1 Composition of FAO Agricultural Land by Region

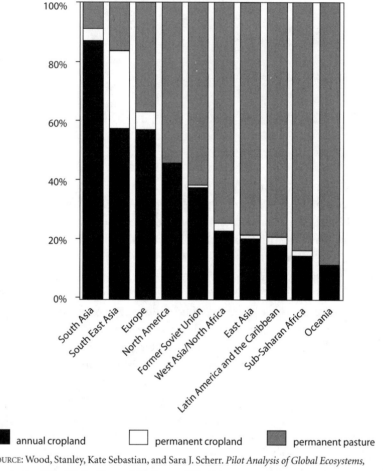

SOURCE: Wood, Stanley, Kate Sebastian, and Sara J. Scherr. *Pilot Analysis of Global Ecosystems,* International Food Policy Research Institute and World Resources Institute, 2000. Available online at http://www.ifpri.org/pubs/books/page/agroeco.pdf

Asia's less productive croplands, which also tend to be the most poverty-stricken areas, remained largely untouched by the benefits of the Green Revolution. As a result, certain regions of numerous countries continue to wage a grim struggle against the specters of chronic malnutrition or starvation. For the period 1990 to 1997, for instance, the United Nations reported that numerous Asian countries continued to have high percentages of underweight children, including Bangladesh (56 percent of all children), India (53 percent), Cambodia (52 percent), Nepal (47 percent), Myanmar (43 percent), and Vietnam (41 percent) (UN Children's Fund 1999).

Moreover, the very elements that powered the Green Revolution—high levels of irrigation, fertilizer and pesticide inputs, monocropping, conversion of undeveloped land to agricultural use, and so forth—have also produced troubling levels of erosion, salinization (accumulation of salt in soil), water pollution, and deforestation. These trends constitute major threats to the integrity and well-being of Asia's rivers, wetlands, and forests, and the flora and fauna that live therein. Moreover, they jeopardize some of the productivity gains that the continent's agricultural sector has achieved in recent decades. If these gains do erode in any significant or large-scale way in the coming years, the results could be catastrophic for the people of Asia and other developing regions around the world. As a result, increased investment and research into agricultural practices that are both productive and environmentally sustainable is seen as imperative to Asia's future.

Recent Agricultural Trends in Asia

The Green Revolution
Spurs Record Agricultural Growth

The global Green Revolution phenomenon of the 1960s and 1970s replaced low-input, labor-intensive agricultural practices with modern, high-input, mechanized farming systems. These systems quickly generated remarkable increases in agricultural productivity around the world. Indeed, the Green Revolution expanded global food production so rapidly that the world was able to accommodate a doubling of its human population even as it reduced the incidence of starvation and malnourishment. In Asia and other regions, the Green Revolution even enabled some developing nations to exorcize the specter of famine that had long lurked over them. Moreover, the revolution generated ripples of expanded economic activity and development in a host of nonagricultural sectors. In India, for instance, where agriculture still accounts for about a third of national income and approximately two-thirds of the labor force, the Green Revolution had a major impact on growth and employment in nonfarm sectors across the country (Asian Development Bank 2001b).

The central crops involved in this era of intensification and agrotechnological advancement were wheat, rice, and maize (corn), long-time staples of the Asian fields. Between 1970 and 1990, improved wheat strains were spread across more than 90 percent of planted acreage in Asia and Latin America (International Food Policy Research Institute 1998). These and other robust seed strains were augmented by tremendous investments in irrigation networks, chemical fertilization, and pest control. The results of this investment in modern agricultural tools were startling. All across Asia, harvests produced under these new high-input regimes eclipsed those that had been possible using traditional seeds and practices. In China, for example, grain yields nearly quadrupled between 1952 and 1996, according to China Statistical Yearbooks. In Southeast Asia, food production grew faster than anywhere else in the world during the 1980s (UN Conference on Trade and Development 1994).

As transformative as the Green Revolution was, however, it did not reach every corner of Asia. "[Some areas] were bypassed either because the soil, water, typography, and labor endowments were unsuited to the demanding set of farm management practices called for to make Green Revolution seed varieties perform (e.g., well-timed fertilization and irrigation and chemical pest control) or because the physical and institutional infrastructure to deliver fertilizers and chemicals—and low-interest credit—to poor farmers was missing" (Paarlberg 2000). Indeed, some small landholders found themselves caught in "poverty traps" because they did not have sufficient capital or collateral to obtain high-yield seeds, fertilizer, and other vital elements of the Green Revolution mix, or they could not gain access to facilities for timely food storage and distribution (Unger 2002).

In Central Asia, meanwhile, investment in irrigation projects and the other trappings of modern agriculture from the 1950s through the 1980s was driven by the Soviet Union's focus on maximizing productivity on its state-controlled farms. Just as the Green Revolution changed the face of agriculture in South and East Asia, major Soviet investment in chemical fertilizers, irrigation, and mechanization transformed the landscape of Uzbekistan, Kazakhstan, and other Central Asian satellites of the Soviet empire. Ecological disaster was the result. Indiscriminate application of fertilizers, defoliants, and pesticides ruined large areas of farmland and contaminated rivers and lakes. In addition, unsustainable diversions of water enabled Central Asia to double its area of irrigated land between 1960 and 1990, but left a grim environmental legacy. The ecosystems of the Aral Sea basin, for example, were shattered after Soviet authorities approved huge diversions of water from the Amu Darya and other feeder rivers to the thirsty cotton fields of Uzbekistan. According to some estimates, at the height of irrigation the Aral Sea was losing 90 percent of its source water to irrigation diversions. These diversions, combined with appalling levels of agrochemical contamination, have reduced the Aral Sea to a polluted, shriveled shell of its former self (Lloyd-Roberts and Anbarasan 2000).

More recently, the 1991 collapse of the Soviet Union had a debilitating impact on the economic underpinnings of the region's agricultural systems. As centrally planned economies crumbled and state subsidies for agriculture were terminated, crop and livestock production levels—which had bloated to

Livestock waste fouls water resources in many regions. OGONIOK LOUCHINE/CORBIS SYGMA

unsustainable levels during the subsidy-heavy Soviet era—plummeted across the region. From 1991 to 1996 in Kyrgyzstan, for example, populations of cattle, poultry, pigs, and other livestock fell precipitously (Asian Development Bank 1998).

"The privatization process [brought] considerable changes in the structure of agricultural production—away from monoculture production on large-scale collective and state farms towards multiproduct, small-scale farming on private lands," explained the Asian Development Bank. This transition, while

Postharvest Losses
in Asian Agriculture

Continual increases in the world's demand for food have produced two main responses from governments: attempts to slow human population growth in order to reduce future food demand, and intensification of agricultural production in order to increase future food supplies. Intensification of agricultural production puts a great deal of stress on the environment. It leads to increased use of pesticides and herbicides, decreased soil quality, conversion of forest and wetlands to agriculture, damage to watersheds from runoff, and the deterioration of rural communities. Experts suggest that another alternative to addressing food shortages might be to reduce postharvest losses of agricultural commodities, which have been estimated to reach 40 percent of harvest totals in some cases (UN Food and Agriculture Organization 1997; Satin 1997).

Agricultural products pass through a number of stages before they reach market. Each stage involves operations that can lead to losses. Common sources of postharvest losses include harvesting, cleaning, and packing processes; consumption by insects, rodents, birds, and molds; damage during transportation and storage; and quality deterioration and spoilage. The extent of postharvest losses varies greatly depending on the type of crop, the country and climatic region where it is grown, and the measurement method used. As a result, it is difficult to come up with a good estimate of total postharvest food losses, though experts agree that the amount is significant. For example, a 1997 survey of rice production in Southeast Asia found losses ranging from 1 to 3 percent during harvest, from 2 to 7 percent in handling, 2 to 6 percent in threshing, 1 to 5 percent in drying, 2 to 6 percent in storage, and 2 to 10 percent in transport. The estimated total loss was between 10 and 37 percent of the rice grown in Southeast Asia, not counting losses by retailers and consumers (ibid.).

Retailers and consumers constitute another source of postharvest losses of agricultural commodities. Consumers— particularly those living in more affluent nations—increasingly demand cosmetically perfect produce. The growing emphasis on qualitative factors means that a great deal of the food that is brought to market is wasted. A review of food waste in the United

States found that 27 percent of the total food available for people to consume, or 43 billion kilograms, was lost after harvesting and distribution—through waste by retailers, food service, and consumers (Kantor et al. 1997).

Postharvest losses have implications beyond reducing the amount of food available to meet world demand. Such losses also imply a waste of the factors of food production, such as arable land, water used for irrigation, seeds, fertilizer, and human labor ("Disappearing Food: How Big Are Postharvest Losses?" 1998).

Given the uncertainties surrounding the measurement of postharvest losses, experts do not know to what degree the losses can be prevented, and estimates of the volume of food that could be salvaged vary considerably. However, studies indicate that potential gains that might accrue to overall food supplies make postharvest losses a subject worthy

of additional study. Ultimately, making meaningful reductions in postharvest losses will require an integrated approach to agricultural management, including the use of new technology for handling and storage of produce, and the implementation of efficient harvesting and packing practices.

Sources:

"Disappearing Food: How Big Are Postharvest Losses?" 1998. *Earthtrends,* World Resources Institute web site, http://earthtrends.wri.org/ conditions_trends/feature_select _action.cfm?theme=8.

Kantor, K. S., et al. 1997. "Estimating and Addressing America's Food Losses." *Food Review* 20, no. 1.

Satin, M. 1997. *Agroindustries and Post-Harvest Management Service.* Rome: FAO.

UN Food and Agriculture Organization. 1997. "Estimated Post-Harvest Losses of Rice in Southeast Asia." Rome: FAO.

difficult, has not been without benefits. The decline in farming intensity relieved pressure on land resources that had been scoured, carved, and saturated to the breaking point by the excesses of the Soviet era. The region's collective and state farms have dwindled away, replaced by small-scale farms that have shown a greater inclination to embrace ecologically sound and sustainable production methods, such as planting diversified crops and using organic waste instead of fertilizer for soil quality enhancement (Asian Development Bank 1998). Moreover, these private farms have registered impressive increases

Part of Asia's Green Revolution, this rice field at Phuoc Thoi, South Vietnam, is an experimental station planted with "miracle rice," a specially developed strain that produces more grain to a stalk and more crops per year. BETTMANN/CORBIS

in productivity, despite the widespread problem of land degradation. In Uzbekistan, for example, meat production on private farms doubled on a per hectare basis between 1992 and 1995, while milk production increased by almost 60 percent, egg production rose by 50 percent, and wool production increased by 1,500 percent (UN Development Programme 1996).

The Green Revolution's Environmental Legacy

In Eastern and Southern Asia, meanwhile, recognition of the ecological toll of the Green Revolution was slower in coming. After all, by mandating a shift toward more intensive farming systems on existing agricultural lands, the Green Revolution had succeeded in dramatically increasing production of wheat, rice, and other crops in the developing countries of Asia. Moreover, its emphasis on maximizing yields from existing agricultural resources has been credited with helping to slow the conversion of forests, wetlands, meadows, and other environmentally fragile lands to crop and livestock production. But reducing pressure for land conversion was one of the few ways in which the revolution proved environmentally benign. In most other respects, "the environmental implications of the green revolution strategy, and indeed the long-term sustainability of the green revolution itself, were ignored. It is only now that there is (some) realization of the environmental impact of the policies adopted to boost agricultural output in the 1960s" (Asian Development Bank 2000b).

Emerging environmental problems associated with the Green Revolution's focus on maximizing crop productivity include soil erosion, salinization, water pollution from pesticides and fertilizers (especially nitrogen-based fertilizers), unsustainable rates of water consumption for irrigation, and other forms of land degradation. These problems—traced to wasteful irrigation programs, heavy chemical application rates, emphasis on monoculture, shortened fallow periods, and other agricultural practices—are believed to have had an adverse impact on wildlife habitat and biodiversity in myriad regions of Asia. Moreover, the damage wreaked by these practices has been magnified by governmental subsidy policies that encourage farmers to wring every last cent out of their landholdings now—by saturating their fields with heavily subsidized chemicals, for instance—rather than establishing practices that are environmentally sustainable over the long term (ibid.; Consumers' Association of Penang 1997).

In India, for instance, land degradation resulting from water erosion, wind erosion, salinization, and waterlogging has become a grave issue. With respect to agricultural land alone, it was estimated that more than 83 million hectares had suffered some degree of degradation by the early 1990s, with more than one-third of the affected land classified as severely degraded (UN Development Programme et al. 1993). By the end of the twentieth century, it was estimated that about 100 million hectares of the country's 160 million hectares of arable land were degraded, with 50 million hectares degraded so severely that they were no longer productive (Ravindranath and Iyer-Raniga 2000). These trends place even greater pressure on remaining farmlands, and constitute an alarming problem for a country that is growing by 18 million people annually.

Arable land degradation is also a rising concern in China, the world's most populous nation (though India is expected to overtake it in the mid–twenty-first century). In China the extent of agriculturally productive land decreased between 1957 and 1990 by an area equal to all the cropland in France, Germany, Denmark, and the Netherlands combined (UN Economic and Social Commission for Asia and the Pacific 1995). Between the late 1950s and the late 1990s, China lost an estimated 40 million hectares of arable land, nearly one-third of all the land currently under cultivation. Prior to the 1980s,

Villages Bypassed by Green Revolution Struggle for Survival

The Green Revolution dramatically improved the lives of millions of Asian people. But social, economic, and health gains associated with this era of agricultural growth and expansion were not distributed equally to all corners of the continent. In fact, some rural areas were bypassed entirely. In the mountains of northern Yunnan province in China, for example, where poverty-stricken communities had long used every scrap of soil they could find for potatoes and other crops, isolated farmers continued to carve a meager farming existence out of the forbidding terrain. Indeed, existence was so tenuous for some farmers that they cultivated patches of soil perched on steep inclines, using supporting ropes in order to avoid falling into the wind-scoured gorges below. In this and other regions like it, hunger and malnutrition remained chronic conditions long after the Green Revolution had produced bounties of rice, maize, wheat, and other crops in other locations (Yencken et al. 2000; Asian Development Bank 2000).

Farmers in this remote pocket also relied on common grazing lands to sustain their sheep herds, their only meaningful source of cash income. But overgrazing produced severe erosion that clogged mountain streams with sediment and removed topsoil from plots that were only marginally productive in the first place. Cognizant that these activities—played out in numerous other communities to one degree or another—were laying the groundwork for permanent ecological most of those losses were due to erosion, salinization, and other types of environmental degradation, but since then the country's well-publicized efforts to modernize and generate economic growth have spawned countless housing developments, highways, and other forms of infrastructure, many of which have been placed on productive land (Hertsgaard 1998). In addition, floods and other natural disasters have damaged significant areas of farmland (Wood et al. 2000).

Such losses provide ammunition to analysts who argue that China is steadily losing the battle to grow within environmental limits, and that it could eventually become so dependent on imported foods that world food markets will go into upheaval, triggering escalating levels of malnutrition and famine around the world (Brown 1995). But efforts to ascertain China's future ability to feed itself have been stymied somewhat by uncertainties about the true extent of China's arable land. Some studies suggest that China may be under-representing its actual level of arable land by as much as 50 percent in order to make its crop yields per hectare appear higher. But some studies also

devastation, the Chinese government imposed restrictions on agricultural and livestock use of many steep slopes and began reforesting some areas. But these new policies, imposed after several particularly devastating floods that were blamed in part on deforestation and erosion in catchment areas, turned some farming communities into welfare enclaves. "The dilemma, of course, is that the peasantry of areas like Dacai [in Yunnan Province] would starve if denied access to their eroding potato patches and pastures. The central government accordingly is promising to deliver supplementary foodstuffs to affected villagers for a period of at least eight years, and extending beyond that wherever necessary. Whether Beijing is successful in enforcing the closure of mountain slopes or, indeed, is willing to institute a permanent system of welfare dependency remains an open question" (ibid.). Moreover, China's central government has stipulated that poverty-alleviation funds must be matched by local governments, many of which can do so only by liquidating forests and other natural resources (Wood et al. 2001).

Sources:

Asian Development Bank. 2000. *Rural Asia: Beyond the Green Revolution.* Manila: ADB.

Wood, Alexander, Pamela Stedman-Edwards, and Johanna Mang. 2001. *The Root Causes of Biodiversity Loss.* London: Earthscan.

Yencken, David, John Fien, and Helen Sykes, eds. 2000. *Environment, Education and Society in the Asia-Pacific: Local Traditions and Global Discourses.* London: Routledge.

indicate that it could be losing arable land at an even greater rate than it admits, and that land degradation might be affecting a greater proportion of land than reported (Hertsgaard 1998).

Modern Asian Agriculture
Buffeted by Financial and Weather Forces

Asian agriculture struggled in the late 1990s, with production growth hampered by a pronounced economic downturn across the region and destructive weather events—most notably the drought-inducing El Niño weather phenomenon. In fact, the rate of overall agricultural production growth in the Asia and Pacific region declined during this period, with the average 3.2 annual rate of production growth for the period 1996 to 2000 falling well short of the 4.6 percent rate attained during the preceding five-year period (UN Food and Agriculture Organization 2001a).

The slowdown in China's production growth is the single most important factor behind this trend. China maintained high rates of agricultural growth throughout most of the 1990s, with an average annual rate of production increase of 6.3 percent between 1991 and 1997. But Chinese agricultural production growth decelerated markedly to an estimated 4 percent in 1998 and 2.9 percent in 1999. Provisional estimates for 2000 point to an increase of about 3 percent as well. This slowdown has been attributed to a series of natural disasters that have bedeviled major farming areas, as well as reductions in harvested area because of reduced state procurement of cereals (ibid.).

Other countries in the southern and eastern sectors of the continent, including Bangladesh, India, Malaysia, Cambodia, and Thailand, have also been periodically rocked by floods and droughts in recent years (by contrast, Vietnam's success in adopting "flood-adaptive" agricultural practices enabled it to post impressive and largely uninterrupted levels of agricultural growth throughout the 1990s). Currency devaluations and inflation brought about by the Asian financial crisis further added to the pain caused by parched earth or overflowing banks. In Indonesia, for instance, the amount of rice that could be purchased with the daily minimum wage fell by more than two-thirds between January 1997 and October 1998, sparking food riots and an upsurge in malnutrition among the country's impoverished population (ibid.).

Asia's Growing Livestock Sector

Asia has been at the forefront of what some analysts have dubbed the "Livestock Revolution," a global expansion in production and consumption of meat, milk, and poultry. This surge has been most pronounced in the developing countries of Asia and Latin America. In these places, economic growth and market reforms have given millions of people the financial wherewithal to add milk, pork, and chicken to the diets of their families. To meet this demand, livestock production around the world has approximately tripled over the past thirty years. By comparison, crop output roughly doubled during the same period (Pinstrup-Anderson et al. 1999).

Asia is a key area in this livestock growth. At the close of the 1990s it had 96 percent of the world's buffalo, 30 percent of its sheep, and 30 percent of its goats. Moreover, China alone held 64 percent of the global pig population (Wood et al. 2000). But while the rise in consumption of milk and meat has improved nutrition in Asia's developing countries, these same countries are still grappling with the challenge of raising livestock in a safe and environmentally sustainable fashion.

In some Asian countries, the environmental damage caused by poor livestock management will be difficult to reverse. During the Soviet era in Kyrgyzstan, for example, massive dairy herds were confined on state and collective farms that were not outfitted with even basic waste treatment equipment. Since independence, addressing this problem has proven a slow and expensive process. "Most farms even lack equipment to collect the manure and to spread it on fields. As a result, liquid wastes from animals are a major contributor to river contamination. . . .On the meat processing side, livestock is slaughtered under unsanitary conditions that affect worker safety and the quality of the meat product. Wastewaters from slaughter houses are routinely discharged into rivers" (Asian Development Bank 1998).

Overgrazing by livestock has also been blamed for ruining large swaths of grasslands and other natural habitat. In India, for example, it is argued that excessive grazing has stunted natural regeneration in more than half of the forests in the country and contributed to the country's terrible difficulties with soil erosion. "Specifically, overgrazing impedes regeneration, retards growth of vegetation, and leads to extinction of good palatable grass, which is then replaced by less palatable and inferior grass. Excessive trampling makes the soil compact and impervious and prevents circulation of air and water, thus exposing the soil to erosive agents like wind and water" (Asian Development Bank 2001b).

Currently, Asia's developing countries are striving to install the same type of "factory farm" industrial livestock operations that are present in the United States and other developed nations. Indeed, these countries had made significant investments in the technologies necessary to operate industrial-scale pig and poultry operations near urban centers, where transport and distribution options are numerous (Wood et al. 2000). But even in the United States, which has a much more advanced regulatory structure, these concentrated industrial-scale installations can pose significant local pollution and public health problems. These problems include exposure to animal-borne diseases (including avian flu and salmonella), microbial contamination from unsafe handling of foods, unhealthy accumulations of pesticides and antibiotics in the food chain, contamination of rivers and other natural areas from animal waste and agrochemicals, and heavy reliance on water resources (for both direct input and waste disposal) that are limited in many regions (Delgado et al. 1999; Wood et al. 2000; Asian Development Bank 2000b). These assorted risks have prompted widespread calls for increased investment in modernization and mitigation processes and equipment throughout the Asian livestock sector, as well as increased regulation of waste discharges and other environmentally destructive elements of farming operations. But establishing these safeguards in the continent's rural farming communities will undoubtedly be accomplished in incremental fashion, because of the tremendous costs involved (Asian Development Bank 2000).

Asia a Dominant Player in Global Aquaculture

Aquaculture operations in Asia and other regions have enjoyed tremendous growth over the past two decades. Global aquaculture production has risen more than 300 percent since 1984, with annual growth routinely hovering around 10 percent throughout the 1990s (UN Food and Agriculture Organization 2001b). This rapid rate of growth has made aquaculture an increasingly vital part of the world food supply. Indeed, by the close of the 1990s, aquaculture accounted for nearly one-third of all fish consumed by humans around the world, and that percentage is expected to rise as aquaculture expands and continued overfishing and environmental degradation reduce wild fish catches (Organization for Economic Co-operation and Development 2001).

Asia currently occupies a dominant place in world aquaculture production. China alone accounted for about 22 million metric tons of farmed fish, shrimp, and shellfish, nearly 70 percent of world production, and Asia as a whole contributed nearly 90 percent of the global total (UN Food and Agriculture Organization 2001b). But environmental problems associated with aquaculture—and especially the intensive, large-scale facilities that are proliferating in Asia and elsewhere—are attracting increased attention. One of these harmful effects is loss of ecologically important coastal lands. Other drawbacks associated with aquaculture operations include reduction of genetic diversity in farmed species, interbreeding of wild and cultured stocks, pollution from aquaculture operations, and the threat of disease transfer from cultured to wild stocks.

"In the end, aquaculture's contribution to the global food supply will likely turn on how well innovations can help fish farms more closely mimic natural ecosystems, with better recycling of nutrients and less waste generation. That will mean fewer inputs and impacts, without eroding aquaculture's profitability and versatility" (Mock et al. 2001).

Major Environmental Problems in Asian Agriculture

All across Asia, rural and urban communities are grappling with environmental problems associated with agriculture, whether those operations are located nearby or hundreds of miles upstream. The specifics and severity of these problems vary, shaped by cultural traditions, climate, regulatory environment, economic factors, and other influences. But stripped to their basic elements, nearly all of these problems concern one or more of the following types of environmental degradation: conversion of diminishing natural areas, soil degradation and erosion, unsustainable water use, and poisoning of land and water from agrochemicals.

Land Conversion

In 1997 the UN Food and Agriculture Organization estimated Asia's total area of cropland at 483 million hectares. India held the largest area of cropland, at 170 million hectares (the Asian Development Bank places the extent of Indian cropland at 160 million hectares), followed by China (135 million hectares), Indonesia (31 million hectares), Kazakhstan (30 million hectares), and Pakistan (22 million hectares) (UN Food and Agriculture Organization, *FAO-STAT Online Statistic Service* 1999). But these figures do not tell the full story, for significant sections of these arable lands, scarred by years of misuse, are not as productive as they once were. This degradation, combined with continued population expansion and growing demand for new urban, industrial, and transport infrastructure, is putting fierce pressure on Asia's remaining natural and seminatural areas.

Indeed, Asian land use is in a perpetual and feverish state of flux. For example, South Asia's total agricultural area has remained at around 223 million hectares for more than twenty years, which would seem to indicate an environment of stability and sustainability. But in reality, the region has lost significant expanses of arable land to urbanization, natural disasters, and environmental degradation during that time. At the same, however, it has generated large areas of cultivated land in other locations through deforestation and other land conversions. These opposing trends have effectively canceled each other out since the early 1980s, enabling the region to claim roughly the same total farmland area (Wood et al. 2000).

This same dynamic of simultaneous land use changes is evident in China, although acquisition of new land for cultivation has not kept up with farmland losses over the years. In 1995, for instance, China lost some 798,000 hectares of cultivated land to horticulture, reforestation, development, or natural disasters such as floods and droughts. (According to China's State Land Administration, most of these losses were directly attributable to severe weather or conversion of cropland to horticulture; conversions for infrastructure, settlements, and industry accounted for only 10 to 15 percent of cropland loss.) However, China's farmers also expanded the extent of cultivated land by approximately 389,000 hectares by converting natural areas and developed lands previously devoted to other purposes. These activities produced a net loss of 409,000 hectares of cultivated land (Wood et al. 2000).

Asian forests have borne the brunt of the continent's unslaked thirst for new cropland. From Bangladesh to the Korean Peninsula, countless forest ecosystems have been sacrificed to make way for fields of rice, wheat, and other crops. Between 1951 and 1980 alone, the Forest Survey of India estimates that more than 2.62 million hectares of forest area were converted for agricultural purposes across the country (Asian Development Bank 2001b). In Malaysia, meanwhile, efforts to alleviate poverty prompted swift expansion of agricultural areas during the 1970s and 1980s. During that period, government-supported land development initiatives resulted in the conversion of 1.64 million hectares of pristine lowland forests on the Malaysian Peninsula—20 percent of the region's forested area—to oil palm and rubber plantations and other agricultural activities. This entrenched pattern of trading biologically rich forests for valuable cropland remains in place today (World Wildlife Fund—Malaysia 1993).

Asia's growing agricultural sector also brings pressure on forests in indirect ways. For example, rural farming communities rely heavily on wood for cooking and heat. This dependence places significant additional pressure on those forests that are not cleared for cultivation. In India, for instance, it has been estimated that the rural population requires about 157 million tons of fuelwood annually. But annual production of fuelwood is less than 60 tons. Farming communities make up the difference by engaging in illegal cutting and logging on a massive scale (Asian Development Bank 2001b).

Asia's heavy demand for new cropland has also led some countries to turn their gaze to lands that are only marginally suited to raising food. In Japan and South Korea, for example, rampant urban and industrial development of relatively flat coastal areas has pushed farmers further inland, up into forested hills that are more vulnerable to erosion. In Southeast Asia, economic opportunity has convinced some tribespeople to clear and plow hilly upland areas. And in countries such as Indonesia and China, declining productivity on traditional farming lands that have been wrung dry by heavy chemical applications and other environmentally destructive practices has forced an exodus to land that is ill suited for cultivation (UN Environment Programme 1999).

Soil Erosion

It has been estimated that agricultural activity has led to the degradation of soil on 27 percent of all land in South and Southeast Asia (van Lynden and Oldeman 1997). This degradation takes many forms, but soil erosion is among the most pervasive and dangerous to the long-term health of both natural ecosystems and human populations. In the latter realm, the harmful effects of soil erosion include reduced crop productivity stemming from the loss of nutrient-rich topsoil, increased levels of siltation that can reduce the capacity and productivity of downstream reservoirs and irrigation systems, and heightened vulnerability of lowland areas to flooding (Asian Development Bank 2000b).

Shielding arable land from further soil erosion has emerged as a critical priority in many regions of Asia, from the foothills of the Himalayas to China's "breadbasket" provinces of the south to the forested margins of Indonesia, Malaysia, Vietnam, Cambodia, and the Lao People's Democratic Republic (ibid.). In Kyrgyzstan, for example, an estimated 5.4 million hectares of Kyrgyzstan's 10.5 million hectares of arable land have been compromised by erosion (Asian Development Bank 1998). In India, meanwhile, almost 6 billion tons of soil are lost to erosion every year, and more than a quarter of the land area has been classified as severely eroded (Ravindranath and Iyer-Raniga 2000).

Water is recognized as the primary cause of soil erosion in Asia, with poorly managed irrigation systems a particularly egregious factor. But wind erosion is also extensive and severe, especially in arid and semiarid regions or those that have removed forests and other natural windbreaks. In Pakistan and India, it is estimated that wind erosion has damaged approximately 25 million hectares of farmland (UN Development Programme 1997).

Water Use

Asia irrigates a far higher percentage of its cropland than other regions of the world, in large part because nearly 40 percent of the continental population (approximately 1.32 billion people) live in areas prone to drought and desertification (ibid.). Globally, about 5 percent of agricultural land (approximately 264 million hectares) is irrigated. But South Asia irrigates 35 percent of its croplands, and Southeast Asia and East Asia use irrigation on 15 percent and 7 percent of their cultivated lands, respectively (Wood et al. 2000). Irrigation rates are highest in arid Central Asia, where Uzbekistan irrigates 88 percent of its cropland and Kyrgyzstan waters three-quarters of its farm fields. But reliance on irrigation is also high in other countries. In Japan and South Korea, more than 60 percent of rice fields are irrigated. In Vietnam, the waters of the Mekong basin enable farmers to irrigate 3 million hectares of the nation's 7.9 million hectares of cropland. Asia's two largest countries are also heavily reliant on irrigation networks, with China posting a 38 percent irrigation rate and India irrigating 34 percent of its cropland (UN Food and Agriculture Organization 1999; UN Food and Agriculture Organization 2001a).

But this state of affairs is in jeopardy for a number of reasons. In Central Asia, China, Pakistan, India, and other places, improper irrigation has resulted in large-scale salinization of previously fertile land and serious disturbances to aquatic ecosystems (Asian Development Bank 1998; Postel 1989). Moreover, population growth, economic expansion, and contamination of freshwater resources by agricultural, industrial, and household sectors have all reduced per capita availability of water. Indeed, freshwater scarcity is increasing so quickly across the continent that some analysts believe that by 2010, freshwater shortages will approach crisis levels in many Asian countries, creating conditions in which "there will simply not be enough water to meet everyone's needs for all or part of the year" (Asian Development Bank 2000b). Countries such as China and India have embarked on ambitious and controversial dam projects to address this growing threat, but "a large share of the water that is needed to meet new demand must come from water saved from existing uses through comprehensive changes in policies related to water and institutional reforms. Such changes will not be easy, because both long-standing practice and cultural and religious beliefs have treated water as a free good and because entrenched interests benefit from the existing system of subsidies and administered allocations of water" (ibid.).

Fertilizers and Pesticides

Many farming regions of Asia became heavily dependent on agrochemical applications during the Green Revolution. These fertilizers, pesticides, and defoliants contributed to record-setting yields of wheat, rice, and other crops, but inappropriate levels of use have left invisible but serious scars on the land. Heavy fertilization has been blamed for increased eutrophication of waterways and widespread soil acidification, and runoff from treated fields has contaminated many rivers, lakes, and wetlands with chemical agents. In Uzbekistan, for example, application rates of mineral fertilizers on cotton fields are so high that it is estimated that only 35 to 40 percent of the applied nitrogen and 15 to 20 percent of the phosphorus will be assimilated, with the rest ultimately finding its way into aquifers, rivers, and other freshwater resources (Asian Development Bank 1998). In addition, many pesticides are toxic to species "other than those directly targeted, such as soil microorganisms, insects, plants, fish, mammals, and birds, that might not only be beneficial to agriculture or other human activities, but that are part of a biodiversity valued by society for recreational, cultural, ethical or other reasons," observed one study. "Although regulations in many countries have promoted the development of more-specific, less toxic, and more rapidly decomposing pesticides, many of the more damaging pesticides are still marketed in countries where regulations are more lax. Human health concerns include the effects of ingesting chemical residues contained in foods, but also the ill-effects on farm workers of pesticide handling and application, particularly in countries where safety standards are not well established, understood, or enforced" (Wood et al. 2000).

Fertilizer use in Asia remained high in the late 1990s. From 1995 to 1997, Asia used an annual average of 139 kilograms of fertilizer per hectare of cropland. The highest rate of application was in economically rich Singapore, where applications averaged an astounding 3,247 kilograms of fertilizer per hectare. Other high application rates endured in the Republic of Korea (693 kilograms per hectare), Japan (440), China (265), and Vietnam (206) (UN Food and Agriculture Organization 1999). Application rates are also influenced by the crop being raised. For example, the average fertilizer application rate for wheat in Asia ranges from less than 20 kilograms per hectare in Myanmar and Nepal to more than 300 kilograms per hectare in Japan (Harris 1998; Wood et al. 2000). Finally, levels of fertilization are directly linked to governmental subsidies. In India, for instance, fertilizer subsidies constituted the single largest subsidy item in the federal budget; in 1996 they accounted for almost half (47 percent) of all federal subsidies (Srivastava and Sen 1997).

Statistics on pesticide applications in Asia are less comprehensive and reliable, in part because of the thriving black market for DDT and other illegal pesticides that persists in Southeast Asia. But even without calculating illegal applications, the data that exists paints a troubling picture of excessive use. Asian countries known to make extensive use of pesticides include the Republic of Korea (13,829 kilograms per hectare of cropland in 1996), Turkmenistan (6,744 kilograms), Sri Lanka (6,261 kilograms), and Malaysia

(5,982 kilograms) (Wood et al. 2000). The lowest application rates for pesticides can currently be found in Central Asia, which is still recovering from Soviet-era saturation of the land. When the Soviet Union collapsed, economic privatization and restructuring combined to make purchase of agrochemicals a much more expensive proposition. As a result, the availability and use of pesticides, defoliants, and fertilizers plummeted across the region. In Kazakhstan, for example, only 36,000 tons of inorganic fertilizers were used on 0.3 million hectares of agricultural land in 1995, compared with 665,000 tons on 9.2 million hectares before independence. Before 1990 about 18 million hectares of land were treated with herbicides and pesticides; five years later, application of those chemicals on cultivated land was negligible (Asian Development Bank 1998).

Genetically Modified (GM) Crops and Asia's Future

The arrival of genetically modified (GM) foods in the international marketplace heralds a new chapter in the history of Asian agriculture. But perspectives on the probable impact of this new technology on Asia's economic prosperity, food security, and environmental health vary widely (Pinstrup-Anderson and Schioler 2001). Advocates believe that GM crop technology can revolutionize Asian farming yet again. Proponents contend that the low productivity of animal agriculture in some regions of Asia could be increased through the introduction of improved breeds, feeds, and vaccines. They also insist that if Asia were able to raise pest- and drought-resistant strains of wheat, rice, and other crops, it would be able to dramatically curtail its use of ecologically destructive irrigation, fertilization, and pest-control programs that reduce soil fertility and contaminate rivers, marshes, and aquifers. In addition, it has been noted that "natural rural ecosystems are under assault today in much of Asia...due to a population-linked expansion of the land area devoted to low-productivity crop farming (especially shifting cultivation) and livestock grazing. If agribiotechnology could help farmers in these countries produce more food on land already in use, one result would be fewer additional trees cut, fewer watersheds damaged, less rangeland and hillside plowing, less soil lost, less habitat destroyed, and more biodiversity preserved" (Paarlberg 2000). Given these potential benefits, analysts such as the Nuffield Council on Bioethics have concluded that "the probable costs of the (mostly remote) environmental risks from GM crops to developing countries, even with no controls, do not approach the probable gains of GM crops concentrated on the local and labor-intensive production of food staples" (Nuffield Council on Bioethics 1999).

Other observers, however, see GM crops as a potentially dire threat to Asian aspirations of melding economic prosperity with environmental conservation. One concern is that poor farmers in Asia and other regions of the world may be unable to afford transgenic (genetically modified) crops, which are currently being developed and commercialized almost entirely by private firms in the United States and other economically advanced nations. "If credit to purchase the seeds is available only to commercial farmers with significant holdings of high-potential land (or only to the politically connected) an initial result could be further marginalization of the poor" (Paarlberg 2000). Another economic worry is that GM crops developed in affluent countries could erode exports of crops raised in Asia by traditional means (Asian Development Bank 2000b).

On the environmental front, objections to transgenic crops have centered on the possible risks associated with the escape of genetically modified foods into the environment. Members of the environmental community have raised the specter of unplanned breeding between GM and non-GM life forms, including wild species. The hypothetical biohazards of such unions range from insect populations resistant to the toxins in pesticides to the creation of herbicide-resistant "superweeds" to the eventual disappearance of some wild species of flora and fauna. Another frequently cited area of concern is the potential effect of GM-food consumption on human health, such as increased risk of allergic reactions or accumulation of toxins in tissue (Paarlberg 2000; Pinstrup-Anderson and Schioler 2001).

Irrespective of the arguments for and against transgenic crops, Asia remained a minor player in the field at the close of the twentieth century. In 1999 only twelve countries were growing transgenic crops, and the United States, Argentina, and Canada accounted for 99 percent of the global area devoted to GM fields, with 70 percent, 17 percent, and 12 percent, respectively. Indeed, China is the only Asian country that has formally launched a GM crop-raising program (Wood et al. 2000). "Even in Asian countries with the strength to develop biotechnology programs, such as India, research emphasis is often placed on export crops. The [profit-driven] private sector is unlikely to change its focus. . . .If Asian countries are to tap more fully into the biotechnology revolution, they will need to expand their own national and regional capacity to undertake some of this research" (Asian Development Bank 2000b).

Indeed, at the dawn of the twentieth century, developing countries in Asia and elsewhere generally have "limited scientific and institutional capacity to manage these powerful new technologies safely. So even if developing countries have much more to gain from the GM revolution in farming, they may, at the same time, find it more challenging to pursue those gains safely and equitably. . . . What the developing countries need, most of all, is larger investment in their own indigenous scientific and institutional capacity, so they can shape this powerful new technology to suit their own distinctive local needs and circumstances" (Paarlberg 2000).

Keys to Sustainable Agriculture Growth

Asian agriculture is poised at a critical point in its history. Over the past few decades, it has risen to the challenge of feeding a rapidly expanding population while simultaneously reducing malnourishment in many poor areas. But the environmental price paid for these productivity gains has been significant, and continued population growth and economic expansion make continued advances in yield size a necessity. Indeed, flat or declining levels of crop and livestock production have the capacity to "jeopardize national food security and increase child malnutrition in many countries, cause significant new unemployment and poverty (particularly in agriculture and the rural nonfarm economy) and slow nonagricultural growth" (Asian Development Bank 2000b).

Nurturing continued agricultural growth in a framework of environmental sustainability will be a major challenge for Asian nations both great and small. After all, "expansion options are limited, soil and water resources in agricultural areas are often already stressed, pesticide resistance is increasing, and growth in yields seems more difficult to achieve" (Wood et al. 2000). Given that reality, organizations such as the World Resources Institute and the International Food Policy Research Institute say that the "strategic cornerstones" of enhanced farming productivity in Asia and other regions of the world are likely to include: a combination of conventional breeding and biotechnology-based innovations designed to improve the yield potential of crops and livestock; refined crop selection and crop rotations; sustainable soil, fertilizer, pesticide, and water management practices that place greater emphasis on soil and water conservation; strengthened regulatory and enforcement mechanisms governing pesticide import, production, and use; reforms in the pricing and allocation of water and other inputs; and improved training of agricultural workers exposed to pesticides. "A common need underlying all of these strategies is that for improved knowledge. Ultimately this calls for continued investment in agricultural and natural resource research that can help design more productive and more environmentally beneficial farming systems and production technologies" (ibid.).

Mitigation of environmental problems associated with agriculture in Asia is going to be enormously expensive. But implementing environmentally sustainable agriculture practices is essential to the long-term health and prosperity of the continent's human populations as well as its flora and fauna. And many analysts note that some relatively low-cost measures can set Asian farmers well along the path toward reducing their "ecological footprint" on the land they cultivate. For instance, organic agriculture excludes synthetic chemical inputs in favor of a farming system that relies on natural, organic inputs. In addition, "low till farming" has grown in popularity in several major agricultural regions of South Asia in recent years, especially among farmers of limited economic means and modest landholdings. Proponents say that this practice greatly reduces water use and plowing (which consumes time and resources) while increasing yields. Under low till regimens, farmers sow wheat in rice straw left standing from a previous harvest rather than in soil that has been repeatedly plowed over. The roots of the rice straw provide channels for wheat roots to grow, habitat for beneficial insects to prey on invasive insects, and a natural fertilizer of organic matter for the wheat crop ("Plow Less, Grow More," 2001).

Another model of sustainable agriculture that has rapidly gained favor in some Asian territories is integrated pest management (IPM). These programs provide an alternative to pesticides in stopping crop loss from pests and disease. They emphasize biological suppression of insects and other pests by nurturing environmental conditions that keep pest populations down (such as by providing fertile settings for insects, birds, and other species that prey on pests). Such systems have enjoyed marked success in the Philippines (for rice crops), Malaysia (rice and various vegetables), India (cotton), Pakistan (sugarcane and mangoes), Indonesia (soybeans), Bangladesh (brinjal), and Pakistan (fruit trees). "Presently, biological control represents an underused natural resource that humans can make use of to benefit environmental protection and preserve biodiversity," commented one assessment. "It is also the cornerstone of sustainable agriculture. Despite this, the biological control agents run high risks of being destroyed by modern agricultural practices that rely heavily on harmful chemical pesticides" (Consumers' Association of Penang 1997).

As with so many other sustainability practices, the key to IPM implementation and acceptance is to make it financially worthwhile. "Farmers are not irrational. On the contrary, they maximize income and minimize risk in a dynamic context and often under harsh conditions and serious constraints. They degrade resources when there are good economic and social reasons for doing so, i.e., when the benefits they obtain exceed the perceived costs that they, as individuals, must bear" (Asian Development Bank 2000). For that reason, proponents of IPM and other aspects of sustainable agriculture emphasize the financial rewards—such as savings in pesticide and application costs or increased yields—that can accrue from such practices (Wood et al. 2000). In Vietnam, for instance, IPM techniques are reportedly being applied by more than 90 percent of the Mekong Delta's 2.3 million farm households, prompting a dramatic fall in insecticide applications in the region from 3.4 per farmer per season to just 1. This not only saves farmers the expense of purchasing and applying insecticide but also greatly reduces the volume of chemicals entering local waters (International Rice Research Institute 2000). In Indonesia, meanwhile, a survey of 2,000 farmers trained in applying IPM techniques found that rice yields had increased by an average of 0.5 ton per hectare, and the number of pesticide applications had fallen from 2.9 to 1.1 per season. Moreover, rice fields cultivated under IPM were being recolonized by wild plant and animal species that had been erased from the region in earlier years by pesticide poisons (Wood et al. 2000). These sorts of advances, which are proliferating in farming communities all across the continent, constitute perhaps the clearest indication yet that China, India, Japan, and the other nations of Asia are finally recognizing that food security and environmental sustainability are ultimately inseparable issues.

Sources:

Asian Development Bank. 1998. *Central Asian Environments in Transition.* Manila.

———. 1997. *Emerging Asia: Changes and Challenges.* Manila: ADB.

———. 2001a. *Environments in Transition: Cambodia, Lao PDR, Thailand, Viet Nam.* Manila: ADB.

———. 2000a. *The Growth and Sustainability of Agriculture in Asia.* Manila: ADB.

———. 2001b. *India: Mainstreaming Environment for Sustainable Development.* Manila: ADB.

———. 2000b. *Rural Asia: Beyond the Green Revolution.* Manila: ADB.

Brown, Lester. 1995. *Who Will Feed China?* New York: W. W. Norton.

Consumers' Association of Penang. 1997. *State of the Environment in Malaysia.* Penang: CAP.

Delgado, C., et al. 1999. "Livestock in 2020: The Next Food Revolution." Discussion Paper no. 28. Washington, DC: International Food Policy Research Institute.

Guo, X. 2000. "Aquaculture in China: Two Decades of Rapid Growth." *Aquaculture Magazine* 26, no. 3.

Harris, G. 1998. "An Analysis of Global Fertilizer Application Rates for Major Crops." Paper presented at the Agro-Economics Committee Fertilizer Demand Meeting at the International Fertilizer Industry Association Annual Conference, Toronto, May 1998.

Harrison, Paul, and Fred Pearce. 1999. *AAAS Atlas of Population and Environment.* Berkeley: University of California Press.

Hertsgaard, Mark. 1998. *Earth Odyssey: Around the World in Search of Our Environmental Future.* New York: Broadway.

Huang, J., and S. Rozelle. 1994. "Environmental Stress and Yields in China." *American Journal of Agricultural Economics* 76, no. 4 (November).

International Food Policy Research Institute. 1998. "Technological Opportunities for Sustaining Wheat Productivity Growth toward 2020." Washington, DC: IFPRI.

International Rice Research Institute. 2000. *Something to Laugh About.* Los Banos, Philippines: IRRI.

Lloyd-Roberts, Sue, and Ethirajan Anbarasan. 2000. "The Aral Sea: Back from the Brink?" *UNESCO Courier* 53, no. 1 (January).

Manning, Richard. 2000. *Food's Frontier: The Next Green Revolution.* New York: Farrar, Straus and Giroux.

McHughen, Alan. 2000. *Pandora's Picnic Basket: The Potential and Hazards of Genetically Modified Foods.* New York: Oxford University Press.

Mock, Greg, Robin White, and Amy Wagener. 2001. "Farming Fish: The Aquaculture Boom." *World Resources 1998–1999,* updated July 2001 for *EarthTrends,* World Resources Institute, http://earthtrends/wri/org/conditions_trends/feature_select-action.cfm?theme=8.

Nuffield Council on Bioethics. 1999. *Genetically Modified Crops: The Ethical and Social Issues.* London: NCB.

Organization for Economic Co-operation and Development. 2001. *Environmental Outlook 2001.* Paris: OECD.

Paarlberg, Robert. 2000. "Promise or Peril? Genetically Modified Crops in Developing Countries." *Environment* 42, no. 1 (January–February).

Pingali, P. L., M. Hossain, and R. V. Gerpacio. 1997. *Asian Rice Bowls: The Returning Crisis?* Wallington, UK: CAB International.

Pinstrup-Anderson, Per, and Ebbe Schioler. 2001. *Seeds of Contention: World Hunger and the Global Controversy over GM (Genetically Modified) Crops.* Baltimore: Johns Hopkins University Press.

Pinstrup-Anderson et al. 1999. "World Food Prospects: Critical Issues for the Early Twenty-First Century." Washington, DC: IFPRI.

"Plow Less, Grow More." 2001. *Environment* 43, no. 10 (December).

Postel, Sandra. 1989. *Water for Agriculture: Facing the Limits.* Washington, DC: Worldwatch Institute.

Ravindranath, M. J., and Usha Iyer-Raniga. 2000. "Living Traditions: India." In David Yencken, John Fien, and Helen Sykes, eds., *Environment, Education and Society in the Asia-Pacific: Local Traditions and Global Discourses.* London: Routledge.

Srivastava, D. K., and T. K. Sen. 1997. *Government Subsidies in India.* New Delhi: National Institute of Public Finance and Policy.

State Land Administration. 1996. *Statistical Information on the Land of China in 1995.* Beijing: State Land Administration.

Unger, Jonathan. 2002. *The Transformation of Rural China.* New York: M. E. Sharpe.

UN Children's Fund. 1999. *State of the World's Children 1999.* New York: UNICEF.

UN Conference on Trade and Development. 1994. *UNCTAD Commodity Year Book*. New York: UNCTAD.

UN Development Programme. 1996. *Human Development Report 1996*. New York and Oxford: Oxford University Press.

———. *Human Development Report 1997*. 1997. New York and Oxford: Oxford University Press.

UN Development Programme, United Nations Environment Programme, and United Nations Food and Agriculture Organization. 1993. *Land Degradation in South Asia: Its Severity, Causes and Effects upon the People*. Rome: UNDP, UNEP, and FAO.

UN Economic and Social Commission for Asia and the Pacific, and Asian Development Bank. 1995. *State of the Environment in Asia and the Pacific 1995*. New York: UNESCAP and ADB.

UN Environment Programme. 1999. *Global Environment Outlook 2000*. London: Earthscan.

UN Food and Agriculture Organization. 1999. *FAOSTAT Online Statistic Service*. Rome: FAO.

———. 2001a. *The State of Food and Agriculture 2001*. Rome: FAO.

———. 2000. *The State of World Fisheries and Aquaculture 2000*. Rome: FAO.

———. 2001b. *The State of World Fisheries and Aquaculture 2001*. Rome: FAO.

van Lynden, G. W. J., and L. R. Oldeman. 1997. *Assessment of Human-Induced Soil Degradation in South and Southeast Asia (ASSOD)*. Wageningen, the Netherlands: UN Environment Programme, Food and Agriculture Organization of the United Nations, International Soil Reference and Information Centre.

Wood, Stanley, Kate Sebastian, and Sara J. Scherr. 2000. *PAGE (Pilot Analysis of Global Ecosystems): Agroecosystems, a Joint Study by the International Food Policy Research Institute (IFPRI) and World Resources Institute (WRI)*. Washington, DC: IFPRI, WRI, December.

World Resources Institute. 2000. *World Resources 2000–2001, People and Ecosystems: The Fraying Web of Life*. Washington, DC: WRI.

World Wildlife Fund—Malaysia. 1993. Malaysian National Conservation Strategy. 4 vols. Kuala Lumpur: WWF Malaysia.

6

Freshwater

The continent of Asia faces serious freshwater supply issues that defy easy or swift solution. Challenges confronting the region include rehabilitation of major rivers that have been ruined by decades of heavy pollution, increasing the efficiency of vast agricultural operations that are severely depleting and polluting groundwater aquifers, and addressing fundamental inadequacies in water distribution, water treatment, and other infrastructure elements that currently waste large volumes of water and leave millions of Asian people without access to safe drinking water. Moreover, these problems besiege a region that is riddled with poverty (three out of four of the world's poor live in Asia), acutely vulnerable to weather-related disasters, and is experiencing rapid population growth that threatens to overwhelm already degraded and oversubscribed ground and surface water systems. Experts believe that the continent's struggles to survive this growing water crisis are likely to become even more desperate in the coming decades, as soaring population numbers and expanding industrialization trigger even greater demand for finite freshwater supplies.

Freshwater Supply and Use

Asia is not without resources to address the growing demand for freshwater. It houses several of the world's largest watersheds, including those of the Ganges, Yangtze, Yellow, Mekong, Irrawaddy, Amu Darya, Syr Darya, and Indus rivers. These rivers have been the lifeblood of millions of Asians for centuries. Major lakes dot the continent as well, including the Dongting-hu in China, Tonle Sap in Cambodia, Lake Toba in Indonesia, the Kasumigaura in Japan, and Lake Songkhla in Thailand. These lakes have been harnessed by local populations for drinking water, irrigation, fishing, and recreation. Finally, Asia possesses major underground freshwater reservoirs in Bangladesh, India, Nepal, Myanmar (Burma), China, and other regions.

Table 6.1 Top Ten Countries in Inland Fisheries Production

Country	Production in 1998 (tons)	Percentage of world production (65% for top ten countries)
China	2 280 000	28.5
India	650 000	8.1
Bangladesh	538 000	6.7
Indonesia	315 000	3.9
Tanzania, United Rep.	300 000	3.7
Russian Federation	271 000	3.4
Egypt	253 000	3.2
Uganda	220 000	2.8
Thailand	191 000	2.4
Brazil	180 000	2.3

SOURCE: UN Food and Agriculture Organization, http://www.fao.org.docrep/003/x8002e/x8002e04.htm

These aquifers currently provide nearly one-third of the continent's total drinking water (one lone aquifer in eastern China currently provides drinking water for an estimated 160 million people) and are the foundation for thriving agricultural operations in China and India, among other nations. In addition, the countries of China, India, Bangladesh, and Thailand are among the ten top countries that account for 65 percent of the world's total inland fishery catch (see Table 6.1).

Together, the continent's total renewable water resources (average annual flow of rivers and recharging of groundwater) easily exceed the volume of annual total withdrawals across Asia, although some individual regions are very water-stressed, a situation that is often exacerbated by tremendous seasonal variations in water availability. Indeed, rainfall and population density vary tremendously across the continent, creating regions of both great water abundance and severe water scarcity. Per capita availability of water in Papua New Guinea, for example, is between 175,000 and 200,000 cubic meters, while other countries, including Afghanistan, the Republic of Korea, Pakistan, and Sri Lanka, all have less than 3,000 cubic meters. Even China and India, which draw on some of the world's largest river basins, have less than 3,000 cubic meters per capita, because of their vast populations (State Environmental Protection Administration of China 1997; World Resources Institute, 1998). These shortfalls in freshwater availability, which are often exacerbated by indifferent stewardship of ecologically fragile rivers, lakes, wetlands, and aquifers, can significantly hamper economic development, although in some instances, disregard for the environment has helped some countries realize economic gains in the short term. For example, the Amu Darya and Syr Darya rivers have been harnessed for irrigation of cotton crops; subsequent cotton harvests have been immensely profitable but have come at the price of ruining large sections of the basins.

Another major factor in Asia's growing freshwater plight is its disproportionate share of the world's total population. The continent contains only 16 percent of the globe's total land area, but it is home to the world's two most populous countries—China and India—and approximately 55 percent of the world's total population. In order to feed this expanding population, most Asian nations have embraced sprawling agricultural operations that require huge volumes of water. Half a dozen Asian nations—China, India, Indonesia, Korea, Pakistan, and Sri Lanka—irrigate more than 30 percent of their total cropland, and irrigated agriculture accounts for 60 to 90 percent of annual freshwater withdrawal in most nations. Moreover, the regions of East Asia and South Asia far outscore any other world regions in irrigation intensity (see Figure 6.1), and not surprisingly, Asia's cropping intensity is the world's highest (see Figure 6.2). In some countries, this percentage is even higher (in Afghanistan, for instance, irrigation accounts for 99 percent of all water withdrawals) (UN Food and Agriculture Organization 1997 and 1999).

Most Asian nations rely on underground aquifers to one degree or another to maintain these agricultural operations, but few have imposed any measures to protect these invaluable resources from overexploitation or pollution. In Vietnam, for instance, many aquifers have become contaminated with saltwater, agrochemicals, or industrial pollutants or rendered useless as a result of withdrawal rates that far exceed natural levels of replenishment.

Figure 6.1 Global Irrigation Intensity, 1995–1997

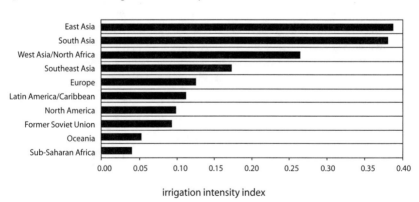

irrigation intensity index

NOTE: The irrigation index is the irrigated area divided by the total area of cropland.

SOURCE: Compiled from FAOSTAT 1999.

Figure 6.2 Global Annual Cropping Intensity, 1995–1997

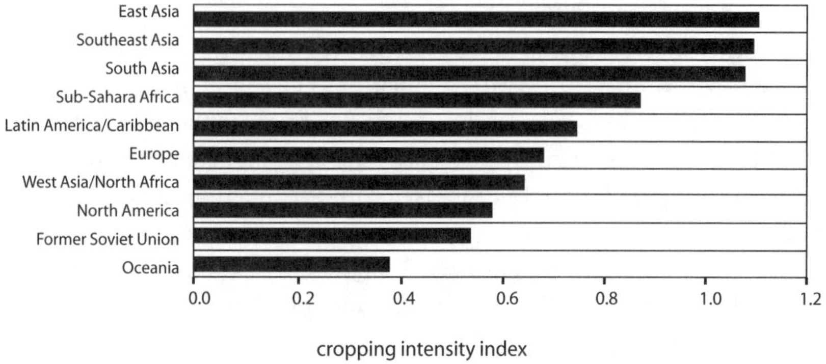

NOTE: The cropping intensity index is the harvested area of annual crops divided by the total area of annual cropland.

SOURCE: Compiled from FAOSTAT 1999.

Elsewhere, large Asian cities such as Jaipur, India, and Shenyang, China, have been forced to conduct frantic—and expensive—searches for alternate supplies of water after fouling their own groundwater beyond repair.

Endemic poverty is another important factor in Asia's inability to provide untainted water in many regions. "In general, the question of access to safe freshwater largely depends on the level of development of a particular country," observed the Asia-Pacific Center for Security Studies. "Industrialized countries in the region—for example, Japan, Singapore, and Taiwan—clearly have fewer problems with providing their populations with access to safe freshwater. Less developed countries . . . face much greater challenges in this regard. . . .In developed countries, access to water is considered an entitlement; this mentality does not necessarily prevail in developing countries where access to safe drinking water is often a luxury, sometimes available only to the affluent" (Asia-Pacific Center for Security Studies 1999). Indeed, many Asian families have to spend a considerable portion of their meager income just to purchase potable water from vendors who take ruthless advantage of the laws of supply and demand. This scenario plays itself out most frequently in rural areas, but poor residents of many major cities face similar situations. "About one-third of Bangkok's population has no access to public water and has to depend on water vendors for their supply," stated the Asia Media Information and Communication Centre (AMICC). "In Jakarta, water vendors service the needs of about 30 percent of the population, charging up to five times the cost of piped water" (Asia Media Information and Communication Centre 1997).

Freshwater availability is also complicated by Asia's vulnerability to devastating weather phenomena. These relatively common events—cyclones, storm surges, earthquakes, droughts, floods, and volcanic activity—compromise the integrity of freshwater resources and put additional financial pressure on already cash-strapped nations. In 2000, for example, terrible floods washed over most of Southeast Asia. In Cambodia and Vietnam alone, overflows from the Mekong River killed 400 people, destroyed the homes of millions more, and damaged an estimated quarter-million hectares of farmland. When such disasters occur, regional governments are routinely forced to divert large portions of their limited financial resources to address disaster-related expenses, leaving little funding for environmental measures that might protect freshwater supplies in the future, such as installation of water treatment facilities, enforcement of antipollution laws, or restoration of wetlands and forest areas. In addition, some scientists speculate that Asia's freshwater supplies may be at even greater risk from natural disasters in the future, as global warming–induced climatic changes become more prevalent. These experts cite the impact of the El Niño and La Niña weather phenomena, which created severe drought conditions in Indonesia, Papua New Guinea, and several other Asian nations during the 1990s, as evidence of this threat.

The combined weight of these various factors—economic impoverishment, exploding population numbers, susceptibility to natural disasters, and environmental degradation—have scarred freshwater systems all across the continent. An estimated 850 million Asians do not have access to safe drinking water, and an additional 2 billion—well over half the continent's population—live without access to safe sanitation facilities (only 10 percent of the sewage produced in all of Asia is treated at the primary level). Not surprisingly, the widespread biological and chemical contamination of water supplies has taken a terrible toll on numerous Asian communities. The World Health Organization (WHO) estimates that diarrheal diseases attributable to polluted water kill an estimated 1.5 million children every year in the seven Asian countries where water conditions are most appalling, and it speculates that perhaps 80 percent of the diseases on the continent are waterborne viruses that originate in polluted wells and waterways. Moreover, the impact of waterborne diseases also extends into the economic realm; according to *World Resources 1998–1999*, the annual cost to human health of water pollution in Asia has been estimated as high as $3.9 billion.

The prognosis for reversing this deadly state of affairs is not encouraging, especially in areas where water resources are already in high demand. "In many parts of Asia, 'water-stressed' people are forced to live, not only without the minimum supply of water for daily necessities, but also with no guarantee that the meager trickle they get is always safe to drink," summarized one study of the region. "Spiraling population and economic growth puts increasing pressure on limited water supplies. Groundwater is threatened by increasing use. . . .Combined with periodic droughts and floods and unregulated industrial pollution, the unprecedented demand on water supplies, that are today already sporadic and of poor quality, will deplete almost half of the available resources by the turn of the century" (Asia Media Information and Communication Centre 1997).

The Freshwater Crisis in China

Asia's ability to triumph over its freshwater supply problems will depend in large part on the actions of China and India, the world's largest nations by population and the region's heaviest users of water by volume. China's freshwater management challenges mirror those of the larger continent. It has more than 20 percent of the world's population within its borders but has access to only 6 to 7 percent of the globe's total freshwater. China is also floundering in its efforts to build urban infrastructures that can accommodate the needs of its rapidly growing industrial populations. China's economic expansion, wrote reporter Jacques Leslie, "has created enormous waves of social change, such as tens of millions of destitute rural migrants to the cities and the rising expectation among city dwellers of running water, indoor toilets, and diets rich in water-intensive beef and pork" (Leslie 2000).

In addition, much of China's economic and population growth is sprouting in regions that are lacking in water resources. For example, northern China—which receives only about one-quarter of the nation's annual rainfall—is home to about 40 percent of the country's population, accounts for about half of its total industrial output, and contains almost three-quarters of its farmland. Desperate to meet the considerable appetites of these various constituencies, the region is devouring its existing water resources at an unsustainable rate. "Why is China running out of water?" wrote journalist Marq De Villiers. "The answer is the same as for the rest of the world: it isn't running out. It's only running out in places where it's needed most" (De Villiers 2000).

In recent years, mounting evidence of China's unsustainable consumption of its freshwater resources has come to light. By the mid-1990s, nearly half of China's 640 major cities were grappling with at least periodic water shortages. The economic consequences of these water shortages in metropolitan areas

The Three Gorges Dam Project

China's Three Gorges Dam is the world's most controversial dam project. The construction of this massive dam in the midsection of the Yangtze River—China's most storied waterway, and its longest at more than 3,900 miles (6,300 kilometers)—has galvanized fierce opposition from a wide array of critics, including scientific, environmental, and human rights organizations. These opponents characterize the dam as an ecological and humanitarian nightmare. But China has forged ahead with the dam, the largest and most expensive hydroelectric project in history, and hopes to complete it by the target date of 2008.

Certainly, the Chinese government already has devoted a great deal of time, effort, and prestige to the Three Gorges project. The estimated price tag of the dam, which is supported by export credit agencies of Canada, Switzerland, France, and Germany and financed in part by several major U.S. American banks, ranges from $30 billion to $75 billion. This breathtaking investment will create a dam of extraordinary physical dimensions. Authorities say that when the dam is completed, the concrete and steel structure will stand 610 feet high and more than 6,800 feet long—more than five times as wide as the Hoover Dam. Each of the dam's two dozen spillway bays will have the average capacity of America's the Missouri River, and the wall itself will create a 600-square-mile reservoir stretching back more than 370 miles up the Yangtze River Valley.

The Chinese government officials and other supporters of the Three Gorges Dam project tout the future dam as an asset that will provide immeasurable benefits to the country. They contend that the dam will make the Yangtze—which currently accounts for nearly 80 percent of China's waterborne trade—an even more valuable method of transportation. It will increase navigation far upstream and transform Chongqing, located 1,300 miles inland, into a major Chinese port able to accommodate ocean freighters. "A hinterland that is truly the heartland of the nation [will] have its products shipped to world markets with a speed and economy it has never known before," agreed journalist Simon Winchester (Winchester 1996). Proponents also say that the Three Gorges Dam will tame the floods that periodically savage the Yangtze basin. As recently as 1998, for example, a Yangtze flood exacerbated by upstream deforestation claimed more than 3,600 lives, rendered 12 million Chinese homeless, destroyed 3 percent of the nation's crops, and cost an estimated $4.8 billion. Moreover, the Chinese government estimates that the dam will provide the nation with an important new source of clean energy. Indeed, the dam is expected to generate up to 18,000 megawatts of power, the equivalent of 40 million tons of coal and four times the power capacity of any European facility currently in operation.

When the Three Gorges dam comes online, China's electricity supply will be boosted by an estimated 10 percent in one fell swoop.

But opponents charge that the Three Gorges Dam will take an unacceptable toll on the Yangtze region, one of the most densely populated and historically significant areas of the world. Critics note that the project fails to comply with many of the recommendations and guidelines set forth by the World Commission on Dams. For example, the dam and its reservoir will ultimately flood hundreds of towns and villages, drowning ancient archaeological treasures and displacing 1.2 to 1.9 million people, according to various estimates. Many of these victims will be forcibly resettled in inhospitable regions that are less conducive to farming and other activities that were their livelihoods. "Resettlement on this scale is impossible," charged the International Rivers Network. "Not only are communities destroyed, but the cities and towns that are forced to absorb the migrants face economic and social upheaval" (International Rivers Network 2001).

Dam opponents also warn that the Three Gorges project could have major unintended health consequences—including increased incidences of malaria, encephalitis, Keshan disease, and schistosomiasis—as billions of tons of industrial wastewater and sewage from cities along the Yangtze contaminate the reservoir. The human health impacts associated with the Three Gorges reservoir could create a "Chernobyl of hydropower," warned an article in the British Medical Association journal *The Lancet*. "There are currently no programs in China to combat the dam's threats to public health, and no funding for treating the area's wastewater or mitigating the environmental problems it will cause" (Sleigh and Jackson 1998). In addition, many analysts warn that huge quantities of silt could become trapped behind the dam, eroding dam performance and safety, depriving downstream areas of fertile, erosion-preventing silt, and increasing the flow of the river downstream of the dam in ways that might actually increase regional vulnerability to flooding. "And beyond this danger, the lessening in the overall flow of the river will allow the tidal effects of the sea to seep farther back in the estuary, changing fishing patterns and altering the salinity of the soils and the groundwater," observed Winchester. "The effects of the dam, in this one very specialist area of interest, are legion." (Winchester 1996).

Many environmentalists and scientists, meanwhile, lament the disruptive effect the dam will have on the habitat of countless fish, reptiles, and riverine mammals, including rare freshwater dolphins, Siberian cranes, and Chinese sturgeon. "The dam will block the flow of nutrients and migration routes for countless fish species, as well as the black finless porpoise and the already endangered Baiji dolphin—the legendary goddess of the Yangtze River," stated the IRN. Critics also note that the reservoir waters will submerge one of the most scenically spectacular stretches of the Yangtze's entire length.

Even international security experts have expressed concerns about the Three Gorges dam. The facility is being built in a region that features several major seismic fault lines, and analysts warn that it would be an inviting target for bombing or sabotage from foreign or domestic groups. If an earthquake or violent attack ever does cause a breach in the dam after its completion, the loss of life and property downstream will be nearly incomprehensible.

Opposition to the damming of the Yangtze River has even erupted in China. In February 1999, some 10,000 resettlers petitioned the Chinese government for assistance, citing rampant corruption, extortion, and falsification of data in the dam resettlement program. One year later, it was revealed that Chinese dam officials had embezzled nearly $58 million in funds set aside for compensating villagers affected by the forced resettlement plan. The $58

million amounted to almost 12 percent of the meager total allotted by the government for that purpose. But despite such embarrassing revelations and continued condemnation by international organizations (and some governments), the Three Gorges project continues to proceed. In fact, many Chinese critics of the project have been arrested or chased into exile by government authorities.

Sources:

Dai Qing, ed. 1998. *The River Dragon Has Come!: The Three Gorges Dam and the Fate of China's Yangtze River and Its People.* Armonk, NY: M. E. Sharpe.

De Villiers, Marq. 2000. *Water: The Fate of Our Most Precious Resource.* New York: Houghton Mifflin.

Sleigh, Adrian, and Sukhan Jackson. 1998. "Public Health and Public Choice: Dammed off at China's Three Gorges?" *Lancet* 351 (May 16).

"Three Gorges Dam, Yangtze River, China." International Rivers Network, (www.im.org.wcd/threegorges.shtml), (accessed March 13, 2001).

Winchester, Simon. 1996. *The River at the Center of the World.* New York: Henry Holt.

Zich, Arthur. 1997. "China's Three Gorges: Before the Flood." *National Geographic* (September 1997).

are significant; according to one estimate, urban water shortages cost China an estimated $11.2 billion annually in industrial output (World Resources Institute 1998). Water shortages are also increasingly commonplace in rural areas. This is especially true in the country's northwest sector, where an esti-mated one-third of all wells have run dry. Hundreds of small towns and vil-lages containing an estimated 50 million rural Chinese now suffer from regular shortages of potable water. Many experts attribute this grim trend to China's massive infusions of water into irrigation networks. According to some estimates, as much as 70 percent of the total water used in China is fun-neled directly into agricultural operations, most of which are notoriously in-efficient (as much as half of the water diverted for irrigation is lost to seepage or evaporation).

Not surprisingly, China's large-scale diversions of water have also had a devastating impact on the health and vitality of many rivers, as well as the fish and wildlife that depend on the waterways for their existence. For example, northern China's Yellow River now fails to reach its mouth for months at a time because of massive upstream water diversions for industrial and agricul-tural purposes. These diversions have reduced the Yellow to a ghost of its for-mer self by the time it reaches Shandong Province, an important corn- and wheat-growing region on the Yellow Sea that relies on the river for half of its irrigation water. The Yellow River first failed to reach the sea in 1972, and since 1985 it has dried up before reaching the river's mouth every year. Moreover, the length of this dry period is steadily growing. In 1996 the river failed to reach the sea for 133 days, and during the drought year of 1997, it failed to reach the river mouth for 226 days. These extensive dry periods have ruined downstream ecosystems, devastating the populations of numerous aquatic animal and plant species.

The Chinese government has taken several steps to address its impending water supply crisis, most notably a major campaign of dam-building and water transfers that will harness several major river systems for increased ir-rigation, drinking, and industrial use. But many observers allege that the dams and transfers are being erected with little or no regard for environmen-tal consequences, and that China's ability to meet its ever-growing water needs will ultimately hinge on adopting much more efficient water use prac-tices and restoring degraded waterways. Moreover, China's steadily expand-ing population is shrinking the amount of available farmland and heightening the need to make additional productivity gains. But the chief means of registering those productivity gains—fertilizer—is one of the pol-lutants most responsible for the deplorable ecological state of its rivers, lakes, seas, and groundwater aquifers.

If China is unable to halt the steady decline in its freshwater supply, the situation could become a grave one with staggering international implications. Without adequate supplies of water, China will ultimately be unable to feed itself. China would then have to import enormous amounts of food to stave off mass starvation. Analysts believe that such large-scale purchases might have a grim ripple effect, pushing world commodity prices to levels that would devastate developing countries in Asia and elsewhere that are already struggling to feed their peoples.

Freshwater Issues on
the Indian Subcontinent

Another region of Asia in which freshwater supply issues are assuming critical importance is the Indian subcontinent. India has long fed itself by virtue of massive water development projects that have bent the nation's waterways and aquifers to its will. These projects—built during the "Green Revolution" of the 1960s and still primarily oriented toward irrigation—enabled India to increase its food production capacity dramatically over the years. But India continues to add 18 to 20 million people to the global population annually, and the nation's track record as caretaker of its freshwater assets does not inspire confidence. Today, analysts warn that the nation does not possess the freshwater resources to accommodate its current population growth or economic expansion. Indeed, water shortages are already affecting the Indian people in fundamental ways across large areas of the country. Many Indian households already spend one-quarter of their income on water for drinking and bathing, and most Indians (57 percent of urban Indians and 96 percent of rural Indians as of the mid-1990s) do not have access to sanitation facilities.

As in China, agriculture accounts for the single greatest drain on freshwater resources in India. By some estimates, Indian farmers account for 85 percent of all renewable water consumption in the country, which leads the world in total irrigated area. Most of this land was converted to irrigated farming in the last half-century. During that time the total amount of irrigated area in India rose from 22.6 million hectares in 1951 to nearly 90 million hectares in 1996, as the country tapped into both groundwater aquifers and monsoon-dependent rivers with unbridled enthusiasm. For example, the number of shallow tube-wells used to draw groundwater to the surface increased from 3,000 in 1960 to more than 6 million by 1990.

Today, however, studies suggest that time is running out for India's underground lakes after decades of large-scale withdrawals. "India's volume of annual groundwater overdraft is higher than any other nation's. Almost everywhere in the country, water withdrawals are proceeding at double the

A family travels by boat across floodwaters to reach their home in Hajaribag, Bangladesh. AFP/CORBIS

rate of recharge, causing a drop in aquifers of three to ten feet per year; in the state of Tamil Nadu, groundwater levels have dropped as much as ninety-nine feet since the 1970s, and some aquifers there have become useless [because of seawater intrusion]" (Leslie 2000). Even India's own National Environmental Engineering Research Institute has admitted that "overexploitation of ground water resources is widespread across the country" and warned that water tables in important agricultural regions were plummeting "at an alarming rate" (National Environmental Engineering Research Institute 1997). The seriousness of this situation is compounded by the state of many of India's rivers, which have been rendered useless as sources of drinking water by decades of mistreatment. If India continues to drain its aquifers at its present rate of consumption, observers warn that the economic and environmental consequences will be severe. "Lakes and rivers dry up as the aquifer recedes," stated the International Water Management Institute. "The costs of pumping become so high that the pumps are shut down and the whole house of cards collapses. It is not difficult to believe that India could lose 25 percent or more of its total crop production under such a scenario."

In neighboring Bangladesh, meanwhile, the availability of potable water is even more uncertain. The impoverished people of Bangladesh—the most densely populated country in the world, with 890 people per square kilometer—have always been acutely vulnerable to floods that overwhelm the nation's rivers and other surface water resources. These natural disasters, coupled with contamination of major rivers, has made most surface resources unusable for drinking water. In the 1970s most of Bangladesh turned to groundwater for its potable water, and the country quickly registered a dramatic drop in the incidence of water-related disease and important gains in crop productivity. But scientists have since discovered that much of the country's groundwater contains extremely high concentrations of arsenic. This substance occurs as the result of natural geological phenomena, but it is exposed or produced when water tables decline and aquifer walls are exposed to oxygen, so a more moderate abstraction rate may not have produced the arsenic danger that now exists (World Resources Institute 1998). Today, an estimated 20 to 40 million people in Bangladesh and the Indian state of West Bengal are believed to be relying on this arsenic-laced water for drinking, cooking, and farming, and observers such as the World Bank publicly worry that the situation may ultimately emerge as "perhaps the largest mass poisoning in history." Various international and national nongovernment organizations (NGOs) and government agencies launched programs to respond to this problem in the late 1990s, but the region's limited supply of safe surface water has thus far made long-term solutions elusive. For many rural peoples, their only alternatives are groundwater pumps that bring up arsenic-contaminated water or surface water sources that are incubators for various waterborne diseases.

Pakistan is also struggling to make better use of dwindling freshwater resources. In order to be successful in this regard, it must institute fundamental changes to its agriculture-based economy, which has been draining huge amounts of water from underground aquifers over the last several decades. In Pakistan, the number of wells tapping into groundwater resources rose from 25,000 in 1964 to almost 360,000 by 1993. The water from these wells enabled Pakistan to establish major agricultural operations across the country, but many of those operations use water inefficiently; in addition, flawed irrigation practices have ruined millions of acres of farmland in the country. In fact, by some estimates overirrigation has ruined an estimated 42 million acres of farmland in Pakistan and India combined.

But Pakistan's halting efforts to enact more efficient water-use policies and practices through land reform and other measures have been hampered by successive years of drought at the turn of the century. These drought conditions, which extended throughout central Asia, have become so severe that in the spring of 2001 desperate Pakistani officials began exploring the possibility of melting glaciers in the mountains of the Himalayan, Karakoram, and Hindu Kush ranges to relieve future shortages. The notion of accelerating the melt rate of these glaciers, the major source of surface freshwater for the region, was quickly decried by a chorus of scientists, environmentalists, and other critics who expressed shock at the potential environmental and economic repercussions of any such action. Detractors argue that any glacier-melting program would transform regional ecosystems—including major river networks—in a host of ways that could never be anticipated.

As India and its neighbors grapple with looming freshwater shortages, observers worry that long-standing tensions between the nations may explode over the issue. These tensions do not stem exclusively from freshwater distribution issues—India and Pakistan, for instance, have long been enmeshed in a bitter fight for sovereignty over the region known as Kashmir—but the region's complex water rights situation is seen by some as a potential trigger issue to wider conflict. However, most border countries in conflict—including India and Pakistan—have historically managed to maintain their water agreements even during periods of active hostility.

When the British Empire partitioned the subcontinent in 1947, it gave Pakistan most of the canals and farmland of the Indus Basin, but India's status as upstream riparian gave it practical control of the river. "It was a solution pregnant with the possibilities of rancour," observed Marq De Villiers (De Villiers 2000). In the intervening years, water rights have emerged as a perennially contentious issue in relations between India and Pakistan, as well as India and Bangladesh (which was a province of Pakistan—under the name of East Pakistan—until 1971). But for the most part, the principals have exercised restraint when negotiating over water rights. The Indus Water Treaty of 1960 signed by India and Pakistan remains in force, despite serious political and ethnic tensions between the two nations, and in 1997 Bangladesh and India signed a formal Ganges Water Sharing Treaty after years of diplomatic wrangling. Analysts also note that the governments of India and Pakistan put major political differences aside and worked together during the drought of 2000, when millions of Pakistanis and Indians faced water shortages that threatened their very lives. Despite such encouraging episodes, however, political observers say that continued diminishment and degradation of regional water resources has the potential to trigger violent interstate conflict in the future.

Asia's Imperiled Waterways

Asia is home to many of the world's grandest rivers. Waterways such as the Yangtze, Mekong, Indus, Brahmaputra, Ganges, and Irrawaddy are among the planet's greatest natural treasures, notable not only for their size and volume but also for the terrific array of biodiversity that they support. Many of these rivers, nourished by timeless cycles of monsoon and drought, are also deeply interwoven in the history, culture, and religious belief systems of the Asian communities through which they pass. But without exception, these magnificent river systems—along with countless smaller rivers, streams, lakes, and wetlands across the length and breadth of the continent—have suffered enormously from years of exposure to agrochemical and industrial pollutants and massive discharges of human and animal waste. Not surprisingly, those bodies of water in closest proximity to pollution sources (factories, crowded cities, farming operations, etc.) have endured the most abuse. In the Philippines, for example, Southeast Asia's largest freshwater lake (Laguna Lake) has been ruined by untreated effluents from the thousand Manila-area factories that ring its shores and the discharge of mind-numbing quantities of untreated human waste from the capital's residential areas. But the impact of rampant air and water pollution also extends into the most remote corners of the continent. Airborne pollution has even contaminated the snow-fed rivers of the Himalayas with toxic materials over the past half-century.

The chief culprits in the deterioration of Asia's rivers, lakes, and aquifers are the continent's economic impoverishment, its continued exponential population growth, and its willful refusal to address environmental issues. The combined weight of these realities has thus far prevented much of Asia (with notable exceptions, such as the economically advanced nations of the Pacific Rim) from erecting the necessary infrastructure and legal measures to safeguard and conserve its freshwater resources. And even developed nations like Japan do not have freshwater systems that are models of ecosystem or biodiversity health.

Less than 50 percent of the domestic wastewater generated in Asia is treated before it is discharged into local waterways. This state of affairs is even more appalling in major metropolitan areas; according to some studies, more than 95 percent of wastewater from Asian cities is discharged into rivers, seas, or fields without any treatment at all. Consequently, Asia's rivers contain three times as many bacteria from human waste (fecal coliform) as the world average, and more than ten times the limit of OECD (Organization for Economic Cooperation and Development) guidelines. The reported median fecal coliform count in Asia's rivers is also fifty times higher than World Health Organization guidelines (UN Environment Programme 1999). This epidemic of waterway contamination from human waste is most severe in Southeast Asia, but it is present to some degree or another across the entire continent.

Pollution from industrial and agricultural sectors is also endemic across much of Asia. According to the Asian Development Bank, toxic pollutants from industrial activity have boosted the region's levels of lead in surface water to twenty times the amount found in rivers and lakes in OECD countries. In rural areas, meanwhile, livestock waste, fertilizers, pesticides, and other agrochemicals have created a poisonous stew in countless river systems and underground aquifers. The consequences in this area have ranged from incidences of profound eutrophication to acute shortages of potable water.

Other villains in the desecration of Asia's rivers are deforestation and wetland drainage or conversion. Deforestation contributes to the siltation of rivers, while drainage and conversion of wetlands—which act as sponges during heavy rainfall—have reduced basins' ability to regulate flows and increased the likelihood of major floods. Both activities are widespread across the continent and particularly pervasive in Myanmar (Burma), Thailand, Cambodia, the Philippines, and other nations in southern Asia. According to some estimates, forest cover in Asian countries has dropped from 70 percent of total land area in the mid–twentieth century to less than 25 percent at the end of the century. Deforestation of watersheds—whether to clear land for farming or for the value of the timber itself—has dramatically increased the sediment load in many Asian rivers, which are particularly vulnerable to erosion because they run through areas of steep topography and heavy rainfall. In fact, a 1996 Global Environment Monitoring System study indicated that two-thirds of the globe's total sediment transport from inland areas to oceans is taking place in Southeast Asia. This increased sedimentation has had a negative impact on the health and vitality of countless aquatic species, and on the fishing communities dependent on them.

In addition, deforestation of important rainfall catchment areas has heightened human vulnerability to flooding, which in turn has triggered profound man-made changes to the character of many river systems. "Deforestation in Asia . . . is a major regional issue and, when coupled with the natural patterns of high wet-season and low dry-season river discharge, has direct and profound impacts on floodplains and their inhabitants," explained scientist David Dudgeon. "In essence, large-scale changes in flow are an inevitable result of deforestation. In turn, they encourage the construction of dams to protect against floods, which further alter the hydrological regime. . . .It is clear that many . . . animals have declined in abundance due to human modification of the natural flood-pulse cycle in riverine wetlands" (Dudgeon 2000).

These various factors have left scars on every major waterway on the continent, but the scope of degradation varies from country to country. Many of China's waterways, for instance, are in a nightmarish state. The nation contains 30,000 miles of major rivers within its borders, but 80 percent of those rivers are too polluted to support fish. The condition of the Huai River basin, home to more than 120 million Chinese, is all too typical. The Huai has endured decades of industrial vandalism at the hands of paper, tanning, and dyeing factories, which pour massive amounts of untreated effluents into the river each day. In 1994, one particularly poisonous flood of industrial toxins turned the river black, sickening thousands, leaving hundreds of thousands of others without drinking water, and killing an estimated 26 million pounds of fish. Yet despite public outrage over the incident, many upstream factories continue to operate as before, pouring toxic chemicals into the Huai without penalty (Hertsgaard 1998).

Elsewhere, China's Zhu Jiang River has been transformed into a vast conveyer belt for human and animal waste, agrochemicals, and industrial solvents. Forced to carry an estimated 1.4 billion tons of sewage a year—most of it untreated in any fashion—much of the river is now devoid of aquatic life. And China's Yangtze River is so heavily contaminated with runoff of chemicals from industrial factories and nitrogen-based fertilizers from farm fields that it now threatens much of the marine life in the East China Sea, the source of one-quarter of China's annual seafood harvest. By some estimates, the Yangtze alone now carries between 9 and 18 percent of the total riverborne nitrogen that is being deposited on the world's coastlines. Fisheries all the way down to Thailand, Malaysia, and Indonesia are already feeling the effects of this massive infusion of nitrogen, which increases crop yields but destroys downstream fishing grounds by consuming life-giving oxygen. "China is the world's most striking illustration of man-made nitrogen's power to create and destroy," wrote journalists Frank Langfitt and Heather Dewar. "It has helped feed the world's most populous nation and eased lives of hardship unimaginable to most Westerners. But it is ruining the nation's rivers, bays, and coastal waters. And worse looms. In 20 years, experts say, Asia will be the dominant source of nitrogen pollution to Earth's air and water, producing more than all the rest of the world's nations combined and almost as much as all of the planet's natural processes" (Langfitt and Dewar 2000).

The state of waterways in most other Asian countries is similarly grim. In the Philippines, cyanide, mercury, and other heavy metals used in gold mining have poisoned numerous rivers, and waterborne diseases rank as the third-leading cause of death (and the second-leading cause of infant mortality). In Malaysia, unchecked discharges of industrial waste and human sewage led the government to label forty-two of its rivers officially "dead" by 1989. In Thailand, the level of pollution in many rivers—whether it takes the form of industrial heavy metals, fertilizers, pesticides, human fecal matter, or other pathogens—often exceeds government standards by as much as 100 times. In Indonesia, a 1999 Ministry of Health study found that more than 40 percent of all water provided to urban communities is contaminated with fecal waste.

India, meanwhile, has fouled many of its rivers by using them to dispose of human sewage and toxic pollutants from factories and farming operations, while at the same time proving indifferent stewards of its all-important aquifers. A late 1990s study conducted by India's Central Pollution Control Board surveyed twenty-two major industrial zones and found that the groundwater in every one was unfit for human consumption. Even the River Ganges, the nation's holy river, is used as a dumping ground, as more than 100 towns and cities dump huge volumes of raw sewage into its waters every year. And in South Korea, hundreds of factories located along the shores of the Naktong River routinely discharge heavy volumes of toxic wastes directly into the stream, flouting regulations with impunity. Similar scenarios play out elsewhere across the nation daily (Postel 1997). Even Japan, an economic powerhouse that touts itself as a world leader in environmental stewardship, has a mixed record in the realm of water protection. It has made significant improvements in water quality over the past two decades by targeting industrial activity that was contaminating rivers and lakes with heavy metal pollution. But 30 percent of Japan's total water area (rivers, lakes, inland seas, etc.) still fails to meet environmental quality standards for organic pollution, and many aquatic ecosystems have suffered collateral damage from a half-century of enthusiastic commercial, residential, and industrial development.

Dam-Building on the Increase in Asia

Asia is in the midst of a sustained dam-building campaign that will dramatically transform the economies, social systems, and ecosystems of the continent. When the twentieth century drew to a close, dam projects were on the decline across much of the globe, in part because most major rivers in Europe, North America, and other regions had already been dammed, and in part because of growing awareness of the important role that free-flowing rivers play in maintaining the health of the environment. But many Asian countries—eager for economic development and increasingly desperate to shore up dwindling freshwater supplies—have embraced major dam and channelization projects, swayed by the undeniable benefits they provide in such realms as flood control, shipping, agriculture, and power production. Indeed, major dam projects have helped boost the economic fortunes of myriad regions across Asia. But critics point out that the impact of these works is never entirely benign. Many dams currently in operation in Asia have disrupted fragile ecosystems, and others have dislocated entire communities from their ancestral homes.

The first dams built in Asia were designed primarily for flood control purposes. These dams succeeded in limiting the seasonal flooding to which so much of Asia is prone, but it also triggered large-scale settlement and development of regions that had formerly been flood plains. As a result, floods have become less frequent but markedly more punishing, exacting a greater toll in economic damage and human mortality when they do occur. By 1950 approximately 1,500 dams more than 15 meters high had been built across Asia, constituting about 30 percent of the global total. But China then embarked on a sustained period of dam-building that touched every major river system in that vast country. This appetite for dam-building continued unabated in the 1980s and 1990s, as China looked to hydroelectric power as a way of relieving its longtime reliance on coal, the chief reason for the nation's atrocious air quality. By the turn of the century, more than 80,000 dams of varying sizes and uses were in operation in China, according to the World Commission on Dams (WCD).

This half-century campaign of dam-building has provided countless Chinese cities with hydroelectric power and supplied water to nourish its crop-producing provinces. But Chinese authorities show little inclination to rein in their dam construction appetites, especially given the nation's relentless population growth. In fact, China has begun construction of a dam that will, when completed, be the largest hydroelectric dam on the planet. The Three Gorges Dam will straddle the mighty Yangtze River, creating a 600-square-mile reservoir for irrigation and generating an estimated 18,000 megawatts of power. But the dam—scheduled for completion in 2008—has been assailed by a wide array of scientists, environmentalists, human rights activists, and economists for alleged shortcomings in conception and design. Critics of the project charge that it will have a catastrophic environmental impact on the river and the upper Yangtze River valley, that it will force at least 1.2 million Chinese people to relocate from their homes, and that the dam itself will be vulnerable to a breach or collapse that would cause unimaginable destruction to heavily populated downstream areas. In 1994 hydrologist Daniel Beard, head of the U.S. Bureau of Reclamation, stated: "There is no more visible symbol in the world of what we are trying to move away from than the Three Gorges Dam" (Winchester 1996). The Chinese government dismisses these concerns, however, and is proceeding with construction. It is also going ahead with three major water transfers from the Yangtze to the Yellow River. Critics contend that these expensive projects—partially responsible for the thirty-eight different large dams that are currently under construction in the Yangtze basin (Revenga 2000)—will further devastate the rivers (and much of the land in between) and will not solve growing water scarcity problems in China's northern provinces. Critics believe that gains in water conservation from reduced consumption and improved infrastructure (replacement of leaky pipelines, etc.) would better ensure long-term sustainable use of existing water resources and also avoid large-scale environmental degradation.

Globally, India is second only to China in both the number of major dams it maintains (nearly 4,300, about 9 percent of the global total) and the size of its population (approximately 1 billion). The two are inextricably intertwined, for India's dam-building policies are geared almost exclusively toward feeding its burgeoning population. Historically, the vast majority—better than 95 percent—of these dams were built solely or mostly for irrigation purposes. The Indian government has been successful in these efforts, reaching food self-sufficiency. But these projects have also extirpated countless regional ecosystems and placed the long-term environmental viability of the country in serious doubt. The World Commission on Dams also estimates that between 20 and 40 million Indians have been displaced by these dam projects over the decades.

India is currently struggling with basic upkeep and operational issues for many of these dams and their affiliated water-diversion facilities. Common problems besetting these existing operations include leaking irrigation canals and serious salinity or waterlogging of significant areas of tilled land.

Narmada River dams, India. BALDEV/CORBIS SYGMA

Nonetheless, India continues to erect new dams at an ambitious pace in order to provide food, potable water, and electricity for its expanding population. The best known of these new dam initiatives is the Sardar Sarovar Project (SSP), a spectacularly huge undertaking in the remote Narmada Valley of India. This project, which will consist of 30 major dams, 135 medium-size dams, and 3,000 small ones if completed as planned, has been fiercely opposed by indigenous peoples who would be displaced by the dams and their reservoirs.

Supporters of the SSP claim that if the dam network is completed, it will be an enormous boon to the Indian people, generating much-needed clean hydropower, irrigating nearly 2 million hectares of farmland, and providing safe drinking water for millions of people. Opponents dismiss those figures as wildly exaggerated, pointing to a litany of other completed Indian dam projects that have exceeded initial cost estimates and failed to realize predicted productivity levels. Critics also charge that the Narmada River dams will have severe negative environmental repercussions for the region, and that the Indian government has offered inadequate reparations to the estimated 200,000 villagers who will be displaced by the project. (The grassroots organization Narmada Bachao Andolan [NBA] places the number of affected villages at half a million.)

Bolstered by a coalition of human rights and environmental organizations, these villagers initiated a series of legal maneuvers and protests that blocked construction for six years and convinced the World Bank and several international corporations to withdraw their support. In October 2000, the Indian Supreme Court cleared the way for construction to proceed, even though environmental impact studies required under Indian law had yet to be completed. Since then, construction on the controversial project has resumed despite ongoing protests. But opposition from grassroots organizations and international NGOs has been so strong that many observers believe that the government is scaling back its plans for the Narmada Valley and preparing new measures to reduce the social and environmental impact of those dams that are eventually built.

Blueprints for other major dam-and-canal projects in Asia are also likely to become a reality over the next two decades. Indeed, dam-building schemes are proliferating from water-wealthy Nepal, home to 6,000 rivers with a hydropower potential assessed at 83,000 megawatts, to Southeast Asia's Mekong River basin. The latter region is seen as a particularly lucrative area for dam-building. In years past, poverty, remote and rugged terrain, and decades of regional warfare hindered dam-building efforts on the Mekong, a richly biodiverse river that courses through China, Myanmar (Burma), Laos, Thailand, Cambodia, and Vietnam for 2,600 miles before flowing into the South China Sea. But the nations of Thailand, Laos, and Cambodia, slowly emerging from years of crippling warfare and internal strife, have all formulated plans to build dams on the Mekong and its tributaries as they scrape up the necessary funding, and China reportedly is considering erecting dams in the upper reaches of the Mekong.

In fact, more than 200 potential dam sites have been identified for the Mekong basin, and some analysts predict that more than a dozen large dams could be erected across the mainstream within the next decade. The construction of such dams for hydropower and irrigation would further alter the basin and damage riverine species in all sorts of ways, from disruption of breeding migrations to flooding of habitat already feeling pressure from encroaching human populations. It will also have major consequences for the region's rural poor. The Tonle Sap, for example, provides fish to millions of people in the basin; the erection of dams would alter the river enormously, vastly diminishing the aquatic resources upon which those populations depend.

The proposed Sambor Dam project in Cambodia presents a fairly representative microcosm of the choices and tradeoffs that Southeast Asia will be making in the coming years. This $4 billion hydroelectric project will provide a much-needed source of power and usable water to the country. "Project backers say [that it] would generate revenue for a nation that ranks among the poorest on Earth and one still reeling from decades of war and terror," noted one International Wildlife report. But as the organization also pointed out, the completed dam will "flood 310 square miles, displace 60,000 people and endanger wildlife that still includes tigers, wild buffalo, bears, elephants, and crocodiles. It would also have a profound impact on the 1,000 aquatic species found in the Mekong—from the largest-known freshwater stingray to migratory catfish that are important commercially" (Mecir 1999).

Another hugely controversial dam project in Asia is the San Roque Dam on Luzon, an island in the northern Philippines. If this dam on the lower Agno River in Pangasinan Province is completed on schedule in 2003, it will become the tallest dam (200 meters/650 feet) and largest private hydropower project in Asia, generating 345 megawatts of power and irrigating more than 87,000 hectares (214,900 acres) of rice fields. Proponents of the dam also tout the San Roque as an essential flood control tool, for in its lower reaches the Agno frequently escapes its banks during the rainy season. But detractors claim that the dam's reservoir may produce dangerous concentrations of heavy metals and other toxic materials from upstream polluters, and they rail against the forced removal of tribal groups from ancestral lands. Critics also charge that the dam's location on a geographic area susceptible to earthquakes and frequent typhoons makes it particularly vulnerable to breaching. If such a nightmare came to pass, the ruptured dam could flood downstream areas containing an estimated 1.5 million people.

Sources:

Abramovitz, Janet N. 1996. *Imperiled Waters, Impoverished Future: The Decline of Freshwater Ecosystems.* Washington, DC: WorldWatch Institute.

Asia Media Information and Communication Centre. 1997. *Water: Asia's Environmental Imperative.* Singapore: Asia Media Information and Communication Centre.

Asia-Pacific Center for Security Studies. 1999. *Water and Conflict in Asia.* Honolulu: APCSS.

Brown, Lester. 1995. *Who Will Feed China? Wake-up Call for a Small Planet.* New York: W. W. Norton.

De Villiers, Marq. 2000. *Water: The Fate of Our Most Precious Resource.* New York: Houghton Mifflin.

Dudgeon, David. 2000. "Large-Scale Hydrological Changes in Tropical Asia: Prospects for Riverine Biodiversity." *BioScience* 51, no. 9 (September).

Fisher, W. F., ed. 1997. *Struggling over India's Narmada River.* Armonk, NY: M. E. Sharpe.

Gaan, Narottam. 1998. *Environmental Degradation and Conflict: The Case of Bangladesh-India.* Colorado Springs, CO: International Academic Publishers.

Gleick, Peter H. 2000. *The World's Water, 2000–2001.* Washington, DC: Island.

Hertsgaard, Mark. 1998. *Earth Odyssey: Around the World in Search of Our Environmental Future.* New York: Broadway.

Hirsch, Philip, and Carol Warren, eds. 1998. *The Politics of Environment in Southeast Asia: Resources and Resistance.* London: Routledge.

Humphrey, Caroline, and David Sneath. 1999. *The End of Nomadism Society? Society, State, and the Environment in Inner Asia.* Chapel Hill, NC: Duke University Press.

"Japan's Dirty Secret: As Deadly Toxins Poison the Environment, the Government Is Doing Its Best to Avoid the Issue." *Time International,* May 29, 2000.

Langfitt, Frank, and Heather Dewar. 2000. "China's Prosperity Turns Seas Toxic." *Baltimore Sun,* September 2.

Leslie, Jacques. 2000. "Running Dry." *Harper's Magazine* 301 (July).

Mecir, Antonin. 1999. "Taming the Mekong, Killing the Past." *International Wildlife* (January).

National Environmental Engineering Research Institute. 1997. "Water Resources Management in India."

Ohlsson, Leif, ed. 1995. *Hydropolitics: Conflicts over Water as a Development Constraint.* London: Zed.

Postel, Sandra. 1997. *Last Oasis: Facing Water Scarcity.* New York: W. W. Norton.

———. 1999. *Pillar of Sand: Can the Irrigation Miracle Last?* New York: W. W. Norton.

Revenga, C., et al. 2000. *Pilot Analysis of Global Ecosystems: Freshwater Systems.* Washington, DC: World Resources Institute.

———. 1998. *Watersheds of the World: Ecological Value and Vulnerability.* Washington, DC: World Resources Institute/Worldwatch Institute.

Smil, Vaclav. 1993. *China's Environmental Crisis.* Armonk, NY: M. E. Sharpe.

State Environmental Protection Administration of China. 1997. *National Report on Sustainable Development.* Beijing: SEPA.

"Three Gorges Dam, Yangtze River, China." International Rivers Network, http://www.im.org.wcd/threegorges.shtml (accessed March 13, 2001).

UN Environment Programme. 1999. *Global Environment Outlook 2000.* London: Earthscan.

UN Food and Agriculture Organization. 1999. *Irrigation in Asia in Figures.* Rome: FAO.

———. 1997. *Water Resources of the Near East Region.* Rome: FAO.

Winchester, Simon. 1996. *The River at the Center of the World.* New York: Henry Holt.

World Commission on Dams. 2000. *Dams and Development: A New Framework for Decisionmaking.* London: Earthscan.

World Resources Institute. 1998. *World Resources 1998–1999: A Guide to the Global Environment.* New York: Oxford University Press.

7

Oceans and Coastal Areas

The health and vitality of Asia's biologically rich oceans and coastal areas have been compromised by an array of closely intertwined forces, including extraordinary population growth, rampant development, appalling levels of pollution, and unsustainable fish harvesting. Experts warn that these issues will have to be addressed quickly and decisively if the region hopes to maintain its ocean resources for future generations.

Concerns Grow about Status of Asian Fisheries

The nations of Asia control a vast swath of the world's oceans. Blessed with 288,500 kilometers of coastline on the Pacific and Indian oceans, the continent's claimed Exclusive Economic Zone (EEZ) amounts to 11.84 million square kilometers (under the UN Law of the Sea, all coastal nations have sovereign control over the waters and seafloor that lie up to 12 miles offshore, as well as dominion over seas extending 200 miles from inhabitable land).

Asia's ocean waters are patrolled by more than 1 million trawlers and other decked fishing boats, as well as countless dugouts and other small vessels employed by subsistence fishermen hailing from Thailand, Vietnam, Malaysia, China, and other states. The immense size of this fleet, coupled with the introduction of modern fishing gear and technology, has transformed Asia's coastal waters into the world's leading fishery by volume. According to the UN's Food and Agriculture Organization (FAO), the continent's total marine fisheries production increased by an average of nearly 3 percent annually from 1975 to 1995. By 1990 the region accounted for 38 percent of the global marine fish catch, with eight Asia-Pacific nations ranked among the world's top fifteen in catch volume (UN Food and Agriculture Organization 1991). Asia continued to register record harvests of its oceans' bounty for much of

Trawlers in Guangzhou, Canton, China. GIPSTEIN/CORBIS

the 1990s as well. The FAO reported that the average annual marine fish catch in Asia from 1995 to 1997 reached 28.35 million metric tons. It also estimated the average total export value of Asia's fish catch from 1996 to 1998 at more than U.S.$8.2 billion, even though most fish caught in its coastal waters were consumed domestically.

Of all the Asian countries that cast nets into the oceans, China unquestionably has the biggest impact on fish stocks. (See graph of marine fishery production in Figure 7.1) The world's most populous nation, China accounts for about 20 percent of all global marine capture fisheries (15 metric tons), according to the FAO. In addition, China's wild marine fish catch is augmented by massive harvests of fish from inland waters and the globe's largest aquaculture industry (UN Food and Agriculture Organization 2001). But marine scientists and conservationists agree that Asia's wild fish stocks and aquaculture programs face potentially crippling threats. Overfishing is endemic in many areas, and fishing nations such as Japan, South Korea, and Taiwan are all suspected of routinely flouting a 1992 global ban on large-scale driftnet fishing (using nets of over 2 miles in length). Fleets in the region have also engaged in practices that threatened the overall ecological balance in the seas. For instance, Japan has been catching and importing large quantities of sashami-grade tuna (bluefin and bigeye) all over Southeast Asia and the South Pacific, despite scientific warnings that overfishing of these and other top predators are throwing entire marine ecosystems into disarray. In addition, rampant pollution from industrial, agricultural, and municipal sources is not only despoiling important marine ecosystems but also jeopardizing aquaculture operations that have helped relieve poverty in China, India, Bangladesh, the Philippines, and other coastal areas. Moreover, essential marine nursery areas such as mangrove forests and coral reefs have suffered extensive damage from pollution and coastal development.

Critics contend that if these problems are not addressed through meaningful changes in industry practices and public policy, Asia's leading marine fish stocks face almost certain collapse. This would be a calamitous event for millions of Asians who rely on fish as a dietary staple and their chief means of economic support. In some areas, warning signs have already been detected. In China, for instance, Michael Berrill writes that

> the fisheries . . . are showing the usual signs. Fewer and smaller fish of the target species are being captured, and boats are bringing in less and less each year. . . . The regulations are inadequate and poorly enforced. Fisheries biologists determine the size of an allowable catch and estimate a maximum sustainable yield, which is at least partially ignored in order to keep the fishers employed. This model of management hasn't worked elsewhere and does not work here either. Meanwhile, as the favoured yellow croaker and hairtail species disappear, they are replaced by smaller, less valuable species. Traditions run deep; not only

Figure 7.1 Marine and Inland Capture Fisheries Production: Top Producer Countries in 1998

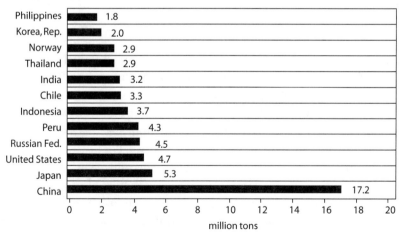

Country	million tons
Philippines	1.8
Korea, Rep.	2.0
Norway	2.9
Thailand	2.9
India	3.2
Chile	3.3
Indonesia	3.7
Peru	4.3
Russian Fed.	4.5
United States	4.7
Japan	5.3
China	17.2

NOTE: For statistical purposes, data for China do not include Taiwan Province and Hong Kong Special Administrative Region

SOURCE: UN Food and Agriculture Organization

have generations fished for their living, but families often live on their boats. The end of the fishing will mean extraordinary loss for these people, and other jobs will be hard to find. (Berrill 1997)

The twin threats of marine pollution and overharvesting are hurting fisheries all across Asia to one degree or another, but conditions vary significantly from region to region. For instance, in the Northwest Pacific—which includes the East China Sea, Yellow Sea, Sea of Japan, Sea of Okhotsk, and the northern portion of the South China Sea—a classic case of "too many ships chasing too few fish" seems to be unfolding. "In the East China Sea the total fishing power of Chinese vessels increased by a factor of about 7.6 between the 1960s and 1990s," reported the FAO. "Catch-per-unit-effort declined over the same period by a factor of 3. In coastal areas such as the East China and Yellow Seas, there has been a shift in catches from large high-valued fish to lower-valued smaller fishes. . . . Reduction of fishing effort in some areas is considered an urgent priority" (UN Food and Agriculture Organization 1997). Further north, catches of valuable commercial species such as Alaskan pollack, Japanese sardine, anchovy, and shellfish all declined by various degrees during the 1990s. Some of this decline has been attributed to natural factors, but overharvesting and global warming have also been cited as potential influences (warming ocean temperatures have been blamed for reductions in plankton and other vital links in the ocean food chain). Meanwhile, industrial pollution from the region's heavily populated coastal areas and agrochemicals carried downriver from inland farms have been blamed for compromising marine ecosystems in the Sea of Japan, the Yellow Sea, and other historically productive fishing grounds.

The threat of marine pollution and overfishing is also acute in Southeast Asia, where fish account for as much as 90 percent of all animal protein in the diets of coastal residents of Indonesia, Malaysia, Philippines, Thailand, and Vietnam. Over the last several decades, the open-sea fleets of these coastal states, which demarcate Asia from Australia and the Pacific Ocean from the Indian Ocean, have scooped so many fish out of the sea that some important wild stocks are mere shadows of their former selves. For instance, populations of bottom-dwelling fish species in the Gulf of Thailand fell by 90 percent from the 1960s to the early 1990s (UN Food and Agriculture Organization 1997), and the tuna trade in the Philippines archipelago declined significantly during the same period. According to the FAO and other observers, uncertainty about the future of the region's fisheries is further exacerbated by a paucity of scientific research programs devoted to tracking fishery populations and overall marine ecosystem health.

With catch rates flattening—and in some cases declining noticeably—tensions in the region between open-water trawler operators and inshore fishermen have steadily increased, giving rise to episodic violence. Indeed, armed clashes between these two camps have periodically reddened Southeast Asia's waters ever since high-tech trawlers armed with massive driftnets first appeared off the coast of Thailand in the early 1960s. "The introduction of trawlers into South-East Asia and surrounding regions in the 1960s and 1970s sparked often violent conflict," noted one report.

In Malaysia, inshore fishers, having learned of the effects of motorized trawlers upon the livelihoods of their fellow fishers in Thailand a few miles to the North, burned the very first trawler to arrive and threatened the life of its skipper. In the early 1970s, the conflicts escalated, culminating in a naval battle involving some 50 boats. . . . In the early 1980s, the Malaysian government bought in certain measures to prohibit trawlers from inshore waters—but also embarked upon a programme of halving the numbers of inshore fishers and expanding the deep water fleet. Since then, foreign trawlers, some of them armed with automatic weapons, have continued to encroach upon Malaysian waters and local fishers have seen their catches decline. (Fairlie et al. 1995)

But while trawlers continue to operate in Malaysian and other Southeast Asian waters, negative publicity about their toll on marine ecosystems and coastal fishing communities has sparked restrictions or outright bans on trawler activity in some regional waters. Other measures to reduce fishing pressure in Southeast Asia are also being considered, including closed or shortened seasons for some species, closure of sensitive marine areas, restrictions on nets and other equipment, and reductions in fleet size. But analysts worry that implementation of meaningful conservation initiatives will not mean much if global warming triggers a change in water temperatures in the region.

Over in the Indian Ocean, the Bay of Bengal and other areas have historically been rich repositories of fish and other marine life. As a result, the fleets of South Asia and other fishing nations were able to harvest 3 to 4 million metric tons of fish and shellfish annually from those waters during the 1990s. But as in other parts of Asia, the harvesting capacity of these huge open-water fleets—India alone had more than 20,000 mechanized trawlers in its fleet in the mid-1990s, including 100 major deep-sea fishing vessels—pose a threat to the livelihoods of untold numbers of subsistence fishermen for whom fish is their primary source of protein (Hinrichsen 1998). Unchecked population growth in coastal areas is another troublesome issue, sparking increased pressure on nearshore fish stocks and increased degradation of coastal waters.

Some fisheries experts believe that harvest rates in the Indian Ocean may actually increase in the near term without wreaking lasting damage on fish stocks. The reasoning here is that some sectors of the sea "tend to have a lower incidence of fully exploited, overexploited, depleted or recovering fish stocks, and a prevalence of underexploited or moderately exploited stocks" (UN Food and Agriculture Organization 2001). But even optimistic assessments of the status of Indian Ocean fish stocks note that scientific study of the region's marine ecosystems has been lacking, casting a pall of uncertainty over any forecasting efforts. Moreover, any efforts to implement fishery management programs in the region in the coming years face significant hurdles. In the western Indian Ocean and eastern Arabian Sea, for example, "the enormous number of small fishing vessels [primarily from India and Pakistan] . . . makes monitoring of stock status and implementation of fisheries management measures difficult," admitted the FAO. "Almost any form and size of fish that can be caught is saleable. Given the scarcity of alternative employment, fishing intensity will remain high, increasing whenever the catch rates and economic conditions will allow it do so. Small-scale shrimp fisheries are important in both Pakistan and along the west coast of India. Gear restrictions are few and the size and range of fishing effort creates major difficulties for management" (UN Food and Agriculture Organization 1997).

Population Surge Brings
Marine Pollution Problems

Asia's oceans are beleaguered by huge volumes of untreated industrial, agricultural, and municipal pollutants that pour forth from nearly every nation on the continent. The level of marine pollution is directly linked to the continent's rapid economic and population growth, most of which is concentrated in coastal areas. Of Asia's total population of 3.6 billion, an estimated 1 billion live within 50 kilometers of the sea. In some ecologically fragile areas, the crush of population is even more overwhelming.

The impact of this population surge is further exacerbated by profound flaws in infrastructure. Asia has seen staggering numbers of people crowd into metropolitan areas that have nonexistent or inadequate waste treatment facilities. Population densities in some of Indonesia's major cities are approaching 800 people per square kilometer, while population densities along China's 18,000-kilometer continental coastline average between 110 and 834 per square kilometer, with even higher concentrations in Shanghai and other coastal cities (Hinrichsen 1998; Yeung and Hu 1992).

But while discharges of human and animal waste and industrial effluents from these coastal population centers are major problems, the oceans of Asia are also feeling the impact of activities hundreds of miles inland. There, in the densely populated river valleys of China, India, Vietnam, and other countries, pesticides, heavy metals, and other pollutants from agricultural, logging, and industrial operations are carried downstream. As these substances are deposited in the sea, they eventually devastate marine ecosystems, spawning tumor-ridden fish and "red tides" (deadly algal blooms caused by excess nitrogen).

Marine pollution is particularly acute in developing nations, where "impoverished coastal inhabitants have exploited coastal resources with little regard for sustainability . . . [resulting] in the loss of critical ecosystems," declared one UN report. "Coastal erosion, resulting from increased land subsidence from groundwater extraction, and off-shore mining of sand and dredging are two other notable problems in some places" (UN Environment Programme 1999). Numerous other environmental problems confront these nations as well. For example, oil spill containment and clean-up plans are nonexistent in cash-strapped countries such as Thailand, Vietnam, and Myanmar (Burma), all of which have experienced oil contamination of marine areas as a result of discharges from coastal refineries, tanker accidents, discharge of oil-laced ballast water, and tank washings from the many ships that ply Asia's ocean waterways.

Many of these same nations have embraced aquaculture as a means of improving the lives of their most impoverished citizens and relieving pressure on wild fisheries. But the ascension of fish farming has transformed regional ecosystems in a number of undesirable ways. Large stands of ecologically vital mangrove forests have been swept aside to make way for fish pens, and some wild species of fish have suffered losses as diseases and waste generated in aquaculture pens invade their natural habitats. Other marine scientists have expressed concern that cross-breeding of escaped cultured fish with wild stock could reduce the survival capacity of the latter. And some Asian aquaculture operations are making increasing use of antibiotics, hormones, and other chemicals to bolster their output; these chemicals are altering marine environments in ways that are not yet clearly understood.

The link between poverty and environmental degradation is perhaps most evident in South Asia, which includes India, Pakistan, Bangladesh, Sri Lanka, and the Maldives. "All along South Asia's coasts, human numbers overwhelm resources," writes oceans expert Don Hinrichsen. "Mangroves are being cut down for fuelwood, tannin, and building materials. Coral reefs face assaults from coral mining and from sedimentation due to coastal construction, soil erosion, and dredging. Coastal forests, like most of the region's forests, have been replaced by agricultural lands and towns. Overfishing has reached crisis proportions. . . .Most sickness is blamed on the acute lack of clean drinking water and access to sanitary facilities. Every morning, one of the most common sights across South Asia is that of scores of people defecating into drainage canals or by stagnant streams, while a few meters away others bathe, brush their teeth, and wash their clothes" (Hinrichsen 1998). Given this state of affairs, disease and sickness have become epidemic in the slums of Calcutta, Dhaka, and other overcrowded metropolitan areas. The impact of all these people is further heightened by a lack of waste treatment facilities. Together, the Indian cities of Calcutta and Bombay dump more than 750 million metric tons of raw sewage and other municipal waste into coastal waters annually.

Marine pollution threatens ocean waters farther west and north as well. The Gulf of Thailand receives overwhelming volumes of raw sewage and municipal waste carried by rivers that run through Bangkok's crowded streets. China discharges millions of metric tons of untreated or partially treated municipal wastes into the Yellow Sea every day. Elsewhere on the Yellow Sea, South Korea is grappling with increased incidence of red tides, attributed to woefully inadequate water protection measures. In the South China Sea, rare Pearl River Delta pink dolphins are being pushed to the brink of extinction by overfishing (which deprives them of food), extensive coastal development, and public apathy, as well as industrial waste that has contaminated their muscle tissue with high concentrations of DDT and other toxins.

On the other side of the South China Sea, meanwhile, the Philippines' Manila Bay is choked by untreated or partially treated waste from millions of people and thousands of factories. In the East China Sea, 80 percent of the municipal waste generated by Shanghai's 17 million residents enters the water untreated, despite the construction of five sewage treatment plants during the 1990s. In the Sea of Japan, radioactive waste dumped by Japan and Russia in years past continues to linger, mingling with toxic chemicals from industrial operations; as a result, squid native to this sea carry the highest PCB load of any species known in the world (Berrill 1997). Finally, the volume of marine pollution emanating from North Korea into the Sea of Japan and the Yellow Sea remains unknown. But considering the economic straits of that secretive nation, experts believe that treatment of waste generated by military, industrial, and agricultural activity is minimal.

Even topography is playing a role in the deterioration of Asia's oceans. According to some estimates, Southeast Asia alone accounts for more than half of the world's total transport of sediment to the oceans. In these and other areas of Asia, steep gradients, active tectonics, and heavy rainfall combine to send massive amounts of sediment out to sea. In earlier eras, ocean currents dispersed these sediments in patterns that nourished inshore ecosystems. But destructive farming and logging practices have dramatically increased sediment loads in area rivers, which have also been laced with agrochemicals, industrial effluents, untreated wastewater, and other poisons. As a result, river mouths and other marine areas in which sediments concentrate have become less hospitable for fish and other ocean life.

But while the state of Asia's oceans is grim in many respects, marine scientists, conservationists, and economists alike have been heartened by some recent efforts to protect marine resources. In southern Asia, Sri Lanka has implemented meaningful initiatives to preserve its coastal resources. Further east, the Philippines and Thailand have implemented coral reef conservation programs, and Singapore has dramatically improved the state of its coastal waters and rivers. Hong Kong, too, has introduced significant programs to rein in the release of industrial pollutants into coastal waters.

Japan is another nation that has launched vigorous ocean protection programs in recent years. During the 1960s and 1970s the country's coastal waters became extremely fouled with toxins and other waste generated by its factories, farms, and cities. This pollution created red tides, hurt regional fish stocks, and—in one case that made international headlines—became a public health menace. During the late 1960s and early 1970s, ingestion of mercury-polluted fish pulled from Japan's Minamata Bay triggered nervous-system disorders among thousands of Japanese citizens. Some victims died from the poisoned fish, while others were afflicted with tremors, sensory disorders in the limbs, blindness, or deafness. The elevated mercury levels in Minamata Bay fish were also blamed for a wave of terrible deformities among babies born in the region.

The tragic situation at Minamata Bay forced Japan to close the bay to fishing in 1974, erecting a massive net across its mouth to prevent the escape of contaminated fish. It also prompted the Japanese government to turn its attention to the dire state of its coastal waters. As the 1970s progressed, Japan dramatically curtailed the release of industrial pollutants into its waters. Since that time, the nation has continued with efforts to restore and protect its oceans. In the 1990s, for instance, Japan passed legislation putting new limitations on releases of nitrogen and phosphorus into the sea, and it has dramatically improved water quality in the Seto Inland Sea, long a notorious symbol of pollution's destructive effects on the marine environment. In 1997, after years of intensive research and clean-up efforts, Minamata Bay was finally opened to fishing again.

Cyanide Fishing Threatens Asia's Coral Reefs

One of the greatest threats facing Southeast Asia's ecologically vital coral reefs is the practice of "cyanide fishing." Fishermen who have turned to this method of harvesting spray a toxic blend of seawater and crushed cyanide tablets onto reefs, where many fish species concentrate, including ornamental species highly valued by the aquarium stock industry. The poison stuns fish and makes them easy to catch, but it also kills coral polyps and small organisms essential for healthy reefs.

Most of the ornamental fish taken from the water in this fashion end up in the United States. In fact, the United States accounts for 60 percent of the global market in ornamental fish, and it is the final destination for 70 to 90 percent of live coral shipments worldwide. Experts believe that approximately 85 percent of the marine aquarium fish exported to the United States are captured on the reefs of Indonesia and the Philippines (Wood 2001).

The current epidemic of cyanide fishing is usually traced back to the Philippines of the late 1950s and early 1960s. During the latter decade, the island nation was home to a modest three aquarium fish exporters. By the early 1980s, however, nearly three dozen such outfits were operating in area waters, harvesting up to 80 percent of the tropical marine aquarium fish sold worldwide. Over time, fishermen in the employ of these companies became increasingly reliant on cyanide spraying to make their catch; by some estimates, these fishermen have injected more

than a million kilograms of cyanide into Philippine reefs since the 1960s.

Efforts to rein in the use of cyanide temporarily dampened the aquarium trade during the late 1980s, but researchers Chip Barber and Vaughan Pratt note that, by that time, "damage was already widespread. Three decades of cyanide use and other destructive fishing practices had debilitated most Philippine reefs, precipitating a sharp decline in the availability of desired aquarium species. As Philippine aquarium fish stocks declined, however, new source areas were opened. More ominously, trade in live food fish began to surge, driven by increasing demand from increasingly wealthy Chinese consumers, particularly in Hong Kong. Indeed, the live food fish trade has grown faster and become more lucrative than the aquarium fish trade in recent years, triggering a wild rush of fishers—and the spread of cyanide fishing—to still unexplored reefs.... In Hong Kong, according to one observer, the fact that a fish species is endangered actually seems to spur consumer demand for that species" (Barber and Pratt 1998).

Today, cyanide fishing remains a serious problem in both the Philippines and Indonesia, which together supply an estimated 85 percent of the aquarium fish traded in the world market. But it has also been reported in many other Southeast Asian nations, including Cambodia, the Maldives, Malaysia, Thailand, and Vietnam (ibid.). In addition, increasing numbers of fishermen have resorted to dynamite or homemade kerosene-based bombs to pull fish from the reefs. The increase in these deadly—and illegal—fishing practices is usually attributed to the still robust demand for ornamental fish on the world market. In 2000 the UN Food and Agriculture Organization (FAO) estimated the total retail trade value of aquarium fish worldwide at about U.S.$3 billion.

Still, many observers contend that cyanide fishing, dynamiting, and other environmentally destructive forms of fishing can be dramatically curtailed or even eradicated if regional governments take meaningful steps to protect reefs and punish those who use illegal means to gather reef fish. One reason for this confidence is that most subsistence fishing communities oppose the use of cyanide and other poisons that degrade traditional fishing grounds. "The number of hard-core cyanide fishers throughout the Indo-Pacific region probably does not exceed 20,000. In short, cyanide fishing is not a ubiquitous problem like slash-and-burn farming. Nor is poverty the root cause of cyanide fishing, although many cyanide fishers are certainly very poor" (ibid.). Marine scientists and conservationists have also been heartened by the response of some regional governments. The Philippines, for instance, has adopted several measures to address this threat, including improved enforcement, cyanide testing of fish exports, and new community-based resource management initiatives.

Despite those and other actions, though, fishermen who use cyanide or explosives to collect the ocean's bounty remain a scourge. Observers such as journalist John Ryan even contend that "this ragtag fleet of bombers collectively poses the greatest threat to the world's richest underwater habitats. Nationwide [in Indonesia], blast fishing does about $500,000 a day in damage, if you believe the economists who try to quantify such things....Bombs have at least moderately affected three-fourths of Indonesia's reefs. Much of the shallow Indonesian seafloor is now occupied by flattened dead zones, spreading as far as the snorkeler's eye can see.... Throughout eastern Indonesia, many fisheries have already collapsed. Reef bombers and other fishers often travel hundreds of miles, even to Australian waters, on month-long trips, in search of healthy fishing grounds" (Ryan 2001).

Sources:

Barber, Chip, and Vaughan Pratt. 1998. *Sullied Seas: Strategies for Combating Cyanide Fishing in Southeast Asia and Beyond.* Washington, DC: World Resources Institute.

Burke, Lauretta, Elizabeth Selig, and Mark Spalding. 2002. *Reefs at Risk in Southeast Asia.* Washington, DC: World Resources Institute.

Mastny, Lisa. 2001. "A Worldwatch Addendum." *World Watch* (May–June).

Ryan, John C. 2001. "Indonesia's Coral Reefs on the Line." *World Watch* (May–June).

Wood, Elizabeth M. 2001. *Collection of Coral Reef Fish for Aquaria: Global Trade, Conservation Issues and Management Strategies.* Ross-on-Wye, United Kingdom: Marine Conservation Society.

Asia's Endangered Mangrove Forests and Coral Reefs

Mangrove Forests— A Key Element in Marine Ecosystems

Mangrove forests are an essential component of the coastlines of South Asia. These wetland forests, which historically have been found in greater abundance in Asia than any other continent, provide vital habitat for thousands of species of fish, shellfish, and plants, serve as important spawning grounds for hundreds of fish species, and anchor vulnerable coastlines against erosion and seawater intrusion. But Asia is engaged in a grim struggle to protect this all-important resource from being washed away by a storm surge of economic and population growth. Some experts estimate that the continent has already lost as much as half of its mangrove forests to development in recent decades, and conservationists note that only a fraction of Asia's remaining mangroves enjoy any sort of protected status.

No Asian nation has escaped this unfortunate trend. Indonesia, for instance, still has vast holdings of mangrove forest, perhaps as much as 30 percent of the world total. But the nation has lost more than half of this resource to development over the past several decades, and large tracts of forest that remain have already been targeted for logging or aquaculture operations. Elsewhere, Vietnam's own Ministry of Science, Technology and Environment admitted in a 1997 State of the Environment report that the size of the nation's mangrove forests shrank from 400,000 hectares to 250,000 hectares between 1950 and 1983, decimated first by wartime defoliation, napalming, and bombing and then by wholesale conversions of coastal land into shrimp farms. Thailand estimates that it lost more than 50 percent of its mangrove forests to aquaculture and other purposes between 1961 and 1996, and observers note that the undeveloped Andaman Coast is the lone mangrove area in the entire nation that has not been battered by habitat degradation. In Malaysia, an estimated one-third of its mangrove forests have been destroyed by logging, farming, and aquaculture. The remaining mangroves of Myanmar (Burma) are under imminent threat from the state's powerful timber industry, while those in the Philippines have been almost entirely wiped out by development, reduced from 1 million hectares to about 100,000 hectares between 1960 and 1998. In Singapore, meanwhile, the mangrove forests that once graced its shores are mostly a memory.

Valuable Coral Reefs Threatened

Coral reefs are another ecologically priceless natural resource of Asia that face an uncertain future. Primarily found in shallow tropical waters, the globe's most extensive coral reefs can be found in Southeast Asia (about 30 percent of the world total) and the Western Pacific; Indonesia's reefs alone account for nearly 18 percent of the world total; see Table 7.1 for countries accounting for the top 35 reef areas worldwide. Worldwide, these marine ridges are thought to provide vital feeding and breeding grounds for nearly 1 million species of plants and animals, including 25 percent of the total fish catch in the developing world. They also serve as a natural breakwater for coastal areas, blunting the impact of cyclones and other severe storms. The Coral Reef Alliance estimated in 1996 that coral reefs have a value of $47,000 per square foot for their shore protection functions alone.

Unfortunately, coral reefs all around the world are under duress from a variety of forces. In 2000 the Global Coral Reef Monitoring Network estimated that 27 percent of the world's coral reefs were severely damaged (in 1992 the percentage was 10 percent). In Southeast Asia, fully 88 percent of the region's reefs are at risk according to the World Resources Institute (Burke et al. 2002). The problem of dying coral reefs is particularly acute in Indonesia and the Philippines, the two Asian nations with the most extensive reef holdings. An estimated 75 percent of reefs in Indonesian waters—home to about 15 percent of all coral reefs—have been degraded by fishermen who rely on explosives, cyanide, massive drift nets, and other destructive means to catch wild fish. In Philippine waters the combined impact of destructive fishing techniques, pollution, and sedimentation have destroyed extensive sections of reefs as well.

The deterioration of Asia's reefs began in the 1960s, when the first big fishing vessels arrived in Asian waters. Over the years, driftnets utilized by some ships—some up to 40 miles long—have taken a tremendous toll on the region's marine life, snaring massive numbers of both target species and by-catch, while trawlers targeting shrimp, flounder, and other bottom-dwellers have ravaged the ocean floor itself. "[The] extent of damage to seabottom habitats that have been swept by trawling equipment may be light, with effects lasting only a few weeks, or intensive, with some impacts on corals, sponges, and other long-lived species lasting decades or even centuries" (World Resources Institute 2000). Indeed, the extensive damage wreaked on the seafloor by bottom trawling has prompted observers to compare the practice to forest clearcutting. And while the international community has taken steps to curtail trawling activity in recent years, renegade operations remain a problem in many Asian waters. "Most trawlers are now officially banned from the near-shore waters of the Philippines and Indonesia," pointed out one expert. "[But] many violate the law, slipping in under cover of darkness to exploit coralline fisheries. Still others bribe the coast guard and fish with impunity in broad daylight" (Hinrichsen 1998).

Table 7.1 Countries with Largest Coral Reef Area

Rank	Country	Reef Area (in 10 sq km)	Percentage of world total
1	Indonesia	51,020	17.95%
2	Australia	48,960	17.22%
3	Philippines	25,060	8.81%
4	France[1]	14,280	5.02%
5	Papua New Guinea	13,840	4.87%
6	Fiji	10,020	3.52%
7	Maldives	8,920	3.14%
8	Saudi Arabia	6,660	2.34%
9	Marshall Islands	6,110	2.15%
10	India	5,790	2.04%
11	Solomon Islands	5,750	2.02%
12	United Kingdom[2]	5,510	1.94%
13	Micronesia, Federated States of	4,340	1.53%
14	Vanuatu	4,110	1.45%
15	Egypt	3,800	1.34%
16	United States[3]	3,770	1.33%
17	Malaysia	3,600	1.27%
18	United Republic of Tanzania	3,580	1.26%
19	Eritrea	3,260	1.15%
20	Bahamas	3,150	1.11%
21	Cuba	3,020	1.06%
22	Kiribati	2,940	1.03%
23	Japan	2,900	1.02%
24	Sudan	2,720	0.96%
25	Madagascar	2,230	0.78%
26	Thailand	2,130	0.75%
27	Myanmar	1,870	0.66%
28	Mozambique	1,860	0.65%
29	Mexico	1,780	0.63%
30	Seychelles	1,690	0.59%
31	China	1,510	0.53%
32	Tonga	1,500	0.53%
33	Belize	1,330	0.47%
34	New Zealand[4]	1,310	0.46%
35	Viet Nam	1,270	0.45%

NOTES

[1] Including: Clipperton, Mayotte, Réunion, Guadeloupe, Martinique, New Caledonia, French Polynesia, Wallis and Futuna Islands

[2] Including: British Indian Ocean Territory, Anguilla, Bermuda, Cayman Islands, Pitcairn, Turks and Caicos Islands, British Virgin Islands

[3] Including: Florida and Gulf of Mexico, Hawaii, U. S. Minor Outlying Islands, American Samoa, Puerto Rico, U.S. Virgin Islands, Guam

[4] Including Cook Islands, Niue, Tokelau

SOURCE: Adapted from Mark D. Spalding, Corinna Ravilious, and Edmund P. Green in conjunction with the United Nations Environment Programme, *World Atlas of Coral Reefs*, Berkeley: University of California Press, 2001.

Another significant factor in the decline of Asia's coral reefs has been the region's increased reliance on explosives and poisons to harvest fish. In places such as Malaysia and Thailand, subsistence fishermen have turned to dynamite, kerosene, and cyanide to harvest fish. But these desperate measures, prompted by dwindling populations of valuable fish species, are only accelerating the degradation of the marine habitats upon which those same fish rely. Other factors in the decline of Asia's reefs include mining operations that destroy reefs to harvest lime used in cement production, and the proliferating crown-of-thorns starfish, which has destroyed large sections of reef habitat off the coast of Japan and elsewhere.

Scientists, environmentalists, and other interested parties contend that Asia's coral reef ecosystems can still be saved if regional governments implement and enforce meaningful protective measures, including increased patrols of reef areas and creation of special marine reserves. In addition, education and outreach programs are cited as important elements of any plan to protect Asia's coastal resources. "We need to advocate the role of coral reefs and mangroves as natural fish farms, wave breakers, shore defenders, leisure areas, and storehouses of many other goods and services, whether we see them or not," said one conservationist. "Not just those who dive over reefs or daily glean their livelihood there, but all of us need to recognize the hive of activity hidden beneath the sea's reflective surface" (Salm 1994).

Finally, the future of Asia's coral reefs will pivot on the international community's response to global warming. This phenomenon poses a significant threat to reefs, which primarily live in tropical waters that are already at the upper end of their temperature tolerance. Scientists warn that even minor ocean temperature increases could have devastating consequences for reef areas. Supporters of this scenario point to the El Niño weather phenomenon of 1997 to 1998. That event, which created climate disturbances in the Pacific Ocean and elsewhere, elevated sea temperatures throughout much of Asia. These warmer waters are believed to have triggered widespread "coral bleaching," a process wherein reefs lose symbiotic algae upon which they depend for their survival. Reefs off the coasts of southern Japan, Taiwan, Vietnam, Sri Lanka, the Maldives, western India, portions of Indonesia, and the Philippines all succumbed to coral bleaching to one degree or another during the 1997 to 1998 El Niño, with reef losses in some regions approaching 90 percent. Since that time, Worldwatch Institute estimates that "about a third of the bleached reefs show early signs of recovery, having retained or recruited enough live coral to survive. Roughly half could rebound in the next 20–50 years—if ocean temperatures remain steady and human pressures are low. But if the warming continues, scientists predict that as many as 60 percent of all reefs could be lost by 2030" (Mastny 2001).

A Japanese fishing crew pulls a whale aboard its vessel. NEWMEDIA INC./CORBIS

Japanese Whaling Stance Sparks Crisis within IWC

In recent years, Japan has emerged as the global leader in efforts to resume commercial whaling activity around the globe. During the 1990s, Japanese whaling boats killed hundreds of the massive, sea-dwelling mammals on an annual basis under the guise of scientific research, in defiance of a global moratorium on commercial whaling. In addition, Japan has joined other whaling nations in demanding a resumption of commercial hunting of some whale species. This drive, spearheaded by Japan—and bankrolled by the nation as well, according to critics—has triggered bitter and potentially crippling dissension within the International Whaling Commission (IWC), the world's primary whale management organization for more than half a century.

The IWC was formed in 1946 by whaling nations that wanted to speak with a unified voice on trade issues affecting the industry. In subsequent decades, however, numerous whale populations around the globe became endangered from overharvesting, and popular perceptions about the morality of hunting whales changed considerably in the United States, Canada, and other industrialized nations. These trends in turn sparked a dramatic change in the orientation and membership of the IWC. Several nonwhaling nations joined the IWC during the 1970s, some of them actively recruited by the international

environmental group Greenpeace, and the organization "evolved from a resource management body to an anti-whaling organization," according to one observer (Van Zile 2000).

In 1986 the IWC enacted an international ban on commercial whaling, citing plunging populations of blue, bowhead, humpback, sperm, northern right, southern right, and other whale species. Exceptions to the moratorium were made for scientific study (of feeding and migration patterns, exposure to chemical contamination, etc.) and traditional whale hunts undertaken by native communities, but the ban ended most commercial whaling activity.

The IWC's suspension of hunting activity enabled several whale species to make partial or full recoveries, although others remain classified as endangered or vulnerable. For example, blue whales—the largest creatures roaming the earth today—once numbered about 250,000 worldwide, but their current population remains stalled at about 5,000. A number of whaling nations chafed under the open-ended ban, however, and by the late 1990s, Norway and Japan were in open rebellion. Norway, for example, escalated its whale hunting activities within its own waters when the door was closed to international whaling; in 1999 alone Norse whalers took almost 600 minke whales from Norway's coastal waters. Japan, meanwhile, harvested 600 to

700 minke whales each year throughout the 1990s. The nation even took minkes from the seas of Antarctica, which had been given whale sanctuary status by the IWC in 1994 (Chadwick 2001). In 2002, Japan announced that it intended to augment its annual catch of minke whales with 50 Bryde's whales, 50 sei whales, and 10 sperm whales. The latter two species are still classified as endangered by environmental groups. The nation also issued an announcement that it was considering allowing imports of whale meat to resume after an eleven-year hiatus.

Japan has vigorously defended its extensive whaling activity as a necessary component of its scientific research, but critics ridicule that claim. They charge that Japan could glean the same scientific information from a much smaller harvest, and they note that meat from endangered whales has repeatedly been found on Japanese supermarket shelves. For its part, Japan says that it is only abiding by the IWC's governing convention, which requires that whales killed for scientific purposes be processed for human consumption when possible. In addition, the country strongly defends its efforts to repeal the whaling ban. "The whale resource is coming back as a food supply, and it could help problems with hunger around the world," stated one

government official. "People harvest all kinds of animals, in many cases just for sport. Endangered species and depleted stocks have to be protected, but we in Japan can't understand the special concern over whales. There is no reason not to harvest abundant stocks" (Chadwick 2001).

Detractors contend that in recent years, Japan's desire to resume large-scale commercial whaling has prompted it to engage in blatant vote-buying within the IWC. During the 1990s, Japan gave tens of millions of dollars in financial aid to several Caribbean island states that have become a reliable voting bloc for the Japanese government on whaling issues. In fact, many observers believe that these machinations have enabled Japan to swing the balance of power within the IWC over to the prowhaling camp. Certainly, Japan and its allies have registered significant victories in the last few years within the halls of the IWC. In 2000, Japan, Norway, and their allies beat back a proposal to conduct DNA tests for endangered whale meat in Japanese and Norwegian markets and restaurants. During the same period, the IWC's prowhaling bloc defeated various whale conservation proposals linked to the Convention on Biological Diversity and the Convention on International Trade in Endangered Species (CITES). And in 2001, IWC proposals to create new whale sanctuaries in the South Pacific and South Atlantic were thwarted by Japan and its prowhaling allies. In 2002, Japan and its allies were defeated in their attempt to dissolve the IWC-sanctioned Indian Ocean Whale Sanctuary. Another large whale sanctuary, located in the Southern Ocean, is up for review in 2004.

For the time being, the IWC's prowhaling nations have focused their energy on increasing the size of the minke whale harvest. Minke whales are abundant, with a worldwide population of 750,000 to 1 million, and Japan, Norway, and other countries argue correctly that a limited commercial harvest would not jeopardize the viability of the species. But philosophical opposition to any commercial hunting remains strong, and concerns about Japanese stewardship of whale populations were not allayed when a top Japanese fisheries official referred to minke whales as "cockroaches of the sea" in July 2001.

By 2001 the deadlock within the IWC over commercial whaling had become so tense that some observers openly worried that the organization might collapse. In July 2001 the conservation group World Wide Fund for Nature (WWF) announced that a return to limited whaling might be

necessary in order to preserve the IWC. "The anti-whaling nations are having no impact at all at the moment on commercial whaling," stated one WWF official in an Australian Broadcasting Corporation broadcast. "Unless the anti-whaling and whaling countries agree on some sort of ... small commercial whaling, then these whaling countries will simply walk out or destroy the IWC and we'll be back to uncontrolled, undocumented whaling on the high seas" ("WWF Backs Return to Limited Whaling to Save Whales" 2001). With this in mind, IWC scientists are reportedly in the process of devising a management plan for the harvest of up to 10,000 minkes annually, less than 1 percent of the estimated global stock.

Sources:

Chadwick, Douglas H. 2001. "Pursuing the Minke." *National Geographic* 201 (April).

Friedheim, Robert L., ed. 2001. *Toward a Sustainable Whaling Regime*. Seattle: University of Washington Press.

Stoett, Peter J. 1997. *The International Politics of Whaling*. Vancouver: University of British Columbia Press.

Van Zile, Dexter. 2000. "To Whale or Not to Whale?" *National Fisherman* (December).

"WWF Backs Return to Limited Whaling to Save Whales." Reuters News Service, July 31, 2001.

Scientists Warn of Possible
Inundation of Coastal Areas

If left unchecked, global warming could also have a catastrophic impact on Asia's heavily populated coastal areas. Numerous cities, towns, and villages along the coastlines of India, Sri Lanka, Bangladesh, the Maldives, and the coastal states of Southeast Asia would be submerged by even a 1-meter rise in sea levels, cited as a distinct possibility in many global warming forecasts. The subsequent displacement of people in those regions would constitute a refugee crisis of grave proportions. According to the Intergovernmental Panel on Climate Change (IPCC), Bangladesh alone would lose approximately 3 million hectares that are currently home to 15 to 20 million people. Another 7 million Indians would be driven from their coastal homes. And a 1-meter rise in sea level could force as many as 12 million Vietnamese to retreat from the Mekong Delta, the Red River Delta, and other low-lying coastal areas. Similar scenarios have been projected for tens of millions of people in China, the Philippines, Sri Lanka, Burma, Cambodia, and Thailand as well.

The impact of such an inundation on regional ecosystems is equally incomprehensible. The coastal topography of an entire continent would be permanently altered, destroying longtime wilderness habitats and disrupting food chains that have been in place for millennia. "Consider the Sunderbans, one of the most vulnerable coastal wetlands in Asia," writes Don Hinrichsen.

> The largest contiguous mangrove forest in the world, the Sunderbans carpets 100,000 hectares along the Bay of Bengal, partly in India and partly in Bangladesh. It is home to myriad wild creatures, including 315 species of birds; among the endangered species to be found here are the Rhesus macaque, Irrawaddy dolphin, and Bengal tiger. A one-meter sea level rise could well mean extinction for the local populations of many Sunderbans creatures. The Sunderbans tigers, for example, currently number around 350 and are an important reservoir of genetic wealth for their species. The rising waters would probably do away with their main prey animals and drive the tigers into heavily settled areas further inland, where it is unlikely that they would survive. (Hinrichsen 2000)

If Asia experiences a significant rise in sea levels in the coming years as a result of global warming, similarly grim dramas will unfold all across the continent.

Central Asia's Inland Seas

Asia's interior houses two landlocked seas, the Aral Sea and the Caspian Sea. These two massive saltwater lakes, which are located in Central and West Asia, respectively, have both suffered significant environmental degradation over the years, but the Aral Sea is in a much more advanced stage of deterioration. In fact, the medical relief organization Doctors Without Borders has termed the ruin of the Aral Sea "possibly the world's greatest environmental disaster and human tragedy," and the UN Development Programme has described the demise of the Aral as "the most staggering disaster of the twentieth century."

Asia's Disappearing Aral Sea

The Aral Sea was once the world's fourth largest lake. In the 1960s, however, Soviet authorities began diverting its primary water sources, the Amu Dar'ya and the Syr Dar'ya rivers, to irrigate cotton—a notoriously water-needy crop. From 1960 to 1990, the area of irrigated land in central Asia more than doubled, from 3.5 million hectares to 7.5 million hectares, enabling the region to become one of the world's largest producers of cotton. But the people of Central Asia paid a heavy price for their agricultural achievement. The diversion of water to raise cotton became so great that the annual flow of freshwater into the sea dropped precipitously. As freshwater replenishment slowed to a trickle—the Aral lost 90 percent of its source water to diversions according to some estimates—the sea's salinity rose dramatically, destroying much of the Aral's flora and fauna and laying waste to the regional fishing industry (Lloyd-Roberts and Anbarasan 2000).

The most obvious indication that regional water diversions were unsustainable, however, was that the sea itself began to shrink. With each passing year, the Aral's waves receded a little more, withdrawing from shoreline communities in incremental but inexorable fashion. By 1990 the sea had lost one-third of its volume and half of its surface area. It had also lost so much water that it divided into two distinct seas, separated by dry seabed that had been cloaked by saltwater only a few years earlier.

The heightened salinity and diminished size of the Aral Sea decimated shoreline communities, some of which found themselves more than 100 kilometers from the water by the early 1990s. Journalist Marq de Villiers described the view from one town that had formerly sat at water's edge:

> As far as you can see there is nothing but sere sand, white bones of dead cattle poisoned on toxic plants, the rotting hulls of fishing vessels and barges, the pathetic detritus of a once thriving fishing culture. In

the foreground are the broken timbers of what used to be a wharf; beyond that are six or seven ships' hulls, grounded at random, pointing in no way in particular. . . . Farther on are humps in the sand where other hulls have been buried, and beyond that only dunes, sand, salt, and nothingness. . . . Without any exaggeration, the Aral Sea has become the greatest man-caused ecological catastrophe our benighted planet has yet seen, an awful warning of the consequences of hubris, greed, and the politics of ignorance. (De Villiers 2000)

The desiccation of the Aral Sea has taken an enormous toll on the health and economic circumstances of the 3.5 million people who live in the region. The Aral's increased salinity has made it difficult for many families to secure safe drinking water, and toxic salts from exposed seabed have been transferred by air currents throughout the basin, damaging the health of people, livestock, and crops alike. Malnutrition, respiratory and intestinal illnesses, incidents of infant mortality, and other health problems have risen dramatically as a result.

Weather patterns in the region have also been permanently altered by the shrinkage of the sea, which helped moderate seasonal extremes. As the Aral Sea has receded, the region has become even more arid, and summertime and wintertime temperatures have become more extreme. Scientists believe that this trend could continue to worsen in coming years if the southern section of the Aral disappears entirely, as some experts predict.

Since the dissolution of the Soviet Union in 1989, the five nations of the Aral basin—Kazakhstan, Kyrgyzstan, Tajikistan, Turkmenistan, and Uzbekistan—have taken some steps to address the deplorable state of the sea. Some of their proposed solutions, such as replenishment of the Aral Sea via massive water diversions from the Caspian Sea or Siberian rivers, are economically and logistically untenable. Moreover, distrust between these young republics over water use and allocation issues has been a recurring problem. But the countries did establish an International Aral Sea Rehabilitation Fund (IFAS) to coordinate water use, and they have made some progress in instituting water conservation measures and providing potable water to poverty-stricken communities.

Nonetheless, many experts believe that restoration of the Aral Sea is a lost cause. They note that massive financial outlays would be necessary to register significant reductions in water pollution, improve and modernize agricultural practices, and re-engineer communities so that they can replace cotton with less water-intensive crops. According to some estimates, these efforts might require as much as $20 billion, which the poor Aral basin nations clearly do not have. As a result, internal and international efforts to address the decline of the Aral Sea have increasingly focused on addressing humanitarian problems and preserving the remnants of the once-fertile sea by establishing guidelines of sustainable water use.

Tapping Oil Reserves
beneath the Caspian Sea

The Caspian Sea is the largest closed inland body of water on earth, with a surface area of 390,000 square kilometers. This saltwater sea demarcates the line between Eastern Europe and Asia's far western reaches, and it is shared by the states of Iran, Azerbaijan, Kazakhstan, Russia, and Turkmenistan.

For many years the Caspian Sea's principal claim to international fame was that its waters are the source of more than 90 percent of the world's caviar (unfertilized sturgeon eggs). Numerous other species ply its waters as well, including dozens of rare species of fish, hundreds of thousands of seals, and large numbers of migratory birds, including flamingos and white-tailed eagles. But some marine scientists and environmentalists fear that the habitat that has nourished these animals for centuries may be sacrificed in order to reach extensive oil deposits lying beneath the sea.

All the countries that share possession of the Caspian Sea are former components or allies of the now-defunct Soviet Union, and they struggled with the economic repercussions of the Soviet collapse throughout the 1990s. But during that same decade, preliminary exploration indicated that the Caspian basin region might hold between 40 billion and 178 billion barrels of oil, making it second only to the Persian Gulf in terms of total oil reserves. The Caspian waters off Azerbaijan and Kazakhstan were estimated to hold the greatest quantities of oil, and those cash-strapped nations quickly joined forces with an assortment of international oil companies to extract these reserves through on- and offshore drilling operations.

In the rush to bring oil out of the ground, however, there are indications that the Caspian is suffering extensive ecological damage. "Extensive prospecting works in the shelf zones of all states carried out over the last decade have contributed to practically uncontrolled pollution throughout the aquatic area of the sea. The threat of oil pollution relates not only to the areas of offshore oil exploration and extraction or shipping across the Caspian Sea; it is also associated with its transportation by pipelines across the coastal zones. Overall oil losses in extraction, transport and processing amount to 2 percent of its total volume" (Saiko 2001). Oil exploration companies, however, contend that the region's oil reserves can be tapped in an environmentally responsible fashion. In addition, the environmental community was heartened by the 1998 establishment of the Caspian Environment Program, an effort sponsored by the World Bank, United Nations, and other organizations to address the long-standing environmental problems in and around the Caspian Sea.

Indeed, it is widely understood that the Caspian Sea region can ill afford further environmental degradation. The nations of the region are already grappling with numerous ecological problems, including massive pollution of the Caspian Sea with industrial, agricultural, and human waste, both from inland and coastal sources; plummeting fish stocks in the Caspian and other major bodies of water; eutrophication and loss of spawning grounds in the Volga delta; contamination of soil by heavy metals; wind erosion from desertified lands; and salinization and waterlogging of irrigated lands. None of the nations in the region have unblemished records in environmental matters, but Russia's history is particularly troubling; by some estimates, it is responsible for an estimated 80 percent of pollution from oil, pesticides, and heavy metals in the Caspian Sea region (Mekhtiev and Gul 1997; Saiko 2001).

Sources:

Ahmed, M., et al. 1999. *Fisheries Policy Research in Developing Countries: Issues, Priorities, and Needs.* Penang, Malaysia: ICLARM.

Barber, Chip, and Vaughan Pratt. 1998. *Sullied Seas: Strategies for Combating Cyanide Fishing in Southeast Asia and Beyond.* Washington, DC: World Resources Institute.

Berrill, Michael. 1997. *The Plundered Seas: Can the World's Fish Be Saved?* San Francisco: Sierra Club.

Bryant, Dirk, et al. 1998. *Reefs at Risk: A Map-Based Indicator of Threats to the World's Coral Reefs.* Washington, DC: World Resources Institute.

Burke, Lauretta, Elizabeth Selig, and Mark Spalding. 2002. *Reefs at Risk in Southeast Asia.* Washington, DC: World Resources Institute.

Dayton, Leigh. "The Killing Reefs." 1995. *New Scientist* (November 11).

De Villiers, Marq. 2000. *Water: The Fate of Our Most Precious Resource.* New York: Houghton Mifflin.

Fairlie, Simon, Mike Hagler, and Brian O'Riordan. 1995. "The Politics of Overfishing." *Ecologist* 25 (March–June).

Grabish, Beatrice. "Dry Tears of the Aral." 1999. *UN Chronicle* 36, no. 1 (Spring).

Hinrichsen, Don. 1998. *Coastal Waters of the World: Trends, Threats, and Strategies.* Washington, DC: Island.

———. "The Oceans Are Coming Ashore." 2000. *World Watch* (November–December).

Ingwerson, Marshall. "Into the Steppe of Genghis Khan Ride the Conquerors of a Sea's Oil Bounty." *Christian Science Monitor*, August 18, 1997.

Jameson, Stephen, John McManus, and Mark Spalding. 1995. *State of the Reefs— Regional and Global Perspectives.* Washington, DC: National Oceanic and Atmospheric Administration.

Lloyd-Roberts, Sue, and Ethirajan Anbarasan. 2000. "The Aral Sea: Back from the Brink?" *UNESCO Courier* 53, no.1 (January).

Mastny, Lisa. 2001. "A Worldwatch Addendum." *World Watch* (May–June).

McClanahan, T. R., Charles R. C. Sheppard, and David O. Obura. 2000. *Coral Reefs of the Indian Ocean: Ecology and Conservation*. New York: Oxford University Press.

Mekhtiev, A., and A. K. Gul. 1997. "Ecological Problems of the Caspian Sea." In M. H. Glantz and I. S. Zonn, eds., *Scientific, Environmental, and Political Issues in the Circum-Caspian Region*. Dordrecht: Kluwer Academic.

Ryan, John C. 2001. "Indonesia's Coral Reefs on the Line." *World Watch* (May–June).

Saiko, Tatyana. 2001. *Environmental Crises: Geographical Case Studies in Post-Socialist Eurasia*. Harlow, England: Pearson Education.

Salm, Rodney. 1994. "Corals' Hidden Riches." *People and the Planet* 3, no. 1.

Sheppard, Charles, ed. 2000. *Seas at the Millennium: An Environmental Evaluation*. 3 vols. Oxford, England: Pergamon.

UN Environment Programme. 1999. *Global Environment Outlook 2000*. London: Earthscan.

UN Food and Agriculture Organization. 1991. *Recent Developments in World Fisheries*. Rome: FAO.

———. 1997. *Review of the State of World Fishery Resources: Marine Fisheries*. Rome: FAO.

———. 2001. *The State of World Fisheries and Aquaculture 2000*. Rome: FAO.

Weber, Peter. 1993. *Abandoned Seas: Reversing the Decline of the Oceans: Worldwatch Paper 116*. Washington, DC: Worldwatch Institute.

Wilkinson, Clive. 2000. *Status of Coral Reefs of the World*. Cape Ferguson: Australian Institute of Marine Science.

World Resources Institute. 2000. *World Resources 2000–2001, People and Ecosystems: The Fraying Web of Life*. Washington, DC: World Resources Institute.

Yeung, Yue-man, and Xu-Wei Hu, eds. 1992. *China's Coastal Cities: Catalysts for Modernization*. Honolulu: University of Hawaii Press.

Energy and Transportation

—SETH DUNN

Trends in energy and transportation in Asia carry enormous implications for the global environment. The Asian region holds 3.7 billion people—more than 60 percent of the world total—and its population is projected to increase by 41 percent, to 5.3 billion, by 2050. Asian economies, as a whole, account for 33 percent of world economic output, a share that is tied to the strong economic growth in many Asian economies during much of the 1990s and that, despite a recent falloff, is expected to continue to grow.

As Asian nations grow in population and develop their economies, demands for energy services and mobility will inevitably rise, creating significant challenges and opportunities. Simply replicating Western patterns of energy use and transport would likely add to the local, regional, and global environmental pressures confronting Asia. On the other hand, the region has a ripe opportunity to pioneer a more sustainable model that is specific to Asia's unique characteristics while also providing lessons for other parts of the world.

This chapter provides a broad overview of the state of energy and transport in Asia. It describes the availability of various resources, their future potential, and their current trends of use. Particular emphasis is given to the connection between renewable energy and rural energy, the health and environmental consequences of continued coal dependence, and the challenge of meeting growing mobility needs—three issues of special importance and concern to the region.

The State of Energy in Asia

The region of Asia—defined here as the stretch of countries extending east from Pakistan to New Zealand, with the exception of Russia—currently accounts for 28 percent of global primary commercial energy, consuming 2,512

In cities like Shanghai, China, energy demand has escalated rapidly. BOB KRIST/CORBIS

billion tons of oil equivalent in 2001. This amount represents a 33 percent increase from 1991, when Asia held a 23 percent share of global energy use. China looms large in these figures, accounting for a full third of primary energy use in Asia.

Coal

Asia used 1,021 million tons of oil equivalent in 2001. This volume of consumption places it first among regions and accounts for 45 percent of the global total. It also represents a 16 percent increase from 1991, when the Asian share of global coal use stood at 40 percent. Coal is the leading energy source in Asia, with a 41 percent share of the regional total. Coal's top position is a recently resumed trend, as declining coal use and rising petroleum use had given oil a brief stay at the top in the mid-1990s (British Petroleum 2002).

Coal is currently the dominant energy source in China, with a 62 percent share of primary commercial energy use and a 75 percent share of electricity use. Coal consumption in China stood at 521 million tons of oil equivalent in 2001. This represents 51 percent of Asian coal use and 23 percent of the world total, a share second only to that of the United States (which accounted for 25 percent of the global total).

Coal use in China fell by roughly 3 percent between 1991 and 2001. But that ten-year statistic masks significant fluctuations over the course of the decade. Indeed, coal use increased by 27 percent from 1991 to 1996, underwent a comparable drop from 1996 to 2000, then registered a 5 percent rise in 2001. These statistics have attracted considerable press attention and international debate. Some experts have openly questioned the veracity of the official statistics, suggesting that illegally operating mines had been excluded from the figures and thus distorted the size of the reduction posted during the late 1990s. At the same time, however, several factors in the nation's energy economy do appear to be affecting coal consumption patterns, including a reduction in coal subsidies, energy efficiency improvements in industry, and switching from coal to natural gas in households.

Coal also features prominently in the energy economy of India, accounting for 55 percent of primary commercial energy use and 73 percent of electricity use. Coal use in India also accounts for 17 percent of the regional total and 8 percent of the world total. Between 1991 and 2001, coal consumption in India increased by 49 percent, primarily for use in power plants and industry. Other significant coal consumers in Asia include Indonesia, Japan, South Korea, Taiwan, and Thailand.

Asia and the Pacific are also the world's leading coal-producing region, responsible for 45 percent of global coal production. In this region, coal production grew by 18 percent between 1991 and 2001, led by expanded output from China and India in Asia and Australia in the Pacific. By the beginning of the twenty-first century, China and India alone accounted for 31 percent of global coal output. Indonesia, meanwhile, increased production sixfold during the 1990s and now accounts for 3 percent of world coal output.

Projections of future coal use in Asia typically begin with the observation that the region has the largest coal reserves in the world. As of the end of 2001, proven coal reserves in Asia stood at 295 billion tons, just below 30 percent of the global sum. The region's reserves-to-production ratio is 147, meaning that its remaining reserves would last nearly a century and a half under current rates of production. But while resource availability is unlikely to constrain future Asian coal use, environmental pressures and competition from other fuels may do so (ibid.).

Oil

Oil is the second leading energy source in Asia and the Pacific, with a 39 percent share of primary energy use. The region in turn accounts for 27 percent of global oil consumption, using 973 million tons of oil in 2001. This rate of consumption is 12 percent higher than in 1991, when the region's share of the global sum was only 22 percent (ibid.).

These statistics reflect the fact that the Asia-Pacific region was a key engine of growth for global oil use in the 1990s. However, the economic crisis of

1997 to 1998 produced a slackening in Asian oil demand that is still evident. As a result, global oil consumption failed to grow in 2001 for the first time since 1993.

As with coal, a handful of countries drive oil use trends in Asia. Japan accounts for 7 percent of world oil use and a quarter of the regional sum. Japanese oil use actually fell by 2 percent between 1991 and 2001, however, because of its late-1990s economic slowdown. China is also responsible for roughly 7 percent of global oil consumption, but its rapidly expanding automobile network fueled a 97 percent rise in consumption between 1991 and 2001.

Asia has also become a not-insignificant oil producer. Asian oil production rose by 13 percent between 1991 and 2001, and by the end of that ten-year period, the region's annual production of 379 million tons gave it an 11 percent share of the world total, placing it fourth among major regions. Nearly half of this oil is produced in China, which increased oil output by 17 percent during the decade. Some smaller producers—India, Indonesia, and Malaysia—saw minor changes, while others—Thailand and Vietnam—doubled and quadrupled their oil production, respectively.

Proven Asia-Pacific oil reserves in 2001 were estimated at 6 billion tons, 4 percent of the global figure and sixth among the seven world regions. This estimate is essentially unchanged from that of 1991, and gives the region a reserves-to-production ratio of less than sixteen years. Some 55 percent of these reserves are found in China, with the remainder scattered in small amounts through India, Indonesia, and Malaysia in Asia, and Australia in the Pacific.

Rising demand and limited domestic resources have made Asia a prominent oil importer. The region imports 631 million tons per year, nearly 38 percent of worldwide crude imports. Of those imports, 34 percent go to Japan, and another 10 percent to China. More than 90 percent of the oil is imported from the Middle East (ibid.).

Natural Gas

Natural gas is a growing source of energy in Asia and the Pacific. The 275 million tons of oil equivalent consumed in 2001 represent 11 percent of the region's primary energy use, and 13 percent of global natural gas consumption. Asian natural gas use grew by 81 percent between 1991 and 2001, with a 5 percent jump in 2001 (ibid.).

Japan leads the region in natural gas use, with 26 percent of the regional total and 3 percent of the global total. Japanese natural gas consumption rose by 45 percent between 1991 and 2001. Other Asian nations have also registered major upturns in natural gas use. China, for example, which accounts for 9 percent of Asian natural gas use, experienced an 86 percent rise in natural gas consumption between 1991 and 2001.

The Asia-Pacific region has also moved aggressively to tap its natural gas reserves in recent years. Proven reserves of natural gas in Asia and Australia stood at 433 trillion cubic feet in 2001, 8 percent of the global total and third among the major regions. By 2001 it accounted for 11 percent of global natural gas production, with 252 million tons of oil equivalent in 2001. That represents a 71 percent increase from 1991, and an 11 percent share of world natural gas output. Indonesia is the leading producer, with a 22 percent regional share and a 3 percent global share. Indonesian natural gas output rose by 22 percent between 1991 and 2001 (ibid.).

Hydro and Nuclear Power

Hydroelectricity accounts for just above 5 percent of primary energy in Asia, with 129 million tons of oil equivalent consumed in 2001. However, Asian hydropower use grew by 31 percent between 1991 and 2001, and the region's share of world hydropower consumption is now 22 percent. China is Asia's leading user of hydroelectricity, with a 45 percent regional share. It is also the world's third leading user, with a 10 percent global share. Chinese hydropower use rose by 106 percent between 1991 and 2001, though the fate of the controversial and massive Three Gorges Dam, on which construction has begun, remains undecided. Other major users, such as India and Japan, saw slight decreases in hydroelectricity use (ibid.).

Asia is a growing user of nuclear power, with 115 million tons of oil equivalent consumed in 2001. This is slightly less than 5 percent of the total primary energy use in the region, but it accounts for 19 percent of global nuclear power use. Indeed, nuclear power consumption in Asia grew by 66 percent between 1991 and 2001. Japan is the top user of nuclear power in Asia, with 62 percent of the regional total and 12 percent of the global total. But although Japan increased nuclear power consumption by 53 percent between 1991 and 2001, that increased reliance on nuclear energy has provoked significant internal opposition. In fact, a number of planned nuclear power facilities have been voted down or suspended because of local opposition. Elsewhere, however, schemes to boost nuclear power generation are proceeding. In South Korea, which uses 22 percent of Asian nuclear power and 4 percent of the global sum, nuclear energy output doubled between 1991 and 2001, and the nation has four new reactors under construction. And China, which drew no energy from nuclear power at the beginning of the 1990s, consumed 3 percent of the Asian nuclear energy total in 2001 and had ten reactors in various stages of planning and construction as of early 2002. To the west, across the

Taiwan Strait, commercial interests on the island nation of Taiwan resumed construction of two units in 2001 after the government's move to stop the plants in 2000 was declared unconstitutional (ibid.).

Renewable Energy

Renewable energy is an increasingly important energy source in Asia. Renewable energy is defined here as energy derived from natural processes that do not require the exhaustion of finite resources such as fossil fuels and uranium. Large-scale hydropower is also typically excluded, leaving biomass, solar, wind, geothermal, small-scale hydro, and wave energy in the renewable energy category.

Much of the renewable energy used today is noncommercial: its production and consumption do not involve any market transactions. Noncommercial energy, which takes the form of firewood, charcoal, crop residues, and animal waste, is very important in many Asian countries. However, it is difficult to collect data on this type of energy, for it is normally not accounted for in conventional energy statistics.

Commercial renewable energy, which now accounts for 2 percent of commercial primary energy worldwide, is growing quickly and beginning to mature. Installed wind power capacity has increased more than tenfold over the past decade, signaling "wind's emergence as a mainstream energy source" (ibid.).

Asia is a growing factor in wind power's emergence. The region accounts for 9 percent of cumulative installed wind turbine capacity, with 2,348 megawatts (MW) installed in 2001. This represents a 110 percent growth in capacity since 1997. Asia added 550 MW in 2001 alone, a 30 percent increase.

India leads the wind power boom in Asia, with 1,456 MW installed in 2001. Indian wind power capacity has grown by 55 percent since 1997, and it now stands at 62 percent of the regional total and 6 percent of the global total. That makes India the fifth leading wind power user worldwide, and the leader in the developing world. Beginning with only 50 MW installed in 1993, the country experienced a boom driven by investment-based incentives for wind power developers and exemptions and concessions for import duties for wind turbine components (Flavin 2002.) In early 2002, the government of India announced the goal of increasing renewable energy production by an additional 10,000 MW by 2012, with 6,000 MW of the total to come from wind power operations primarily installed in remote villages, where the cost of hooking up to the country's existing energy grid is prohibitive.

China is another Asian country that has invested heavily in wind power, especially via bilateral donor grants and special concessional financing. As a result, it registered a 178 percent upturn in wind power capacity from 1997 to 2001, to 406 MW. That gives China 17 percent of the Asian wind power total and just less than 2 percent of the world total. Japan, meanwhile, has increased wind power capacity to 357 MW, giving it 15 percent of the regional total and slightly more than 1 percent of the global sum.

The use of solar photovoltaic (PV) energy has also increased dramatically over the past decade, both globally and in Asia. Japan is the world's largest solar PV producer and consumer, with its manufacturers producing just under 44 percent of the global output in 2001. Japan had 318 MW of cumulative installed PV power in 2000, 44 percent of the total among OECD nations. Installed capacity increased by more than sixteenfold between 1992 and 2000, thanks to generous government subsidies for PV system purchasers. Another significant Asian investor in solar PV technology has been South Korea, which increased its installed PV capacity by 169 percent between 1992 and 2000 (Sheehan 2002.)

Solar PV consumption is also increasing at a fast pace in the developing regions of Asia, particularly as part of solar home systems that combine PVs with batteries and lighting or other equipment. Indeed, the world's two largest existing markets for solar home systems are in India and China, which have 450,000 and 150,000 systems in place, respectively. China is one of the world's fastest-growing markets, with annual growth rates of 10 to 20 percent. Other notable emerging solar PV markets in Asia include Indonesia, Nepal, Philippines, and Sri Lanka. The region already hosts a number of PV module manufacturers, in India (23 firms), China (7 firms), and Thailand (3), and of PV cell manufacturers, in India (9 firms) and China (7 firms).

The PV market in India is the result of a government program of subsidy, tax, and financial incentives dating back to the 1980s. These subsidies have contributed to most solar home system installations. But while the market's development has encouraged more public agency and private entrepreneur involvement, the number of installations on purely commercial terms and without government subsidies remains small.

The recent growth in the Chinese PV market has been on commercial terms and has taken place primarily in the northwestern provinces and autonomous regions of Qinghai, Xinjiang, Tibet, Inner Mongolia, and Gansu. These isolated regions now have a solar industry and infrastructure in place, helped in part by a number of small donor programs. In these markets, most sales are cash transactions for small (10 to 25 watt) systems.

Geothermal power is another prominent renewable energy source in Asia. The region had 3,075 MW of cumulative installed capacity in 2000, 44 percent of the global total. The Philippines leads the region, and it is the second leading user globally, with 590 MW installed in 2000. This is nearly a tripling of Philippine geothermal power since 1990, and 24 percent of the world sum. Indonesia is the second leading geothermal power user in Asia and the fifth leading user globally, with a 7 percent world share. Indonesian installed geothermal capacity more than tripled between 1990 and 2000, to 590 MW. Japan, with 7 percent of global geothermal power use, increased capacity by 155 percent, to 547 MW.

Asian countries are beginning to better understand the critical role that renewable energy can play in meeting one of their most pressing goals: improving access to rural energy. Of the roughly 2 billion people worldwide living without access to electricity, the number in Asia is an imprecise but significant share. Those lacking modern energy services are typically forced to rely on the unsustainable use of biomass or on dirty, expensive, kerosene lanterns. This inequity in electrical access is detrimental to human health, living standards, and economic prospects, and poses the risk of social unrest—making "power poverty" an increasingly important issue for policy-makers.

Government rural electrification programs have yielded some progress in bringing grid electricity to populations in developing Asia over the past thirty years. But the majority of connections have occurred in or near urban areas, and in Asia the rate of electrification has not kept up with population growth. Between 1970 and 1990, urban access to electricity increased in South Asia from 39 to 53 percent and in East Asia from 51 to 82 percent. But rural access during the same time period increased in these regions only from 12 to 25 percent and from 25 to 45 percent, respectively (Dunn 2001b).

Nor does village access necessarily mean household access: 80 percent of India's villages, for example, are electrified, but a far smaller percentage of homes have power. The rural/urban disparity in access is especially pronounced in countries such as Nepal, where 9 percent of rural households have electric power, compared with 89 percent of urban households, and Vietnam (39 percent and 88 percent, respectively).

Where electric power systems do exist, they are typically more brittle than in industrial nations. Transmission and distribution losses equal roughly 20 percent of power demand in India and Sri Lanka, and more than 30 percent in Bangladesh. In India, power unreliability has led industries to invest in on-site generation, which now accounts for 12 percent of the nation's total installed capacity.

Off-grid renewable energy systems have emerged as attractive choices for rural electrification in Asia. In terms of performance and reliability, these biogas, microhydro, solar PV, and small wind systems compare favorably with the cost of extending transmission lines to unserved areas. They also offer viable alternatives for a range of crucial village tasks, such as ice making; water desalination, purification, and pumping; and the operation of rural schools, police stations, and health clinics.

Developing Asia is also a leading center of the use of biogas digesters. These facilities convert animal and plant wastes into a fuel usable for lighting, heating, cooking, and power generation, and they can be implemented at either the household scale or the community scale, with the plants shared by numerous households. China, India, and Nepal have all developed large manufacturing industries for biogas plants (Martinot et al. 2002).

Of these countries, China is the leading biogas user, with 7.5 million household digesters installed and another 750 medium- and large-scale industrial plants. It may be the case, however, that the number of operational biogas plants has declined in the late 1990s. The Chinese biogas programs began in the 1950s and peaked in the 1960s and 1970s. From that point forward, insufficient education and household training led to declining use until service centers were established in the mid-1980s. India's biogas program is also considerable, with approximately 3 million household plants installed. The Indian program initially focused on technology development, moving later to training of engineers. However, as much as 30 percent of the installed systems are no longer operational. The Nepalese biogas program, meanwhile, installed more than 35,000 biogas plants between 1992 and 1998. That program's success has been attributed to investment subsidies, affordable financing schemes for small and low-income farmers, and an effective after-sales service program (Goldemberg et al. 2002; Martinot et al. 2002).

Small hydropower, which harnesses small rivers and streams with power plants less than 10 MW in size, has long been a component of Asian rural energy development. China alone has 21,000 MW of small hydropower installed, just under half of the global total. The Chinese projects have been driven by government rural electrification programs.

Biomass power projects can also be found in Asia. Methods include the direct combustion of feedstocks to produce power from steam turbines, and gasification—the direct conversion of biomass into a biogas that is then burned in an engine. Although no large-scale gasification projects are yet operating in Asia, a number of small-scale plants (200 kilowatts and less) are operating in India, China, and Indonesia. Most of the biomass feedstocks, meanwhile, are from agricultural and forest industry residues, with the Philippines currently ranking as the region's leading producer in this sector.

Renewables Emerge as Practical Energy Option

In recent years, the attractiveness of renewable energy has been augmented by its ability to support a range of productive activities in rural Asia in the realms of agriculture, small industry, commercial services, and social services such as drinking water, education, and health care. For example, renewable energy sources have become cornerstones of some agricultural water pumping schemes in China and India. But permanent inroads have been difficult to achieve. For instance, the Indian government has yet to embrace biogas technology for water pumping, despite its economic potential, and a biogas-for-water program initiated by the Philippines in the 1980s eventually fell by the wayside.

Despite such setbacks, advocates of renewable energy investment claim that it can be a useful tool to small industries that generate significant local income and employment. Examples of such applications are emerging. On one Philippine island, a wind-solar-diesel hybrid provides twenty-four-hour power for seaweed drying, woodworking, and sewing, with little diesel fuel requirements. In the West Bengal state of India, small local enterprises such as cycle repair shops and health clinics are run by solar- and biomass-powered village-scale mini grids. In a remote Indonesian fishing community, wind turbines help provide income through ice production for freezing fish, grinding corn, creating potable water supplies, and other applications.

Many other examples are emerging as well, though slowly and anecdotally. Studies have shown, for example, that solar-electrified retail stores in Bangladesh operated for longer hours and generated higher incomes than unelectrified stores, with the disparity partly attributed to solar power. The organization Greenstar is developing "solar community centers" in villages with lighting, satellite links, computers, and video equipment to enable sales of local music and crafts over the Internet. Other promising applications include paper-making, wood- and metalworking, drip irrigation, distance education and medicine, and vaccine refrigeration (Dunn 2000).

Confronting King Coal

At the same time that rural energy needs provide a "pull" toward renewable energy in Asia, human health and environmental pressures are creating a "push" away from the region's heavy reliance on coal. At present, coal is an important fuel in several Asian countries. Three nations in the region qualify among the world's "Thirteen Colonies of Coal": those that rely on coal for at least one-quarter of their energy supply. In China, coal accounts for 78 percent of energy and 75 percent of electricity. In India the shares are 57 and 73 percent, respectively; and in South Korea, the proportions are 31 and 35 percent, respectively (Dunn 1999).

The human health hazards of coal, which contains potent carcinogens, are becoming particularly problematic in parts of the region. Lung cancer from air pollution is now the leading cause of death in China, mainly in urban areas. Particulate matter, sulfur dioxide, and nitrogen oxides, long associated with a range of respiratory and cardiovascular problems, are leading sources of air pollution in the megacities of China and India. These countries host the world's ten most polluted cities, nine in China and one in India. All of these cities are, not surprisingly, heavy coal users. Cities such as Beijing, Calcutta, and Shanghai regularly expose millions of children to these coal smogs. In rural China, meanwhile, exposure to coal smoke has increased lung cancer risks by a factor of nine or more. Coal can also contain arsenic, lead, mercury, and fluorine—toxic heavy metals that can impair the development of fetuses and infants and cause open sores and bone decay. In rural China, where an estimated 800 million people use coal in their homes for cooking and heating, thousands of cases of arsenic poisoning, and millions of cases of fluorine poisoning, have been reported (ibid.).

Coal mining and extraction pose health hazards as well. Explosions, falls, and hauling accidents injure or kill several thousand coal miners in Asia each year. In China, more than five miners die for every million tons of coal mined. Perhaps the most serious and chronic threat to miners is pneumoconiosis, or "black lung," a condition caused by continued inhalation of coal dust. Over time, breathing this polluted air can inflame, scar, and discolor lungs and lead to debilitating declines in lung function. In China, where 2.5 million coal miners are exposed to dust diseases, the current annual death toll of 2,500 is expected to increase by 10 percent each year (ibid.).

Heavy coal use is also a major culprit in the creation of acid rain, a phenomenon that first emerged in the developed countries of the Western world. Acid rain is created by emissions of nitrous oxides and sulfur dioxide associated with the burning of fossil fuels. These chemicals mix with water and oxygen in the air to form sulfuric and nitric acids that return to earth in snow and rain, damaging buildings and monuments, ruining forests (especially at higher elevations), and acidifying lakes, streams, and soil.

Acid deposition in the West surged when nations installed major clean air laws to address heavy airborne concentrations of pollution from coal and other fossil fuel consumption. Industries reacted to those regulations by installing high smokestacks that would spread the pollutants over larger areas and to more distant regions. This seemingly simple solution had the unintended consequence of creating acids that fell back to earth as rain, snow, and fog. Acid rain eventually became a major environmental problem in Europe and North America in the 1980s, and though significant gains have been made in combating the problem in recent years, acid deposition remains a chronic issue for numerous ecosystems in those regions.

The West's acid rain debacle is now being replicated with potentially greater repercussions in Asia. A haze the size of the United States has been reported over the Indian Ocean in winter; in summer that cloud has blown inland and produced quantities of acid rain that have reportedly reduced Indian wheat yields. Indeed, by some estimates, fully one-fifth of India's farmland faces acidification. It has also been estimated that acid rain affects nearly 30 percent of China's land area, including some of the country's most economically significant regions. For example, an estimated 60 to 90 percent of rainfalls in Guangdong, a southern province that has been a key to China's robust economic development, are acid rain. According to some estimates, acid rain annually wreaks $U.S.5 billion in crop and other damage across China (World Bank 1997).

Buildings, farmlands, and forests in South Korea, Thailand, Cambodia, and Vietnam are bearing the scars of acid rain as well, with much of the emissions generated by their northern neighbor China. Indeed, China's sulfur emissions may overwhelm fertile soils across China, Japan, and South Korea by 2020. Moreover, other types of ecosystem overload have been linked to heavy coal consumption, including ground-level ozone concentrations that damage forests and crops (each year, ozone cuts wheat yields in parts of China by an estimated 10 percent). Finally, Asia has made the local coal smogs of the past into today's transcontinental travelers: large dust clouds of particulates and sulfur from Asian coal now commonly reach the U.S. West Coast (Dunn 1999).

Developing countries in Asia are struggling to steer clear of the pitfalls of a simplistic response to coal pollution. Yet the folly of focusing solely on coal's air pollutants proves most perverse in developing Asia, where the added mining and processing requirements exacerbate severe land and water constraints in highly populous countries. For instance, Chinese enterprises commonly violate emissions standards and burn high-sulfur coal rather than pay for precious water with which to wash coal. In India, meanwhile, citizens' groups have criticized the government's coal-washing mandate, arguing that it will waste energy, use up large quantities of scarce water and land, and increase pollution at mines (ibid.).

Public concern over acid rain led to another technological quick fix: "clean-coal" technologies, or flue-gas desulfurization and nitrogen-control equipment. Even though this equipment lowered emissions of the targeted

Table 8.1 World Carbon Dioxide Emissions, 1990–2020

Region	Carbon dioxide emissions (million metric tons)			
	1990	*1999*	*2010[5]*	*2020[5]*
Industrialized nations[1]	2,849	3,129	3,692	4,169
Eastern Europe/Former Soviet Union	1,337	810	978	1,139
Developing nations				
Asia[2]	1,053	1,361	2,139	3,017
Middle East[3]	231	330	439	566
Africa	179	218	287	365
Central and South America[4]	178	249	377	595
Total Developing	1,641	2,158	3,241	4,542
Total world	*5,827*	*6,097*	*7,910*	*9,850*

1. Includes the U.S, Canada, Mexico, Japan, France, Germany, Italy, the Netherlands, and the United Kingdom.
2. China, India, and South Korea are represented in developing Asia.
3. Turkey is represented in the Middle East.
4. Brazil is represented in Central and South America.
5. Projections.

pollutants, they, like higher smokestacks, had unforeseen side effects. Clean coal creates added water demands, produces large amounts of sludge and other solid wastes, and decreases energy efficiency, thereby increasing emissions of carbon dioxide, the most significant greenhouse gas (see table 8.1 for a breakdown of carbon dioxide emissions by world region). Critics also contend that clean-coal equipment has failed to demonstrate financial viability in the West (its high capital-investment costs make it less attractive than natural-gas-fired combined-cycle turbines), and that its increasingly high profile is attributable less to economics than to the political clout of the industry (ibid.).

Despite these problems, observers express hope that Asian nations can avoid the West's emergency-room approach to coping with coal and environmental hazards associated with its consumption. If treating coal's symptoms in isolation has not been sufficient for improving human and ecological health in today's industrial West, it is even less likely to do so in Asia. Two policies are central to the process of reducing coal dependence—subsidy removal and energy taxation. Supporters of these steps say that their implementation will address widespread market distortions that imply that coal is cheap, abundant, and irreplaceable, when countries in Asia are beginning to realize that continued coal dependence is increasingly costly, limited, and unnecessary.

China, for instance, will undoubtedly remain heavily dependent on coal for the foreseeable future. But China's coal subsidy rates have been more than halved since 1984, contributing to that nation's slowdown in consumption. Opportunities exist for further reductions as well. Coal subsidies have been estimated at $6 billion in China and India. Bold initiatives in coal taxation have also been instituted in China in the form of a tax on high-sulfur coal that is designed to encourage greater use of natural gas and renewable energy resources. In the Chinese capital of Beijing, meanwhile, city officials have responded to public pressure by cracking down on coal burning. Beginning with the city's 42-square-mile central limits, the government plans to establish coal-free zones wherein local authorities will assist residents in switching from coal to cleaner-burning natural gas. Hundreds of residents in Beijing have mobilized through citizens' groups such as Global Village to supervise implementation of the policies and raise public consciousness of the problem. Since the program was announced, several other Chinese cities, including Shanghai, Lanzhou, Xian, and Shenyand, have announced plans to follow suit with their own coal-reduction programs (ibid.).

Meeting the Transportation Challenges of the Twenty-First Century

Asia faces major challenges in meeting the mobility needs of its rapidly expanding and urbanizing populations and growing economies. Although enhanced mobility can have many beneficial effects on economic development and social welfare, achieving that enhancement through greater reliance on conventional private cars—the U.S. model—can result in the diversion of substantial financial resources to roads and the worsening of air pollution and traffic congestion. These cost and benefit tradeoffs are magnified in Asia.

Some analysts, in fact, argue that the challenges posed by motorization are unprecedented for developing countries. When the world's more developed countries were building their transportation systems, their populations were relatively small. Today's megacities, on the other hand, are already huge and continuing to expand. Governments of developing countries typically have little time or money to build public transportation systems or to expand roads to handle new traffic. They are already experiencing serious traffic congestion, economic and environmental damage, and social problems. These factors make the institution of environmentally sustainable models of transportation a formidable and vexing challenge.

Rapid motorization—and rapid growth in related emissions—are to some extent unavoidable in developing Asia. Rising incomes are major factors in that trend, and once people have personal vehicles, they tend to use them. Nonetheless, there are a number of intelligent policies and strategies available to Asia to slow its growth of transport-related emissions. The twin cornerstones of those strategies are increasing the cost of using conventional private cars and enhancing the quality and choices of alternative transportation modes.

If such goals can be achieved, benefits accrue at both the local and global levels. Local benefits include reduced air pollution, less traffic congestion, and lower expenditures for road infrastructure. Global benefits include slower growth in transportation-related greenhouse gas emissions, which are rising more quickly in the developing world than anywhere else. From 1980 to 1997, transportation energy use and associated greenhouse gas emissions increased by more than 5 percent per year in Asia, compared with 2.6 percent in Latin America and 1 percent in greenhouse gases from all sectors worldwide (Sperling and Salon 2002.)

In choosing a more sustainable transport path, Asia can draw on some of the successful efforts already underway in the region (although experts acknowledge that there is no single city that can stand as a sustainability model for all others). The region can also learn from the experiences of the industrial nations in creating integrated land use and transportation plans, encouraging more efficient forms of vehicle ownership and use, and accelerating the deployment of environmentally sensible vehicle technologies and fuels.

At the same time, however, many cities in Asia are growing at unprecedented rates, with personal vehicles (of admittedly low quality—and characterized by high pollution emissions) increasingly available to people with very low incomes. Policy and investment decisions need to be made soon to avoid many negative social, economic, and environmental consequences. But successful strategies are likely to vary greatly from city to city, according to local circumstances and institutional strengths and weaknesses of each metropolitan area.

The city of Delhi, India, provides an excellent case study for the mobility challenges facing Asia. A rapidly expanding megacity, Delhi is facing urban gridlock and dangerous levels of air pollution. Although vehicle ownership is still a fraction of that in industrial countries, it is remarkably high for a population with a relatively low income (many of these vehicles are small, inexpensive motorcycles and scooters, as opposed to automobiles). Delhi is confronted with the same transportation, economic, and environmental challenges facing other megacities. Its air pollution levels are well above national and World Health Organization–based standards, and transportation is its largest source of pollution. Over the past thirty years, Delhi's population more than tripled, and its number of vehicles increased nearly fifteenfold. By 2000, Delhi had roughly 2.6 million motor vehicles—200 per 1,000 inhabitants, a rate well above that of cities with comparable incomes (Bose 2001).

Moreover, the human and vehicle populations of Delhi are expected to continue to grow at a rapid rate. The city's population is projected to surpass 22 million by 2020. The number of motor vehicles, including cars, trucks, and motorized two- and three-wheelers, is expected to grow at an even faster rate. India's domestic auto industry is predicting car sale increases of approximately 10 percent per year. And with a growing network of roads and rising incomes, vehicle sales and use can be expected to continue to increase sharply.

Shanghai, China, provides another snapshot of Asia's burgeoning mobility needs. Rapid economic growth and rising affluence are leading to far-reaching changes in urban structure, transportation, and energy use. The metropolitan population of 13 million is growing at a relatively slow pace, but the economy is growing and the average annual per capita income, at $4,000, is three times higher than that of the rest of China. The Shanghai economy is projected to grow at more than 5 percent per year through 2020 (Zhou et al. 2001).

Major new investments in Shanghai's transport system are planned, with the aims of lowering the city's population density while supporting economic growth and enhancing the quality of life. These investments include expansion of the city's new airport, construction of a deep water harbor, three new bridges and tunnel river crossings, completion of a 200-kilometer modern rapid-transit rail system, expansion of suburban highways, and construction of 2,000 kilometers of new and upgraded urban roads. Although improving mobility, these investments may also lead to greater energy use and air pollution.

Currently, cars and other motorized vehicles are not as pervasive a presence in Shanghai as they are in other Asian countries. Little land is currently used for roads, and the city posts levels of vehicle ownership that are well below those of other Asian cities with similar per capita incomes. Yet even with this relatively small vehicle population, Shanghai already faces grave transport-related air pollution and traffic congestion issues. According to Shanghai city planners, the number of cars and trucks in the city will quadruple by 2020. That increase is tied mainly to two factors. The first is rapid income growth, which will improve the possibility of car ownership for larger parts of the population. The second is vehicle prices, which are expected to plummet with China's accession to the World Trade Organization. Lower prices are anticipated from increased competition, compulsory reductions in vehicle tariffs, and easier access to vehicle purchases (ibid.).

Public Transport Trends in Asia

Rates of motor vehicle use in Asia are still low compared with those of the developed world, but they are growing rapidly (motorization rates are at the levels and growth rates seen in Europe in the 1950s and 1960s). That is in part due to Asia's highway systems, which are sparse, poorly planned, and in some cases in advanced states of disrepair. In China, for instance, the road infrastructure is about 1 million kilometers, yet only 6,000 can be considered "highway" in the industrial-world sense: most of the network is two-lane, with side-paths for bicycles and tractors. The Chinese rail system has been compared in scope with that of the United States at the time of the Civil War, though in size it is more extensive.

Despite lower levels of private automobile ownership, however, Asia's emissions of pollutants from the transportation sector is growing, and it is already well above the levels posted in the developed world, because of the poor fuel economy of the region's automobile fleet and the high-polluting character of most vehicles.

Even though passenger car use is increasing in Asia, the bulk of mobility demand is still met by train and bus. Rail and bus account for roughly 70 percent of the passenger-kilometers in the region, compared with 5 percent for air and 25 percent for cars. Further, a large number of trips in large urban areas are still made on foot—close to 70 percent in Shanghai, for example. The mixing of pedestrian traffic and vehicular traffic generates massive congestion and high accident rates, especially among the poor.

Rail passenger traffic remains important in a number of Asian countries. Some 57 percent of global revenues for rail are collected in Asia: 20 percent in China and India, 11 percent in Japan, and 6 percent in other countries. Yet a number of those passenger rail systems, especially in China and India, are poorly maintained and have an aging stock. With the continued urbanization of these countries, intercity rail travel can be expected to face increased competition from other modes of transport. In Japan, however, the government has adopted a proactive stance to ensure the continued viability of its rail passenger networks. Rail systems are being upgraded to compete to some extent with passenger vehicles, and high-speed rail systems have been installed to attract passengers traveling longer distances.

Passengers sit on the roof of an Indian Railways local train, plying the Delhi–Rewari route, as it leaves the Palam railway station in New Delhi, India, 2002. AFP/CORBIS

Both developing and industrial Asia face sustainability concerns with freight transport as well. As in other parts of the world, Asia is experiencing a steady shift away from rail transport to truck transport. For example, rail freight's share of total rail and road freight dropped between 1970 and the early 1990s from 95 to 75 percent in China, and from 30 to 10 percent in Japan. This shift has been blamed as a factor in the continent's increasing energy consumption, air pollution emissions, noise pollution levels, and traffic congestion.

Making Asian transportation systems more sustainable will require action on several fronts. Important steps include improving public transport as a viable option for those without access to personal vehicles; improving the planning process for mobility infrastructure; phasing carbon out of transport fuels; and addressing the competition between personal and freight transportation in urban areas. Although there is potential for technological leaps— hydrogen-based fuel cell buses are scheduled to undergo testing in Bangkok, Beijing, Shanghai, and Delhi, for example—institutions will have the major role in determining what sort of transportation systems emerge in the region. Indeed, the same can be said for energy and transport in Asia more broadly. Whether governments and the private sector have the institutional capacity to build infrastructures that meet Asia's expanding power and mobility needs in sustainable fashion is a question that will loom large for both the region and the world in coming years.

Sources:

Bose, Ranjan, et al. 2001. *Transportation in Developing Countries: Greenhouse Gas Scenarios for Delhi, India.* Prepared for the Pew Center on Global Climate Change. Washington, DC: Pew Center.

British Petroleum. 2002. *BP Statistical Review of World Energy 2002.* London: Group Media.

Dunn, Seth. 1999. "King Coal's Weakening Grip on Power." *World Watch* 12 (November–December).

———. 2000. *Micropower: The Next Electrical Era.* Worldwatch Paper 160. Washington, DC: Worldwatch Institute.

———. 2001a. "China, Energy, the Environment, and Climate Change." In Julian Weiss, ed., *Tigers' Roar: Asia's Recovery and Its Implications.* New York: M. E. Sharpe.

———. 2001b. *Hydrogen Futures: Toward a Sustainable Energy System.* Worldwatch Paper 157. Washington, DC: Worldwatch Institute.

Flavin, Christopher. 2002. "Wind Energy Surges." In Janet N. Abramovitz et al., eds., *Vital Signs 2002: The Trends That Are Shaping Our Future.* Worldwatch Institute. New York: W. W. Norton.

Goldemberg, Jose, et al. 2002. "Rural Energy in Developing Countries." *World Energy Assessment: Energy and the Challenge of Sustainability.* New York: UN Development Programme, UN Department of Economic and Social Affairs, and World Energy Council.

"India Plans 6,000 MW Wind Power in Next 10 Years." 2002. *Reuters News Service,* April 3.

Martinot, Eric, et al. 2002. "Renewable Energy Markets in Developing Countries." *Annual Review of Energy and the Environment* 27.

Sheehan, Molly. 2002. "Solar Cell Use Rises Quickly." In Janet N. Abramovitz et al., eds., *Vital Signs 2002: The Trends That Are Shaping Our Future.* Worldwatch Institute. New York: W. W. Norton.

Sperling, Daniel, and Deborah Salon. May 2002. *Transportation in Developing Countries: An Overview of Greenhouse Gas Reduction Strategies.* Prepared for the Pew Center on Global Climate Change. Washington, DC: Pew Center.

World Bank. 1997. *Clear Water, Blue Skies.* Washington, DC: World Bank.

World Business Council on Sustainable Development. 2001. *Mobility 2001.* Geneva: World Business Council on Sustainable Development.

Zhou, Hongchang, et al. July 2001. *Transportation in Developing Countries: Greenhouse Gas Scenarios for Shanghai, China.* Prepared for the Pew Center on Global Climate Change. Washington, DC: Pew Center.

Air Quality
and the Atmosphere

Air pollution is a major environmental problem in Asia. Emissions of myriad pollutants, including sulfur dioxide, nitrogen oxides, chlorofluorocarbons (CFCs), particulate matter, and ammonia have all risen steadily over the past few decades, pushed upward by fossil fuel consumption in the energy, transportation, and industry sectors; environmentally destructive mining practices; and slash-and-burn deforestation. Rapid urbanization, a consequence of positive economic growth, is responsible for much of this surge in emissions, because it drives ever-greater demand for motor vehicles, electricity, and other trappings of improved standards of living. Moreover, most Asian countries remain reliant on coal and other low-quality, high-polluting energy sources. For the most part, the use of these resources is very inefficient, and it continues to take place in an environment in which monitoring and control of emissions is spotty at best. All of these factors contributed to a doubling in per capita commercial energy use in most regions of Asia between 1975 and 1995, a period when industrialized countries were making marked strides in improving their per capita energy use. Between 1990 and 1993 alone, Asian energy consumption grew by 6.2 percent annually, while global energy consumption actually declined by 1 percent a year (Asian Development Bank 1997a).

Some promising national and multilateral efforts to combat these and other environmental quality issues have been implemented in recent years. But as one analyst noted: "[T]he current state of environmental degradation in developing countries in Asia is more serious than it was in developed countries in the 1960s and 1970s because Asian countries must address the global environmental issues that have emerged since the 1980s [such as global warming and stratospheric ozone loss] in addition to those that are

presently emerging, despite the lack of financial resources and technologies"
(Harashima 2000).

In 1999, Asia's myriad difficulties with emissions of air pollutants crystal-
lized in particularly disquieting form. That year, scientists announced the existence of an enormous cloud of pollution over the Indian Ocean. Analysis
placed the size of the cloud at approximately 9 million square kilometers, approximately the size of the United States. This cloud, believed to have been
blown out to sea from the Asian mainland during winter monsoons, consisted of soot, sulfates, nitrates, organic particles, fly ash, mineral dust, and
high concentrations of gases such as carbon monoxide and sulfur dioxide.
Two years later, scientists with the UN Environment Programme (UNEP)
and the Indian Ocean Experiment (INDOEX) announced that they had con-
firmed the existence of a vast brown haze of even greater size—10 million
square kilometers—over the Asian continent (UN Environment Programme
2001). The formation of these cloud phenomena is the clearest indicator yet
of the severe air pollution hazards threatening Asia, and their existence has
injected new urgency into the international drive to curb airborne emissions
in the region.

Air Pollution

Urban Trends Drive Jump in Emissions

Asia is squarely situated on the horns of a dilemma that is also confronting
other developing regions of the world. It is seeking to improve the socioeconomic standing of its peoples while simultaneously protecting the natural
environment. In practical application, however, the latter issue has generally
been an afterthought (just as it was in Europe and North America in earlier
decades), and that remained true in the 1990s, when Asia experienced significant economic growth. "The more rapid the growth in industrial production, the more serious the environmental problems related to industrial
pollution are likely to be since time is required to identify and act on problems, to develop the legislative basis for pollution control and develop the institutional structure needed to implement it. In addition, there are usually
powerful vested interests that oppose the implementation of pollution control and political circumstances often slow or halt such implementation"
(Hardoy et al. 2001).

Indeed, effective management of air quality requires accurate assessment of
environmental conditions, and many Asian countries have limited institutions and policies in place to gather and interpret research data. This fundamental research principle is entrenched in Europe, the United States, and

other developed countries, but "recognition of the principle has been slow to reach the majority in the developing world, which is coming late to the table of economic prosperity" (Jaafar 1999).

Research data from international government institutions and environmental research organizations, however, provide ample evidence that Asia's air quality is steadily worsening. Certainly, the extent of air pollution in many Asian cities is appalling, according to virtually any means of measurement. For example, elevated concentrations of tropospheric or ground-level ozone—formed via photochemical reactions between nitrogen oxides, volatile organic compounds (VOCs), and carbon monoxide—are an unfortunate reality in many urban settings. These high ozone concentrations create smoggy conditions; poison crops and vegetation; damage the respiratory systems of people, livestock, and wildlife; and contribute to global warming.

Particulate levels are also severe in most Asian metropolitan areas. According to a joint analysis compiled by the World Bank, the World Resources Institute, and the UN Environment Programme (UNEP), Asia is home to nineteen of the world's twenty most polluted cities, including the planet's fifteen most polluted cities, in terms of total suspended particulates (which includes particles released during the combustion of fossil fuels), principally gasoline burned in motor vehicles and coal burned for electricity or household heating as well as naturally generated dust particles (World Resources Institute 1998b). In addition, numerous cities have generated serious levels of nitrogen dioxide air pollution that have risen in concert with escalating automobile use, and high sulfur dioxide pollution, which is also attributable to factory and household use of coal and other high-sulfur fuels (Japan Environmental Council 2000).

Emission Trends across the Continent

One notable exception to the troubling state of air pollution that exists in most of Asia is economically advanced Japan, though its record is not unblemished. After years of neglecting its air, water, and land resources, Japan passed a series of laws in the 1960s and 1970s with the express purpose of abating air and water pollution. These mandates produced major improvements in the quality and health of the country's natural resources. Since that time, its dedication to clean air and other environmental priorities has ebbed and flowed somewhat. For example, its heavy reliance on incineration as a waste disposal tool has drawn heavy criticism from environmentalists. Still, its overall body of law on air and water protection is arguably the best on the continent. Moreover, Japan is rehabilitating its reputation as one of the world's worst offenders in terms of carbon dioxide emissions. Japan's 2002 ratification of the Kyoto Protocol requires it to reduce its emissions of carbon dioxide and other greenhouse gases responsible for global climate change to below 1990 levels between 2008 and 2012.

In the past two decades, South Korea has also adopted a number of significant policy measures to reduce air pollution, from beefed up vehicle emissions standards to mandatory use of clean fuels for electricity generation in large cities. It has also made noticeable gains in incorporating environmental stewardship issues into other policy areas, although local ecosystems remain stressed to varying degrees (Harashima 2000).

At first glance, China's air pollution problems appear far more intractable. At least five of the world's ten most air polluted cities are in China, and perhaps as many as eight out of ten (Changhua 1999). This state of affairs is partially attributable to the country's rapidly swelling motor vehicle fleet. From 1984 to 1999, the number of automobiles, trucks, motorcycles, and other vehicles on China's roads more than quadrupled, from fewer than 2.4 million to more than 11 million, and experts estimate that by 2020 China's urban vehicle population could be at least ten times greater than in 1999 (ibid.).

China is also shackled by continued dependence on high-polluting coal in both urban and rural areas in its residential, industrial, and utility sectors. A typical coal-fired power plant in China currently releases about 100 times the sulfur dioxide emitted by a plant outfitted for natural gas, although emissions generated by coal-fired plants do vary somewhat depending on the quality of coal that is used. "Compared to nuclear or hydroelectric power, which emit no sulfur dioxide, coal is 'infinitely dirty'" (McDonald 1999).

At the close of the twentieth century, coal accounted for about 80 percent of China's power generation, and it is almost a certainty that the country will consume even greater quantities of the fossil fuel in the near term. "China's coal dependence is likely to last for decades: virtually the entire national infrastructure runs on coal. The exception is the transportation system, which is based on petroleum and human muscle. But three-quarters of electricity production and virtually all the factories and heating are coal-powered. To replace or upgrade this infrastructure—the hundreds of electric power stations, the hundreds of thousands of boilers in factories and apartment buildings, the millions of honeycomb stoves—is an essential but necessarily long-term project, especially because Chinese of all classes are impatient to have economic progress *today*" (Hertsgaard 1998).

But this consumption comes at a high price. Coal burning is a major contributor to sulfur, nitrogen, and particulate pollution in China's urban environments, and it is the primary source of China's enormous—and growing—volume of greenhouse gas emissions. It also generates the main

A township coal manufacturing plant along the Three Gorges of the Yangtze River in China. KEREN
SU/CORBIS

precursors to acid rain and stratospheric ozone loss (Feng 1999). Indeed, acid
deposition already affects nearly 30 percent of China's land area, including
some of the country's most economically significant regions. For example, an
estimated 60 to 90 percent of rainfalls in Guangdong, a southern province
that has been a key to China's robust economic development, are acid rain. By
some estimates, acid deposition causes $U.S.5 billion in crop and other dam-
age annually across China (World Bank 1997b).

Emissions of sulfur dioxides and other pollutants also constitute a growing
health threat. According to one estimate, smoke and small particles from
burning coal are responsible for more than 50,000 premature deaths and
400,000 new chases of chronic bronchitis in eleven of China's largest cities annually (World Bank 1997c). On a countrywide basis, lung disease, aggravated
by air pollution and the soaring popularity of cigarette smoking, is responsible for one-fourth of all deaths in China (Hertsgaard 1998; World Bank
1997b). And finally, some reports suggest that excessive levels of haze are reducing crop yields by altering rainfall patterns and filtering sunlight.

There are indications, however, that China is beginning to recognize the
scale of the air pollution problems it faces. Sensitive to the growing impact of
pollution on its people and natural resources—and to increasing scrutiny
from the rest of the world—the Chinese government has adopted a host of

Gridlock in Bangkok

Traffic congestion on Sukhumvit Avenue in Bangkok, Thailand MASSIMO MASTRORILLO/ CORBIS

Bangkok, the capital city of Thailand, is among the most polluted cities in the world, in large measure because of explosive growth in the size and use of its notoriously dirty motor vehicle fleet. The number of motorcycles and other registered vehicles rumbling through Bangkok's crowded streets multiplied from 600,000 in 1980 to 2.7 million in 1993, a 4.5-fold increase. Today, Bangkok accounts for more than one-quarter of all the motor vehicles in Thailand (Japan Environmental Council 2000), and it has been described as a "flagrant example of how, even under the worst circumstances, the car has a magnetic appeal for humans. Despite the ungodly traffic jams, Bangkok residents continue to buy motor vehicles" (Hertsgaard 1998).

An estimated 90 percent of Bangkok vehicles are powered by outdated two-stroke engines that emit appalling levels of airborne particulates, hydrocarbons, and lead in their exhaust fumes. Not surprisingly, the financial and social cost of the "chaos and pollution of motor vehicle traffic in Bangkok" is significant. Residents and visitors to Bangkok and surrounding environs are routinely exposed to levels of particulate matter and other air pollution that far exceed World Health Organization (WHO) standards of safety. Studies undertaken by the World Bank and other institutions have concluded that if air pollution by airborne particulates and leaded gasoline were reduced by 20 percent in Bangkok, the annual benefit owing to decreased respiratory system damage and other health improvements would be the equivalent of U.S.$1 billion to $1.6 billion (Japan Environmental Council 2000; World Bank 1997).

The Thai government has taken some steps to address the problem of automobile pollution in Bangkok and other cities. Thailand began offering unleaded gas in 1992 and outlawed leaded gas in 1996. These steps have cut curbside concentrations of lead in Bangkok by 90 percent, and they have also resulted in a drop in carbon monoxide levels even as city traffic continues to worsen as a result of the inexorable addition of new cars, trucks, and motorcycles. Fleet modernization, enforcement of emission standards, and other fuel quality improvements—including requirements for oxygenates in gasoline—have also had beneficial effects (Asian Development Bank

2001). Still, Bangkok air quality remains very poor, and overall transport trends in the city and region do not bode well for the respiratory systems of its residents.

Sources:

Asian Development Bank. 1997. *Emerging Asia: Changes and Challenges.* Manila: ADB.

———. 2001. *Environments in Transition: Cambodia, Lao PDR, Thailand, Viet Nam.* Manila: ADB.

Hertsgaard, Mark. 1998. *Earth Odyssey: Around the World in Search of Our Environmental Future.* New York: Broadway.

Japan Environmental Council. 2000. *State of the Environment in Asia 1999–2000.* New York: Springer.

World Bank. 1997. *Environment Matters: Towards Environmentally and Socially Sustainable Development.* Washington, DC: World Bank.

policies and measures to address pollution emissions in recent years. One of the most important of those initiatives is a drive to shift Chinese reliance away from coal toward natural gas. This effort has had tangible results. For example, 97 percent of Shanghai's residential households had shifted to natural gas by the end of the 1990s, and other major metropolitan areas such as Beijing have dramatically improved their ratio of coal-to-natural gas households as well. "Because of the shift from coal to natural gas in many households, particulate emissions have not risen as much as they would have if the increased energy use had come only from coal," remarked one analyst. "Though China continues to pollute more each day, it is starting to do so more 'efficiently'" (Changhua 1999).

China has also moved to address its terrible problem with sulfur and nitrogen oxide emissions from power plants. Steps taken include integrating desulferization and nitrogen removal technology into some conventional coal-burning power units, shutting down other inefficient, high-emission plants, and developing major new facilities that rely on high steam pressure to generate electricity. It is also exploring a variety of new energy technologies, including integrated gasification combustion cycle power plants, fluidized-bed combustion-combined cycle power plants, liquefied natural gas power plants, and fuel-cell innovations (ibid.). In 1998, meanwhile, China imposed new sulfur dioxide emission limits and fees on mining and other industries in two zones of south and central China that have historically accounted for an estimated 60 percent of the country's total sulfur emissions (McDonald 1999). Moreover, after allowing cars and trucks to operate on leaded gasoline for decades, China belatedly ordered gasoline producers to stop making leaded gasoline by the end of 1999 and directed suppliers to stop selling it in mid-2000. The Chinese authorities have even decided to ease import tariffs on particulate removal equipment.

All of these steps are encouraging to public health and environmental organizations, as well as other nations in Asia and beyond. But these observers also note that China, which emits prodigious amounts of greenhouse gases (GHGs) every day, is not a signatory to the Kyoto Protocol, the 1997 UN agreement that seeks to address the threat of global warming by garnering international cooperation in the reduction of GHG emissions. Many analysts also wonder if China will continue to finance its present environmental improvement commitments—and make necessary investments in pollution abatement in the future—given its other economic, social, and strategic priorities. "[China] brings together two of the most disturbing trends in global environmental affairs: the large, growing population typical of poverty and the high-impact consumption patterns promoted by Western capitalism," observed one analyst. "This combustible union makes China a sort of environmental superpower in reverse. Like the United States, the other environmental superpower, China wields what amounts to veto power over the rest of the world's environmental progress. China and the United States are each responsible for such a large share of global consumption that any international attempts to reduce greenhouse gas emissions, limit oceanic overfishing, or phase out ozone-destroying chemicals simply cannot succeed without their cooperation" (Hertsgaard 1998).

Air pollution difficulties confronting other areas of Asia, meanwhile, differ in their specifics but share the same larger quandary: improving air quality in an era of accelerating population growth, increasing consumerism, and economic flux. In India, for instance, explosive population growth will likely keep the country heavily dependent on coal for the foreseeable future and further exacerbate already polluted conditions in its urban centers. Indeed, Calcutta, Lucknow, New Delhi, Kanpur, Jaipur and other cities are all saddled with extremely high levels of sulfur dioxide, carbon monoxide, nitrogen oxides, and hydrocarbons emitted by industry, power plants, motor vehicles, and household stoves. In fact, the annual mean concentrations of ambient particulate matter in Indian cities are more than six times that of the urban mean in the United States (McGranahan and Murray 1999).

Central Asia, meanwhile, is bristling with outdated and inefficient mining, chemical, metallurgical, and coal operations. Emissions of most major pollutants did subside to one degree or another in the region during the 1990s, when economic and political transitions triggered the closure of many industries. But they remained high enough in many areas to constitute a public health hazard. In Kazakstan, for instance, many industrial towns exceed the minimum allowed standard of pollution by five times or more, and some regions with intensive mining and ore-processing industries have radioactivity levels far above the norm (Asian Development Bank 1998). Indeed, significant expanses of Central Asia, most notably Uzbekistan and Kazakstan, still bear radioactive scars from the Soviet Union's uranium mining and nuclear testing activities. "Owing to its vast expanses of sparsely populated desert territory, Kazakstan was…a major location of former nuclear and other military testing for the Soviet Union.…Between 1949 and 1989, some 490 nuclear tests were conducted in the republic, including 26 above-ground tests, 87 atmospheric tests, and 354 underground tests. This resulted in the release of 45 million curies of radiation into the atmosphere. During the past 40 years, nuclear testing has rendered more than 19 million hectares of land unusable" (ibid.).

The challenge of reducing emissions of airborne pollutants is also formidable in Southeast Asia, where abatement policies, regulations, and technologies are only now being introduced. In Vietnam's urban areas, rising emissions from the transport and industry sectors routinely push air pollution levels above basic health standards. Coal remains the principal fuel for household cooking and heating and industrial power, and pollution abatement devices are nonexistent in industrial facilities, many of which are outfitted with aging, low-efficiency boilers (Asian Development Bank 2001). In addition, urban sprawl and population growth has swallowed up industrial parks and factories that were previously located outside Hanoi and other cities, bringing many residents into proximity with facilities that spew large amounts of hazardous substances each day. "Compounding the poor air quality is the profusion of low-efficiency two-stroke motorcycles and poorly maintained vehicles that run on leaded gasoline, generating high ambient levels of particulates, lead sulfur dioxide, and carbon monoxide. Air pollution is further exacerbated by increasing traffic congestion, reducing traffic speeds, and increasing emissions per kilometer traveled" (ibid.). In addition, Vietnam has asserted that dioxin contained in Agent Orange, a defoliant used extensively by U.S. forces in the Vietnam War, is to blame for generations of birth defects, cancer, and other diseases across the country. Vietnam has demanded financial compensation from the United States for those health problems. But the United States notes that industrial emissions of dioxin and other hazardous chemicals are significant in many areas of Asia, and it wants to conduct its own studies to confirm any linkage between Agent Orange and Vietnamese health issues.

In South Korea and Taiwan, emissions of pollutants by the industrial sector have been a major factor in the precipitous decline of air quality in both countries. Increased use of low-sulfur fuels has relieved some buildup of sulfur oxides, but increased motor vehicle use is rapidly pushing up nitrous oxide emissions in both nations. In 1970, for instance, South Korea's motor vehicle fleet consisted of fewer than 130,000 vehicles; by July 1997 the number of vehicles had reached 10 million. In Thailand, meanwhile, an estimated 100,000 factories—many of them located in Bangkok and other heavily populated areas—belch appalling levels of pollutants into the air (air quality is also atrocious within the confines of many of these factories as well). Small- and medium-sized factories in Thailand have become particularly notorious for their unchecked releases of pollutants into the air and water. Most Thai manufacturing and chemical facilities are not regulated, and in many cases they operate without any pollution control equipment at all. "Thus, even if one can easily imagine their heavy atmospheric pollutant emissions, there are no data from measurements of these emissions. Data are not available even for some large facilities" (Japan Environmental Council 2000). To the south, Indonesia is grappling with the growing environmental impact of annual frenzies of slash-and-burn deforestation as well as high levels of pollution from transport, household, and industrial sectors.

Individual public policy responses within ASEAN (the Association of South-East Asian Nations, consisting of Malaysia, Indonesia, the Philippines, Singapore, Thailand, Myanmar [Burma], Brunei Darussalam, and Vietnam) to the region's growing air pollution crisis have varied considerably. Several countries, including the Philippines, Malaysia, and Thailand, have established and begun enforcing emissions standards for automobiles, factories, and other emission sources. Indonesia has also acted, establishing air pollution standards covering motor vehicle exhaust and the cement, pulp, coal-fired thermal power, and steel industries (Jaafar 1999). Resource-poor countries like Singapore are exploring fuel-cell technology and expanded use of biofuels such as ethanol.

Some observers are skeptical about whether these and other regulatory changes constitute evidence of an evolving sense of environmental steward-ship within ASEAN. They note that genuine commitment to improving air quality requires effective accountability and enforcement mechanisms. Still, there is a general sense that Southeast Asian governments are finally begin-ning to take environmental factors into account in the realm of public policy. This shift may be partly attributable to growing public knowledge of and con-cern with the state of the region's rivers, forests, and air. In 2002, for example, the government of Thailand announced plans to "indefinitely postpone" con-struction of two controversial Japanese-funded coal-fired power plants with a combined capacity of 2,100 megawatts. The key factor in this decision was strong opposition from local communities and environmental activists who argued that the facilities would worsen air and water conditions.

The next pollution abatement step for Southeast Asia is to establish a strong framework of regional intergovernmental cooperation in addressing environ-mental issues. After all, seasonal weather patterns facilitate the transport of air pollutants across borders and from land to sea and back again, making it im-possible for individual countries to solve their air pollution problems alone. At the beginning of the 1990s, such alliances were nonexistent or in early stages of development. But since then, momentum for establishing new pollution abate-ment programs has increased. In February 2001, for example, the World Bank and Asian Development Bank launched a new Clean Air Initiative in partner-ship with eight Asian countries. That initiative is designed to expedite the im-plementation of a variety of energy efficiency and alternative fuel programs.

Major Threats to
Air Quality across Asia

Acid Rain

Acid rain damages crops and forests, corrodes buildings, statues, and other ar-chitecture, and renders lakes and streams uninhabitable for fish and other wildlife. Created by emissions of oxides of nitrogen and sulfur associated with the burning of fossil fuels, acid rain's destructive impact on ecosystems is ac-centuated by its lingering quality. Lakes and forests damaged by acid deposi-tion can take decades to recover, even after emissions of acid rain precursors have been curbed.

In Asia, acid rain is a looming threat to wilderness areas and farmlands alike. It already has been blamed for forest dieback, river and lake degrada-tion, and reduced crop yields in several regions. For example, researchers in India found that wheat growing near a power plant where sulfur dioxide deposition was almost five times greater than the critical load (the amount the soil can safely absorb without harm) suffered a 49 percent reduction in yield compared with wheat growing a mere 22 kilometers away (Pattel 1997). Moreover, sulfur dioxide pollution levels in China, Thailand, the Korean Peninsula, and areas of Indonesia and Japan are already higher than those that caused wide-scale forest dieback and other ecological disasters in Central Europe in the 1970s and 1980s (McDonald 1999).

Alarmingly, continental emissions of sulfur dioxide are expected to double or possibly even triple from 1990 levels—when Asia released an estimated 34 million metric tons of sulfur dioxide, 40 percent more than North America— by 2010 if current trends of coal consumption by India, China, and other nations do not undergo substantial change (Downing and Shah 1997). "Curtailing the already substantial acid rain damage in Asia and avoiding much heavier damage in the future will require investments in pollution control on the order of those made in Europe and North America over the past 20 years" (World Resources Institute 1998).

As it is, Asia is currently home to the world's four most polluted cities and fifteen of its worst nineteen in the category of sulfur dioxide emissions (World Resources Institute 1998b). Acid deposition is particularly severe in South Korea, Thailand, northeast India, and southeast China, which are near or downwind from major urban and industrial centers. But even the remote mountains of Central Asia are accumulating excessive concentrations of sulfur dioxide. The Nepalese city of Kathmandu, for example, has reported daily mean concentrations of sulfur dioxide that are five to seven times above the safety range of World Health Organization (WHO) guidelines (World Health Organization 2000). Even Japan, which dramatically cut its own sulfur emissions in the 1980s through a variety of technological innovations and regulatory mandates, is experiencing increasing difficulties with acid rain because of transboundary pollution from China.

Keys to reducing acid deposition include adoption of flue-gas scrubbers, increased use of low-sulfur fuel—or even better, natural gas or renewable energy sources—and increased energy efficiency. According to the World Bank, implementation of the best available pollution control technologies could cut acid deposition levels across Asia in half from 1990 levels by 2020, even though total energy demand is projected to triple during those years. Of course, the expense of buying and installing that level of environmental protection is formidable: roughly U.S.$90 billion per year throughout the Asia region, or about 0.6 percent of the region's gross domestic product (Downing and Shah 1997; World Resources Institute 1998a).

Particulate Matter and Haze

Concentrations of suspended particulate matter exceed safety guidelines in numerous Asian cities and towns. In fact, Asia is home to all fifteen of the most polluted cities in the world in the area of total suspended particulates, according to a joint report issued by the UN Environment Programme, World Resources Institute, and World Bank (World Resources Institute 1998b). Moreover, twelve of the world's twenty largest cities have particulate pollution over twice that of WHO guidelines, and ten of them are major Asian cities. Levels of smoke and airborne dust in Asia are also about twice the world average and more than five times as high as in most high-income nations (World Health Organization and UN Environment Programme 1992; Asian Development Bank 1997b).

Suspended particulates include a great range of substances and particle sizes. They range from naturally occurring dust and soil particles (which may nonetheless enter the air as a result of human activity, such as driving on dirt roads) to particles that are created from incineration, burning of coal for heating and cooking, exhaust from motor vehicles, and a variety of power generation and industrial processes. Smaller or finer particles, usually generated by fossil fuel consumption, are more harmful to respiratory systems (Elsom 1996).

Particulate matter is also an important component of the haze that bedevils certain areas of Asia, especially during the dry season. These veils of pollution, which also contain sulfur oxides, nitrous oxides, lead, volatile organic compounds, and other pollutants, are generated by the continent's rapidly expanding transport, industry, and energy sectors. In recent years, manmade fires and other activities carried out to clear land for new rice fields, rubber trees, and palm-oil plantations have added significantly to regional haze.

In 1997 the practice of slash-and-burn deforestation reached new heights of environmental catastrophe. That summer, devastating forest fires set on drought-stricken land in order to expand agricultural operations roared out of control throughout the Sumatra and Kalimantan regions of Indonesia. The fires ultimately burned 1.7 million hectares of land, killed more than a thousand people, and triggered smoke-inhalation problems of varying severities for another 20 million. Haze from the fires also drifted over a 3,200-kilometer area that included portions of half a dozen Asian countries, upping the number of people affected to approximately 70 million. Some regions were particularly hard hit by the haze, most notably Singapore, Thailand, and Malaysia. In the Malaysian state of Sarawak, for instance, the fires pushed the air pollution index up to a record 839 (levels of 300 are equivalent to smoking eighty cigarettes a day and are officially designated as "hazardous") (Stockholm Environment Institute 2002). The sooty haze created by the fires is also believed to have inflicted considerable damage on regional economies because it convinced large numbers of international travelers to book their vacations elsewhere. ASEAN placed the damage to regional economies from the fires in 1997 and 1998 at $9 billion, with agriculture, transport, and tourism bearing the brunt of the impact.

In the aftermath of the 1997 fires, Indonesian efforts to characterize the damage caused by flames and smoke as a "natural disaster" for the country were widely dismissed. "[The carnage caused by the fires] transcends country borders and stems directly from human actions—excessive exploitation of forests, the intentional use of fire for clearing land, officially tolerated industrial pollution, and widespread overcrowding—that are all too common in the newly industrializing countries of the world," remarked one environmental researcher. "The only natural element [in the fires] is the drought brought on by an El Niño now developing in the tropical Pacific, the timing and intensity of which may be related to global climate change" (Kates 1997).

On the positive side, the epic scale of the Indonesia fires gave new impetus to the coalescing drive to improve air quality across Southeast Asia. In 2002, the eight ASEAN nations announced a regional antihaze pact that provides for cooperation in fighting fires and monitoring environmental conditions. ASEAN declared that it was "the first such regional arrangement in the world to collectively tackle land and forest fires and its resultant transboundary haze pollution." In addition, some individual countries have implemented new emission abatement policies that incorporate assessment and monitoring capabilities. Brunei Darussalam, located on the island of Borneo, has hammered together a particularly strong haze policy. Regulations specifically prohibit open burning during dry seasons and impose strict limits on emissions from industrial and automotive sources. But analysts acknowledge that without meaningful changes from neighboring countries, transboundary pollutants will continue to compromise the tiny country's air quality (Jaafar 1999).

For its part, Indonesia, which still holds nearly 10 percent of the world's rain forests, has established target levels for land conversion to ensure the protection of remaining forestlands. It has also imposed restrictions on the amount of ecologically significant land that can be burned for plantation agriculture and placed limits on the volumes of agricultural, household, and industrial wastes that can be burned. But Indonesian haze policies do not discriminate between wet and dry seasons (fires during the dry season are particularly bad for air quality), nor do they address emissions from industrial operations, motor vehicles, power facilities, and other significant emission sources. Environmental organizations are also watching closely to see if Indonesia enforces these new emissions and forest protection regulations, which are opposed by politically powerful timber companies and other business interests.

Atmospheric Issues

Asia's Role in Ozone Layer Loss

Over the past three decades, the world's developed nations have made important strides in protecting the stratospheric ozone layer from ozone-depleting chemicals. Preserving the ozone layer from thinning and loss are critically important because ozone in the stratosphere (the area of the atmosphere between 6 and 30 miles above the earth's surface) protects earth life from the full force of the sun's ultraviolet radiation, which can cause cancer and other health problems. Other negative effects associated with increased exposure to ultraviolet radiation include damage to valuable food crops and other vegetation and declines in plankton, the cornerstone of the ocean's food chain. Ozone loss has also been implicated in rising levels of carbon dioxide, the primary cause of global warming.

Historically, chlorofluorocarbons (CFCs)—chiefly chlorine-laced chemicals used in refrigerants and aerosols—have been the most important factor in ozone depletion, in part because of the corrosive nature of the compounds on the stratospheric ozone layer and in part because of the ubiquitous presence of CFCs in global manufacturing processes. But since the discovery in the mid-1980s of the ozone layer's fragile state, most industrialized nations have acted decisively to curb emissions of CFCs and other ozone-depleting chemicals. The 1989 Montreal Protocol, for instance, committed numerous nations to end their use of CFCs, and individual ozone protection policies were implemented throughout Europe and North America.

These measures halted the deterioration of the stratospheric ozone layer, but scientists believe that developing countries such as China, India, Malaysia, and Indonesia hold the key to full ozone layer restoration. Indeed, the failure of China (which accounts for 35 percent of the world's CFC market) and India (16 percent) to phase out dangerous ozone-depleting chemicals threatens the progress made in Europe and North America in recent years ("India Re-Doubles Efforts to Save the Ozone Layer," 2002). Moreover, illegal trade in ozone-depleting substances—a practice that makes it impossible to track all emissions—is a growing problem across Southeast Asia and on the Indian subcontinent.

Thus far, China has made only halting steps to reduce its emissions of CFCs and other ozone-destroying compounds. In 2002, for example, China announced a ban on the production and import of passenger cars with air conditioners that use the CFC Freon, but it has not yet acted to curb CFC emissions generated by the millions of automobiles already winding their way through China's cities and towns. India, meanwhile, has also signaled its growing interest in reducing emissions of CFCs and other ozone-destroying compounds. In 2002 the Indian government announced a joint ozone protection program with the UN Environment Programme. Under the initiative, the country's four largest manufacturers of CFCs pledge to crack down on "rogue emissions" by introducing new and cleaner production technologies. Production by the four companies is scheduled to drop to zero by 2010, after a peak production figure of 23,659 tons at the end of the 1990s. In addition, the program includes an education component designed to reach smaller companies that are part of the CFC supply chain, from consumers to refrigerator manufacturers (ibid.).

Asia's Role in
Global Climate Change

At the same time that airborne pollution degrades the air upon which the earth's people, plants, and animals depend, it also transforms the planet's atmosphere so that it retains greater levels of heat from the sun rather than returning it to space. Under this greenhouse effect, the sun's heat is trapped in the atmosphere under a blanket of greenhouse gases, which include carbon dioxide, nitrous oxide, methane, CFCs, and HCFCs. Sources of greenhouse gases include nitrous oxides from agriculture, emissions of fluorinated gases from industry, and releases of carbon dioxide when forests and other vegetation are lost. Methane emissions from landfills, mining operations, and cattle are also a factor. This is especially so in heavily populated countries such as India and China that have proportional holdings of domestic animals, fields, and rice paddies. But the leading culprit in climate change is carbon dioxide released by automobiles, trucks, factories, and power plants when they burn fossil fuels.

Since the 1970s, industrial emissions of carbon dioxide have grown 60 percent faster in Asia than anywhere else on the planet (Asian Development Bank 1997a). In 1996 the Carbon Dioxide Information Analysis Center reported that Asian nations released 7.452 billion metric tons of the world's total output of carbon dioxide emissions, about 31 percent of the global carbon dioxide emission total of 23.88 billion metric tons. Leading producers of the pollutant on the continent were China (3.364 billion metric tons), Japan (1.168 billion metric tons), India (997.39), and South Korea (4.08). In 1998 these emissions declined very modestly, to approximately 7.36 billion metric tons (Carbon Dioxide Information Analysis Center 1999, 2001).

Asia's contribution to global carbon dioxide emissions—and hence over-all greenhouse gas emissions—are driven by steady population gains and economic development, which in turn have spurred dizzying expansion of the continent's transport sector and ever-greater consumption of coal and other fossil fuels that release greenhouse gases. From 1980 to 1997, for in-stance, transportation energy use and associated greenhouse gas emissions increased at better than a 5 percent annual rate in Asia, compared with 1 percent growth in greenhouse gases from all sectors worldwide (Pew Center on Global Climate Change 2001). In Southeast Asia alone, carbon dioxide emissions increased 69 percent from 1990 to 1998, according to the ASEAN Center for Energy. But the true "greenhouse gas giants" of Asia are Japan—which in 2002 agreed to reduce its emissions of carbon dioxide and other greenhouse gases by ratifying the UN-sponsored Kyoto Protocol—and India and China, which have resisted international calls to reduce their car-bon dioxide emissions. Current trends of population growth and energy consumption in the latter two countries are widely seen as among the planet's most serious impediments to stopping—or even mitigating—global climate change.

As it is, the scientific consensus is that the growing accumulation of greenhouse gases in the atmosphere is triggering fundamental changes to the world's weather and ecosystems. According to the Intergovernmental Panel on Climate Change (IPCC), the planet will warm by an unprece-dented 2.5 to 10 degrees Fahrenheit during the twenty-first century without major reductions in greenhouse gas emissions (Intergovernmental Panel on Climate Change 2001). This transformation is in its early stages, but as global temperatures continue to rise they will become more apparent. Likely manifestations of climate change include increasingly severe and numerous storms, altered rain and snowfall patterns that will make some areas increas-ingly vulnerable to drought or flooding, rising sea levels from melting gla-ciers and polar ice caps that will submerge low-lying coastal areas and islands, increased exposure to diseases, and breathtaking loss of biodiversity as various species of flora and fauna see their habitats destroyed or funda-mentally altered.

Some evidence of global warming is already apparent across Asia, from in-creasing temperatures to shifting precipitation patterns. Scientists have drawn particular attention to the retreat of glaciers all across Central Asia, and in particular in the Himalayan Mountains. The Tien Shan Mountain gla-ciers of Central Asia have lost more than 20 percent of their volume in the past forty years, while the Duosuogang Peak glaciers in the Ulan Ula Mountains of China have shrunk by 60 percent since the early 1970s. In the

Dioxin Pollution in Japan

Over the years, Japan has instituted a number of laws and programs that have measurably reduced its output of a number of air pollutants. But it remains one of the world's major emitters of dioxin, a chemical compound that can accumulate in the tissues of humans and animals, causing cancer, birth defects, and possible sexual development problems.

A key factor in Japan's dioxin output is its reliance on incineration to dispose of trash and other waste materials. With only limited space for landfills, Japan has long favored disposing of garbage and other materials by burning. In fact, approximately 75 percent of the municipal solid waste generated in Japan is currently incinerated. By the mid-1990s the nation had approximately 1,800 household-waste incinerators in operation (by comparison, the United States had fewer than 250), as well as thousands of additional licensed and unlicensed hazardous waste incinerators. According to the Japanese government, approximately 30 percent of the country's incinerator plants were substandard in terms of performance (Japan Environment Agency 1998; "Japan's Dirty Secret," 2000).

In 1997, mounting concern about the levels of dioxin generated by these incinerator complexes led the Japanese government to further strengthen dioxin emission guidelines that it had instituted back in 1990. In 1999, Japan put additional restrictions contained in a "Law Concerning Special Measures against Dioxin" into effect. This law includes provisions for dioxin emission regulation, the monitoring of effects on health and the environment, and the preparation of a comprehensive emission reduction program. In addition, new measures are being drawn up that concentrate on installing equipment to increase the efficiency of combustion and to cool exhaust emissions, since dioxin can be suppressed at certain temperatures. But these pollution-fighting efforts have drawn criticism from municipalities within Japan which claim that implementation of new dioxin control measures has forced them to make drastic cuts in other budget areas.

Indian Himalayas, meanwhile, the immense Pindari Glacier is retreating at an average of 135 meters annually ("The Melting of the World's Ice," 2000).

As global warming intensifies, however, the impact on ecosystems and human communities alike is expected to become much more severe in Asia's developing countries, where "adaptive capacity of human systems is low and vulnerability is high" (Intergovernmental Panel on Climate Change 2001). For example, the IPCC forecasts that there is a "high" probability (67 to 95 per-

Japan is also seeking to solve its dioxin emission problem by pursuing measures that reduce the use and burning of materials that discharge dioxin. Cognizant that plastics and vinyls used as packing material have become the leading cause of dioxin discharges, Japan is encouraging its citizenry to reduce waste by sorting plastic trash and not burning vinyl, and by lobbying businesses to reduce excess packaging of consumer goods. It also has passed a number of measures mandating increased recycling by consumers, municipalities, and some businesses.

Sources:

Howard, Michael C., ed. 1993. *Asia's Environmental Crisis*. Boulder, CO: Westview.

Japan Environment Agency. 1998. *White Paper on the Environment*. Tokyo: Japan Environment Agency.

Japan Environmental Council. 2000. *The State of the Environment in Asia 1999–2000*. New York: Springer.

"Japan's Dirty Secret: As Deadly Toxins Poison the Environment, the Government Is Doing Its Best to Avoid the Issue." 2000. *Time International* (May 29).

cent) that temperate and tropical areas of Asia will experience increasingly severe and numerous floods, droughts, forest fires, and tropical cyclones in a warming world. It also forecasts a high likelihood that rising sea levels and an increase in the intensity of tropical cyclones will displace tens of millions of people in low-lying coastal areas of temperate and tropical Asia.

Other possible impacts of global warming on the Asian continent include diminished food security in many countries caused by decreased productivity of agricultural and aquacultural activities that are buffeted by thermal and water stress, sea-level rise, floods, and droughts (an exception to this grim forecast is made for northern Asia, which may see increased agricultural productivity). The availability of potable water may also decrease in arid and semiarid regions of Asia under global warming, and human communities might also see increased exposure to vector-borne infectious diseases and heat stress. Climate change is also expected to increase energy demand, decrease tourism, and influence transportation in many regions of Asia. Finally, global warming could wreak major havoc on marine, freshwater, and terrestrial ecosystems across Asia.

The Kyoto Protocol

The Kyoto Protocol is a 1997 UN-brokered agreement that calls on developed nations to reduce their emissions of greenhouse gases by a combined

5.2 percent below 1990 emissions levels by 2012. The protocol enters into force when it has been ratified by at least fifty-five parties to the convention, including developed countries accounting for at least 55 percent of carbon dioxide emissions from this group in 1990.

Even proponents of the Kyoto Protocol admit that the agreement is only a first step in addressing the threat of global warming. After all, the IPCC estimates that worldwide emissions of greenhouse gases must decline by 50 to 70 percent to stabilize current concentrations of greenhouse gases in the atmosphere. But supporters of the treaty argue that any progress in reducing GHGs is welcome, and they believe that if the protocol enters into force, it can serve as a model for future GHG abatement negotiations.

In June 2002, Japan formally ratified the Kyoto agreement, joining the European Union as key participants. This was an important development, for Japan is the second-greatest producer of carbon dioxide in Asia after China. But most countries in Asia—including China and India, the third greatest generator of carbon dioxide emissions on the continent—are not obligated to make reductions under the Kyoto treaty, which covers only developed nations. And few Asian nations are taking the initiative in implementing their own GHG-reduction policies. Instead, governments that have displayed a commitment to improving environmental conditions are primarily concentrating on acid rain, haze, and other air quality problems that are having an immediate and clear impact on human health and economic prosperity within their borders.

Sources:

Asian Development Bank. 1997a. *Emerging Asia: Changes and Challenges*. Manila: ADB.

———. 1997b. *Second Water Utilities Data Book, Asian and Pacific Region*. Manila: ADB.

———. 1998. *Central Asian Environments in Transition*. Manila: ADB.

———. 2001. *Environments in Transition: Cambodia, Lao PDR, Thailand, Viet Nam*. Manila: ADB.

Carbon Dioxide Information Analysis Center. 1999. *Global, Regional, and National Annual CO2 Emissions from Fossil-Fuel Burning, Hydraulic Cement Production, and Gas Flaring: 1951–1996*. Oak Ridge, TN: Oak Ridge National Laboratory.

———. 2001. *Global, Regional, and National Annual CO2 Emissions from Fossil-Fuel Burning, Hydraulic Cement Production, and Gas Flaring: 1951–1998*. Oak Ridge, TN: Oak Ridge National Laboratory.

Changhua, Wu. 1999. "The Price of Growth." *Bulletin of the Atomic Scientists* 55, no. 5 (September–October).

Chaudhry, Shivani. 1999. "Giant Pollution Cloud Hovers over Asia." *World Watch* 12 (November–December).

Consumers' Association of Penang. 1997. *State of the Environment in Malaysia.* Penang, Malaysia: CAP.

Downing, R., R. Ramankutty, and J. Shah. 1997. *RAINS-ASIA: An Assessment Model for Acid Rain in Asia.* Washington, DC: World Bank.

Elsom, Derek. 1996. *Smog Alert: Managing Urban Air Quality.* London: Earthscan.

Feng, Therese. 1999. *Controlling Air Pollution in China.* Northampton, MA: Edward Elgar.

Harashima, Yohei. 2000. "Effects of Economic Growth on Environmental Policies in Northeast Asia." *Environment* 42 (July–August).

Hardoy, Jorge E., Diana Mitlin, and David Satterthwaite. 2001. *Environmental Problems in an Urbanizing World: Finding Solutions for Cities in Africa, Asia, and Latin America.* London: Earthscan.

Hertsgaard, Mark. 1998. *Earth Odyssey: Around the World in Search of Our Environmental Future.* New York: Broadway.

Howard, Michael C., ed. 1993. *Asia's Environmental Crisis.* Boulder, CO: Westview.

"India Re-Doubles Efforts to Save the Ozone Layer." 2002. UN Environment Programme Press Release, May 2.

Intergovernmental Panel on Climate Change. 2000. *The Regional Impacts of Climate Change: An Assessment of Vulnerability.* Geneva: IPCC.

———. 2001. *Climate Change 2001: Impacts, Adaptation, and Vulnerability.* Geneva: IPCC.

Jaafar, A. Baker bin. 1999. "Smoke Signals in Southeast Asia." *Forum for Applied Research and Public Policy* 14, no. 4 (winter).

Japan Environment Agency. 1998. *White Paper on the Environment.* Tokyo: Japan Environment Agency.

Japan Environmental Council. 2000. *The State of the Environment in Asia 1999–2000.* New York: Springer.

"Japan's Dirty Secret: As Deadly Toxins Poison the Environment, the Government Is Doing Its Best to Avoid the Issue." 2000. *Time International* (May 29).

Kaiser, J. 1996. "Acid Rain's Dirty Business: Stealing Minerals from Soil." *Science* 272 (April 12).

Kates, Robert W. 1997. "Unnatural Disaster." *Environment* 39 (December).

Kuylenstierna, J. C. I., et al. 2001. "Acidification in Developing Countries: Ecosystem Sensitivity and the Critical Load Approach on a Global Scale." *Ambio* 30.

McDonald, Alan. 1999. "Combating Acid Deposition and Climate Change: Priorities for Asia." *Environment* 41 (April).

McGranahan, Gordon, and Frank Murray, eds. 1999. *Health and Air Pollution in Rapidly Developing Countries.* Stockholm: Stockholm Environmental Institute.

"The Melting of the World's Ice." 2000. *WorldWatch* 13 (November–December).

Pattel, T. 1997. "Rampant Urban Pollution Blights Asia's Crops." *New Scientist* (June 14).

Pew Center on Global Climate Change. 2001. *Transportation in Developing Countries: Greenhouse Gas Scenarios for Delhi, India.* Pew Center.

Sperling, Daniel, and Deborah Salon. 2002. *Transportation in Developing Countries: An Overview of Greenhouse Gas Strategies.* Pew Center.

State Planning Commission. 1997. *China's Energy Development Report.* Beijing: Economic Management Press.

Stockholm Environment Institute. "Regional Air Pollution in Developing Countries: Asia," http://www.york.ac.uk/inst/sei/rapidc/aspoltex.html (accessed June 8, 2002).

UN Environment Programme. 1999. *Synthesis of the Reports of the Scientific, Environmental Effects and Technology and Economic Assessment Panels of the Montreal Protocol.* Nairobi, Kenya: UNEP.

———. 2000. *Handbook for the International Treaties for the Protection of the Ozone Layer.* Nairobi, Kenya: UNEP.

———. 2001. "More Knowledge of Interactions between Asian Brown Haze, Global Warming, and Ozone Urgently Needed." Press release, April 9.

UN Environment Programme, World Meteorological Organization, National Oceanic and Atmospheric Administration, National Aeronautics and Space Administration, and European Commission. 1998. *Scientific Assessment of Ozone Depletion: 1998.* Geneva: UNEP.

World Bank.1997a. *China 2020: Development Challenges in the New Century.* Washington, DC: World Bank.

———. 1997b. *Clear Water, Blue Skies.* Washington, DC: World Bank.

———. 1997c. *Environment Matters: Towards Environmentally and Socially Sustainable Development.* Washington, DC: World Bank.

World Health Organization. 2000. *Guidelines for Air Quality.* Geneva: WHO.

World Health Organization and UN Environment Programme. 1992. *Urban Air Pollution in Megacities of the World.* London: Blackwell.

World Resources Institute. 1998a. "Acid Rain: Downpour in Asia?" *World Resources 1998–1999: A Guide to the Global Environment.* Washington, DC: WRI.

———. 1998b. *World Resources 1998–1999: A Guide to the Global Environment.* New York: Oxford University Press.

———. 2000. *World Resources 2000–2001, People and Ecosystems: The Fraying Web of Life.* Washington, DC: WRI.

Environmental
Activism

In most Asian nations, environmental activism is a fairly recent phenomenon. In fact, there were few organized environmental movements in the region until the 1980s. By that time, however, many countries in East and Southeast Asia had been experiencing high rates of economic growth and rapid urbanization for years. During this period, citizens expressed growing concern that their nations' resource-intensive, export-oriented economic development was causing severe degradation of the natural environment. They suffered from the effects of a variety of environmental problems, including air and water pollution, deforestation, destruction of farmland and watersheds, encroachment on protected areas, and dislocation of indigenous peoples. As scientists and other observers around the world noted that the economic "miracles" in East and Southeast Asia were creating a vast environmental crisis, the people of Asia also began speaking out against the pollution, depletion of resources, and destruction of natural areas that sometimes resulted from this commercial growth.

"By the early 1970s, one could detect a growing, albeit highly limited, public concern in Asia over the inability of the state to address the environmental consequences of postwar population and economic growth," observed scholars Yok-shiu F. Lee and Alvin Y. So in one history of Asian environmental activism. "By the late 1970s, numerous non-governmental organizations emerged throughout East and Southeast Asia, often serving as a vehicle for grassroots communities to express their political dissent and socioeconomic grievances. Since the 1980s, the increasing deterioration of the living and natural environment all over Asia has led to a gradual emergence of environmental consciousness among the citizenry and the evolution of various types of environmental movements throughout the region" (Lee and So 1999).

Environmental consciousness and activism have not developed uniformly throughout Asia. In fact, the character of Asian environmental movements tends to vary widely from country to country, depending on each nation's culture, its stage of democratic transition, the reaction of business and government, and a number of other factors. China, for example, has shown little tolerance for organized environmental activism. In fact, the Chinese government allowed the first citizens' environmental group to incorporate only in 1994. On the other hand, the government of Mongolia works closely with environmental nongovernmental organizations (NGOs)—such as the Mongolian Association for the Conservation of Nature and Environment—to protect nature and wildlife.

In many Asian nations, environmental movements have grown out of other social and political movements, such as anticolonial or national independence movements, feminist movements, or religious movements. As grassroots resistance develops around these issues and becomes established in the culture, people begin to recognize linkages between rapid economic development and environmental degradation. Social and political action turns into environmental activism as citizens realize how resource depletion and pollution can lead to poverty and reduced life prospects. In nineteenth-century India, for example, anticolonial dissent turned into environmental protest over the Indian Forest Act of 1878. Farmers, peasants, and tribal groups—hoping to end destructive European logging practices and restore local control of forests—staged violent protests against government officials and property.

In a number of Asian countries, environmental activism has grown out of the antinuclear movement. The centralized governments of Taiwan, South Korea, and Hong Kong undertook large-scale development of nuclear energy in the 1970s without any public input or debate. But antinuclear sentiments emerged with the liberalization of authoritarian governments and the move toward democratization in the mid-1980s. Citing the potential for harmful accidents and the problems inherent in disposing of nuclear wastes, activists successfully lobbied for input into the decision-making process. In Taiwan, the antinuclear movement allied itself with political opposition groups in convincing the government to scale back its nuclear power development program. In South Korea, grassroots activism and street protests encouraged the government to have a similar change of heart about nuclear energy (Lee 1999b).

Nongovernmental organizations have played an important role in environmental activism in many Asian nations. There are about 200 environmental NGOs in Thailand, for example, which has an article recognizing the right of citizens to participate in the protection of natural resources in its constitution. South Korea also harbors about 200 NGOs concerned with environmental issues, most of which work under the umbrella of the Korean Federation for Environmental Movement. Conservation-related activities of NGOs in Asia include coordinating the efforts of local communities and individuals, assisting governments in creating and implementing environmental policies, and providing public education. In India, environmental NGOs hold people's tribunals to hear cases involving individuals or communities that suffer from the effects of environmental degradation. In Sri Lanka, NGOs were instrumental in preventing logging of the Singharaja Forest and in halting the construction of a thermal plant at Trincomalee (UN Environment Programme 1999).

Although environmental NGOs have experienced some success in Asia, these groups tend to be smaller, less organized, and less confrontational than those found in some other parts of the world. Around 4,500 environmental NGOs exist in Japan, for example, but 90 percent of them operate at the local level; their total membership is estimated at 100,000 (Mason 1999).

Some local NGOs have been able to bolster their efforts by enlisting the support of international environmental groups, such as Greenpeace and Friends of the Earth. In India, for example, a number of local groups that were engaged in protests against the Narmada Dam project sent faxes to inform international environmental organizations about their struggle. Several of the larger organizations responded by pressuring politicians in their home countries to convince the World Bank to withhold funding for the project. Unfortunately, support from international environmental groups can have negative effects on local groups in Asia. For example, these groups may become vulnerable to criticism at home by business and government officials who claim that global environmental initiatives are another way for wealthy nations to take advantage of them. Partly to avoid such criticism, NGOs in some developing countries in Asia have formed regional coalitions, such as the Asia Pacific People's Environmental Network (APPEN) and the Asian NGO Coalition (ANGOC).

The Experiences of Individual Asian Nations

Regardless of their stages of development, the nations of Asia tend to face similar environmental issues in the early twenty-first century. Many developing countries have been adversely affected by the activities of multinational corporations, which sometimes extract resources or establish industrial operations with little regard for the effects on the natural environment and local people. More developed Asian nations have created similar problems for themselves in their rush to match the living standards of the West. As governments embarked on programs of rapid industrialization and economic growth, they paid little heed to the environment. As a result, many Asian nations face severe problems with pollution and resource depletion, though their approaches toward recognizing and addressing those problems differ. This section looks at the movement toward environmental consciousness and activism in seven countries—Thailand, the Philippines, Vietnam, South Korea, Taiwan, China, and Japan.

Thailand

Thailand has experienced double-digit economic growth since the 1970s, but much of this impressive development has taken place at the expense of the natural environment. The main source of Thailand's environmental problems is its estimated 100,000 factories. In an effort to establish manufacturing industries and attract foreign investment, the nation welcomed many multinational corporations, which often took advantage of lax environmental regulations to set up substandard industrial plants. The factories discharged various kinds of wastes that severely contaminated Thailand's air and water. Another problem involves the conversion of land for industry and tourism, which caused a 50 percent reduction in forested area between 1961 and 1988 (Lee and So 1999).

As the people of Thailand—particularly rural people who depended on the nation's natural resources for their livelihoods—suffered from the effects of pollution and resource depletion, they increasingly began speaking out and taking action. An organized environmental movement first started to develop in the early 1970s as a loose network of student ecological clubs. In 1973, when the country was under military rule, these clubs exposed a scandal involving high-ranking officials in the military government who had been hunting illegally in a wildlife sanctuary. The resulting investigation raised public awareness of and interest in environmental issues.

In the mid-1970s, citizens of Thailand continued using environmental issues to highlight government abuses. In 1975, for example, the growing environmental movement focused its attention on illegal mining concessions granted by shareholding government officials to the Thailand Exploration and Mining Corporation (TEMCO), which was operated by the multinational energy company Union Carbide. Student protesters mounted a sustained political battle that ultimately forced the government to withdraw the lucrative mining concessions. Following this success, however, environmental activists became the targets of a government crackdown, and student leaders were forced to take refuge in the forest for the next few years.

Thailand's environmental movement re-established itself in the 1980s, as the military government adopted a more tolerant stance toward dissent and as evidence mounted of severe damage to the environment. In 1982, student-led protests erupted over the proposed construction of the Nam Choan Dam on the Khwae Yai River. The protests convinced the government to postpone the project, and even larger protests occurred when authorities revisited the dam idea in 1986. These protests—which came to involve scientists, religious leaders, celebrities, NGOs, and several international environmental organizations—caused the idea to be abandoned altogether in 1988. The following year, a series of direct actions by farmers aimed at stopping the development of croplands and the destruction of watersheds led to a nationwide ban on logging.

By the late 1980s, the Thai government began to embrace many of the causes that had engaged the nation's environmental activists. Government planning was increasingly concerned with such issues as pollution, the loss of forests and farmland to development, the creation of national parks, and the protection of endangered species. In the early 1990s, the Thai government undertook several initiatives aimed at conserving natural resources and protecting the environment. For example, it strengthened the National Environment Board, established an Environment Fund to provide grants for the operation of wastewater treatment plants and waste disposal facilities, and created several think-tanks to devise development strategies that were compatible with the environment. Thai businesses also began to take a more proactive approach toward environmental issues during this time. But critics claim that enforcement of the new, more stringent environmental regulations has been spotty, and they charge that government officials often place the needs of business above those of local communities.

By the 1990s, there were about 200 environmental NGOs in Thailand. These diverse groups were concerned with a wide range of issues and operated on both the local and national levels. Most tended to be poorly financed and were forced to operate under close government supervision. Even though the Thai government has encouraged public participation in environmental management, it has also stressed the need for harmony and cooperation among competing interests. Critics claim that the government's position on the environment is motivated by its desire to pacify and contain the grassroots movements, which had threatened to topple the military government in the 1980s. Still, NGOs have made some important strides in improving the environmental situation in Thailand. For example, the Hill Area Development Foundation has initiated sustainable development efforts in twenty-eight tribal villages. Many of these villages have become national models of sustainable agriculture and resource conservation ("From Silent Spring to Vocal Vanguard" 1997).

The Philippines

Like many island nations, the Philippines was once graced with a unique and diverse collection of flora and fauna. Dating back to its colonial days, however, the Philippines' fragile ecosystem has suffered severe damage as a result of resource extraction and development by international logging, mining, and agribusiness concerns. Some of the main environmental problems facing the Philippines include deforestation, soil erosion, watershed degradation, loss of biodiversity, deteriorating air and water quality, overfishing, destruction of marine habitat and coral reefs, and industrial pollution. Together, these trends amount to an environmental crisis in the Philippines.

Environmental activism in the Philippines came into existence during the 1970s, when local people began protesting the depletion of the rain forests and coral reefs on which they depended for their livelihoods. A number of communities organized coalitions to fight back against specific, high-impact development projects. The authoritarian government of Ferdinand Marcos, with its close ties to international business interests, used force or coercion to silence many of those protests. But some demonstrations succeeded in fending off the threats facing communities. For example, vocal protests erupted over the Chico River Dam project, which would have subjected 100,000 tribespeople to involuntary relocation. The fierce resistance of the indigenous people led the World Bank to withdraw funding from the project, which was eventually canceled. Many protesters were incarcerated by the Marcos government during the struggle against the dam, however, and one prominent tribal leader was killed.

Prior to the overthrow of the Marcos regime in 1986, the Philippine environmental movement was largely integrated with the pro-democracy movement. Groups with environmental agendas—such as the Philippine Federation for Environmental Concerns—also took part in antidictatorship activities, pointing out the intimate connections between ecological degradation and social, economic, and political inequities. Once Corazon Aquino was elected president of the Philippines, however, the environmental movement became a separate force. The new government recognized the role of NGOs and community-based organizations, encouraged their formation, and worked in concert with them to address environmental issues. The Aquino government also undertook a number of important reforms, including restructuring the former Ministry of Natural Resources into the Department of Environment and Natural Resources (DENR). Both the DENR and NGOs received a great deal of environmental aid from foreign countries over the next several years.

By the early 1990s, environmental NGOs had become a significant force in Philippine social and political life. The largest environmental coalition in the country was the Green Forum, which consisted of more than 200 NGOs, grassroots organizations, and church groups. These groups gradually gained more influence over government policy and began promoting sustainable development. In 1992, after Fidel Ramos became president of the Philippines, leading environmental groups successfully lobbied to defeat a politician with ties to logging companies as chief of the DENR. Instead, the NGOs pushed for the appointment of Angel Alcala, an environmentalist from the Haribon Foundation, to the position.

In the late 1990s, environmental NGOs remained an active force in Philippine politics, addressing both local and national environmental issues. Many community groups fought for local control of natural resources and implemented sustainable management practices. For example, some small communities now manage their own fishery or forest resources (Magno 1999).

Vietnam

Vietnam has developed a culture in which individuals, local groups, and the news media often call attention to environmental problems. Thousands of Vietnamese citizens file official complaints against polluting factories each year, and some communities organize protests outside such facilities. The Vietnamese news media helps spread the word about environmental problems, adding to the public criticism and increasing the pressure on the government to take action. For example, Vietnamese newspapers published a series of articles claiming that a monosodium glutamate plant in Dong Nai run by the Taiwanese company VEDAN was poisoning the Thi Vai River with untreated organic waste. The resulting pressure from the Vietnamese government and people eventually forced the company to erect a wastewater treatment plant on the site.

In many cases, the Vietnamese government has responded positively to environmental concerns. For example, the government established national pollution standards in 1994, and since then it has conducted inspections, pressured several plants to improve their compliance, and arranged for some residents of polluted areas to receive monetary settlements. The positive reaction of the government has encouraged even more people to come forward with complaints. In fact, the government's environmental offices in Ho Chi Minh City received 1,000 citizen letters of complaint per day in the mid-1990s (Roodman 1999).

Despite the fact that Vietnam has begun to recognize and address some of its most serious sources of pollution, it continues to face severe environmental problems. For example, the nation lacked both the technical knowledge and the capital to install state-of-the-art pollution control systems, even as it doubled its industrial output during the 1990s. Vietnam receives some assistance in this area from the UN-funded Vietnam Cleaner Production Center, which provides corporations with technical advice on cutting emissions. The center reported that nearly all of its clients have sought assistance after becoming the target of citizen complaints.

Overall, the growing public concern about the environment in Vietnam has led some analysts to believe that citizens' criticism of polluters may evolve into a proactive environmental movement in the future. "By inviting criticism of polluters, the government of Vietnam has wisely accommodated what is evidently a well-spring of civic energy within the nation," commented one analysis. "But the current is bound to build as the country develops. To maintain its legitimacy, the government will need to let the current find its natural course" (ibid.).

South Korea

South Korea was among the many Asian nations that placed a high priority on rapid industrialization and economic growth from the 1960s onward. South Korea largely achieved its goal, boasting an average annual growth in gross national product of around 10 percent during that period. Unfortunately, much of this growth took place with little regard to its effects on the environment, which has led to severe problems with air and water pollution. "The much-lauded high-speed industrialization of South Korea has brought about devastating consequences," Su-Hoon Lee wrote in *Asia's Environmental Movements.* "One such negative consequence is the irrevocable damage to the environment, which is nothing short of an environmental crisis."

Environmental groups first emerged in South Korea in the 1970s, but most of them were loosely organized and isolated groups connected to churches or universities that sought remedies for local environmental problems. The first significant organized environmental group in South Korea was the Korea Pollution Research Institute (KPRI), formed in 1982 by church leaders. The KPRI supported the activities of smaller environmental groups and helped forge links between isolated ones. The KPRI also worked to assist local residents in fighting pollution. In 1985, for example, the organization issued a report on a mysterious illness that had struck 500 residents of the area surrounding the Onsan Industrial Complex near Ulsan. Scientists connected with the KPRI discovered that the residents were suffering from the effects of poisoning by cadmium and other heavy metals that were being discharged by the nearby factories. The report garnered a great deal of negative media attention and raised public awareness of the potential for pollution-related illness in other industrial areas, leading to the formation of many antipollution groups through the 1990s. With more people suffering symptoms of "Onsan illness" each year, the South Korean government eventually relocated 40,000 residents of the contaminated area.

In addition to the antipollution movement, environmental activism in South Korea has also focused on antinuclear movements. Grassroots resistance to the government's nuclear policies first appeared in the late 1980s. Needing electricity to support its rapid industrial growth, the South Korean government pursued an ambitious nuclear energy development program. The nation had eleven nuclear power plants in operation as of 1996, with forty-four more scheduled to come on line over the next three decades. But the eleven existing plants experienced a large number of accidents, and their operation created a nuclear waste storage crisis.

The first large-scale antinuclear protest took place in 1987, when residents of Youngkwang county—home to four nuclear reactors—launched a campaign to persuade the government to compensate them for the loss of fisheries. Two years later, a coalition of twenty-one environmental and social organizations formed the National Headquarters for the Nuclear Power Eradication Movement. That event marked a turning point in the history of the South Korean environmental movement, as it raised public awareness of the environmental issues surrounding nuclear power and drew disparate groups together to create more effective antinuclear campaigns (Lee 1999).

By the early 1990s, many South Koreans expressed serious reservations about their nation's nuclear policies. Antinuclear protesters routinely fought to block the construction of new power plants and sought compensation for damages resulting from existing plants. Large-scale demonstrations also took place whenever the government announced a new potential site for the location of nuclear wastes. Local residents—joined by antinuclear activists—reacted to each announcement by blockading roads, attacking government buildings, and staging riots.

Both the antipollution movement and the antinuclear movement encouraged the people of South Korea to question their government's models for development. As a result, some citizens tended to view environmental groups as militant or extremist. But that public perception began to change in 1990, when information was released showing that the tapwater in the capital city of Seoul had been contaminated with heavy metals. Another incident occurred the following year, when the Doosan Electronics semiconductor manufacturing plant dumped phenol into the Nakdong River, which fed a reservoir that supplied tapwater to the southeastern section of the nation.

As more citizens became involved in direct actions to reverse the effects of pollution and prevent further use of nuclear energy, the movements began to consolidate into a single environmental movement. Increased public interest led to the formation of larger NGOs, such as Green Korea and the Korean Federation for Environmental Movement (KFEM), as well as more ecologically oriented groups. The South Korean government has begun to acknowledge environmental problems and has taken some steps toward environmental protection, but economic growth remains its primary objective. As a result, residents have seen little improvement in the state of South Korea's environment through the turn of the century.

Taiwan

Taiwan provides yet another example of an Asian nation in which rapid economic development led to environmental damage and resource depletion. Some citizens raised concerns about the need to protect the nation's natural resources in the 1970s, but broad public discontent did not become evident until the 1980s, when Taiwan's environmental problems became too obvious to ignore. By that time, Taiwan had begun to suffer serious problems with air and water pollution, accumulation of solid and hazardous wastes, energy and water shortages, and destruction of fragile ecosystems such as coastlines and mountainous regions. Today, surveys show that environmental problems rank high among the concerns of Taiwan's citizens.

Environmental activism in Taiwan since the 1980s can be divided into three movements: antipollution, nature conservation, and antinuclear. All of these movements first formed in order to raise public awareness of mounting problems associated with Taiwan's rapid industrialization. They sought to mobilize the Taiwanese people against threats to their way of life and to convince the government to make environmental protection a priority (Lee and So, 1999).

The antipollution movement in Taiwan started out as isolated protests by groups representing the victims of pollution. As one community successfully forced polluters to clean up their operations or compensate the victims of pollution, nearby communities took note and organized their own demonstrations. By the mid-1980s, such antipollution protests had become so widespread that they turned into a nationwide grassroots movement. The nature conservation movement grew out of the burgeoning antipollution movement, as groups of writers, scholars, and scientists began to organize campaigns to save nonhuman victims of pollution, such as migratory birds,

Residents of Orchid Island, Taiwan, kick painted drums demanding the government save the island from nuclear waste, 2002. AFP/ CORBIS

mangrove swamps, rivers, and forests. People involved in the nature conservation movement formed NGOs such as the Bird Society, which started out as a collection of people who enjoyed bird-watching and grew into Taiwan's largest environmental group. The Bird Society gradually became politicized as its members recognized the damaging effects of Taiwan's rapid industrialization on wildlife and its habitat.

The antinuclear movement in Taiwan first became active in the 1980s, when intellectuals and residents of affected areas joined forces to protest the construction of a fourth nuclear power plant by the state-owned Taiwan Power Company. At that time, Taiwan's three existing nuclear power plants provided 52 percent of the island's electricity, which made the nation the world's second-most dependent on nuclear energy, after France. The government's decision to add a fourth plant was made without any public input or debate.

Over time, the focus of the antinuclear movement expanded to include challenging the state's overall energy and environmental policies. That led to the formation of political opposition parties and contributed to a nationwide push toward further democratization of the government. Today, environmental movements in Taiwan enjoy a great deal of public understanding and support and are seen as being responsible for some significant changes to the government's environmental policies. The state's main priority remains national development, however, so enforcement of the new policies tends to be weak.

China

With its huge population and its double-digit annual economic growth over recent decades, China has suffered tremendous environmental degradation. The effects—which include a decline in water quality and quantity and widespread air pollution—cost the nation a huge amount in lost productivity each year. Yet few Chinese citizens show much concern about the environment, partly because environmental issues receive very little coverage in the state-controlled news media. Most Chinese seem willing to accept the tradeoff between economic growth and environmental damage, believing that it is more important to provide people with jobs and food than to save rain forests or protect wildlife (Hertsgaard 1998).

Some environmental activists raised concerns about specific issues in the mid-1980s. One target of criticism was the proposed Three Gorges Dam project on the Yangtze River. Led by journalist Dai Qing—who published a collection of essays by leading scientists and intellectuals about the dam—opponents of the project eventually included a number of international agencies and environmental groups. But the Chinese government suppressed environmental protests following the Tiananmen Square massacre of 1989 and put several prominent activists in prison, including Dai Qing. The dam was approved by the National People's Congress in 1992, and construction began in 1998.

By the mid-1990s, the Chinese government had once again started to tolerate environmental activism, as long as it focused on solving specific problems rather than criticizing the government's policies and decisions. The government permitted the first formal Chinese citizens' environmental group to incorporate in 1994. That group, Friends of Nature (FON), focuses on public awareness and education and stays away from highly contentious issues. One FON campaign involves the endangered golden monkey of western Yunnan Province, the population of which declined to around 200 individuals because of rubber planting and slash-and-burn farming in ancient tropical rain forests. By raising public awareness and suggesting alternative routes to economic development in the region, the FON campaign managed to halt logging of the monkey's habitat, at least temporarily (Dunn 1997).

In recent years, the Chinese government has allowed the formation of several other environmental groups, including one founded by Dai Qing.

Dai Qing, Leading Opponent of China's Three Gorges Dam

A temporary diversion channel during the construction of the Three Gorges Dam in Sandouping, China. Ca. 2001. LIU LIQUN/CORBIS

Chinese environmental activist Dai Qing was born on August 24, 1941, in Chongquing, China. She was the daughter of intellectuals who worked as spies in Beijing during the Japanese occupation of China in World War II. After her father was executed for his spying activities, Dai was raised by a family friend who was a prominent political and military leader.

Dai earned an engineering degree in 1966 and worked for a guided missile firm for several years. She was married in the late 1960s and had a child before she had reached the government-approved age. As a result, she was forced to give up her daughter while she and her husband spent three years on a rural farm for "reform through labor." Dai reclaimed her daughter upon her release in 1972, but the experience caused her to begin questioning the Chinese system of government.

In the late 1970s, Dai became involved in military intelligence. After posing as a writer in Europe for a spy mission, she found that she enjoyed writing. In 1979 she published a short story that became very popular and launched her writing career. During the 1980s, Dai began working as an investigative journalist and often published stories that were critical of the Chinese Communist Party.

In 1985, Dai was assigned to write a story about cultural artifacts along the Yangtze River. It was during her research for this assignment that she learned about the proposed Three Gorges Dam. This project involved constructing the largest dam on the planet, at nearly 1.5 miles long and more than 600 feet high. Although the dam would generate enough electricity to meet 10 percent of China's needs, which in turn would reduce air pollution from coal-burning power plants, the project also created many potential problems. For example, the related flooding would displace 1.5 million people and allow a buildup of sediments and waste emissions from 3,000 factories along the river's banks that would pose dangers to both people and wildlife.

As Dai learned more about the proposed dam, she became determined to fight it as both an environmental issue and a human rights issue. She particularly resented the fact that the Chinese government withheld information about the dam from people who would be affected by it. She felt that the Chinese people should have a say in the decision of whether or not to build the dam. Toward that end, Dai put together a collection of essays by leading scientists and intellectuals about the environmental issues surrounding Three Gorges Dam. Published in 1989 as *Yangtze! Yangtze!* the book made Dai the first Chinese writer to speak out publicly against the dam project.

At first Dai's book received positive reviews in China. But then the political events that culminated in the Tiananmen Square massacre curtailed the Chinese people's ability to disagree with the government. After the government cracked down on pro-democracy demonstrators, Dai's book was banned in China and she was arrested. The dam project was approved by the National People's Congress in 1992, around the time she was released from prison after spending ten months in solitary confinement.

In 1993, Dai received the prestigious Goldman Environmental Prize for her work in opposing the Three Gorges Dam. The following year, *Yangtze! Yangtze!* first appeared in English translation. The worldwide distribution of her book convinced several international agencies to cut off funding for the dam project, which caused the Chinese government to postpone the start of construction. Work on the dam finally began in 1998, however, the same year that Dai published *The River Dragon Has Come! The Three Gorges Dam and the Fate of China's Yangtze River and Its People*. As construction of the Three Gorges Dam continued, with a scheduled completion date of 2009, Dai hoped that her struggle might call attention to the problems inherent in the Chinese system of government and lead to political reforms.

Source:

Qing, Dai. 1997. *The River Dragon Has Come! The Three Gorges Dam and the Fate of China's Yangtze River and Its People*. Armonk, NY: M. E. Sharpe.

This marks a significant change for the government, and it may signal a recognition of the worsening environmental problems in China. Some observers believe that the central government will increasingly depend on local groups to help monitor lax enforcement of environmental laws in the provinces and support its other environmental initiatives.

Japan

Japan's environmental record has often been the target of international criticism. The nation is the world's leading importer of tropical timber, has been vocal in its support of whaling, and was the last of the more developed countries to approve the Convention on International Trade in Endangered Species (CITES). Yet Japan compares favorably to other industrialized nations in several areas, including recycling rates, industrial energy efficiency, and carbon dioxide emissions. The Japanese government worked to improve its image as a global environmental citizen in the 1990s, particularly in the period leading up to the Kyoto Global Warming Conference of 1997.

Japan has a long history of environmental protest. One of the nation's earliest environmental protests concerned Ashio Dozan, a copper mine located 100 kilometers north of Tokyo. In the late 1800s and early 1900s, peasants organized repeated demonstrations against the mine's poisoning of their water and crops. The peasants lost their battle against the mine, but their struggle helped inspire later environmental groups (Mason 1999).

Japan experienced widespread environmental protests in the late 1960s and early 1970s, beginning with the highly publicized resistance to Tokyo's Narita Airport. Several pollution-related court cases also received a great deal of news media attention, as rulings favored the victims of cadmium poisoning in Itai-itai and of mercury poisoning in Minamata and Niigata. Empowered by the judiciary's new emphasis on public health and environmental protection, more citizens became determined to counteract the negative effects of rapid industrialization. By the early 1970s, some 3,000 citizens' groups had formed to address environmental issues in Japan.

Recognizing the people's growing interest in environmental protection, the Japanese government responded in 1970 by passing fourteen environmental laws aimed at regulating pollution. The following year it established the Environment Agency to monitor compliance and provide aid to pollution victims. These government actions were widely viewed as efforts to address citizens' most pressing environmental concerns. As a result, Japan's environmental movement continued to consist of local groups working on a diverse range of issues. No national movement formed to bring these groups together to work toward larger goals.

The people of Japan experienced a resurgence of interest in environmental issues in the mid-1990s because of a series of events that served to keep such issues in the news. For example, the Kobe earthquake of 1995 raised questions about the government's ability to use technology to overcome environmental dangers. The limitations of technology became the topic of public debate again following nuclear reactor accidents in 1995 and 1997, as well as an oil spill in the Sea of Japan in 1997. The cleanup and support efforts following these disasters also demonstrated the effectiveness of citizens' groups and led to a law making it easier to incorporate NGOs in Japan.

Despite its history of environmental activism, however, Japan lacks a true national environmental movement. Although there are an estimated 4,500 environmental NGOs in Japan today, 90 percent are locally based. They tend to be small in terms of membership, funding, and scope. In addition, they enjoy minimal recognition and acceptance by the general public, and they operate on the margins of the political system. Few of the environmental NGOs engage in direct action or legal action, which may be explained by the Japanese cultural emphasis on social harmony. One exception is the Japan Tropical Action Network (JATAN), a national organization that has employed direct action tactics in an attempt to reduce Japanese imports of tropical timber. JATAN's campaign has garnered some news media attention, but it has had little impact on reducing consumption of tropical lumber in Japan.

Sources:

Dunn, Seth. 1997. "Taking a Green Leap Forward: In China, an Environmental Group Moves into the Mainstream." *Amicus Journal* 18, no. 4 (winter).

"From Silent Spring to Vocal Vanguard." 1997. *UN Chronicle* 34, no 3.

Hertsgaard, Mark. 1998. *Earth Odyssey: Around the World in Search of Our Environmental Future.* New York: Random House.

Kalland, Arne, and Gerard Persoon, eds. 1998. *Environmental Movements in Asia.* Richmond: Curzon.

Lam, Pang Er. 1999. *Green Politics in Japan.* London, New York: Routledge.

Lee, Su-Hoon. 1999a. "Environmental Movements in South Korea." In Yok-shiu F. Lee and Alvin Y. So, eds., *Asia's Environmental Movements: Comparative Perspectives.* Armonk, NY: M. E. Sharpe.

Lee, Su-Hoon, et al. 1999b. "The Making of Anti-Nuclear Movements in East Asia." In Yok-shiu F. Lee and Alvin Y. So, eds., *Asia's Environmental Movements: Comparative Perspectives.* Armonk, NY: M. E. Sharpe.

Lee, Yok-shiu F., and Alvin Y. So, eds. 1999. *Asia's Environmental Movements: Comparative Perspectives.* Armonk, NY: M. E. Sharpe.

Magno, Francisco A. 1999. "Environmental Movements in the Philippines." In Yokshiu F. Lee and Alvin Y. So, eds., *Asia's Environmental Movements: Comparative Perspectives*. Armonk, NY: M. E. Sharpe.

Mason, Robert J. 1999. "Whither Japan's Environmental Movement? An Assessment of Problems and Prospects at the National Level." *Pacific Affairs* 72 (summer).

Roodman, David Malin. 1999. "Fighting Pollution in Vietnam." *World Watch* 12 (November–December).

UN Environment Programme. 1999. *Global Environmental Outlook 2000*. London: Earthscan.

Appendix

INTERNATIONAL ENVIRONMENTAL AND
DEVELOPMENTAL AGENCIES, ORGANIZATIONS, AND PROGRAMS
ON THE WORLD WIDE WEB

African-Eurasian Migratory Waterbird
Agreement (AEWA)
http://www.unep-wcmc.org/
AEWA/index2.html

Albertine Rift Conservation
Society (ARCOS)
http://www.unep-wcmc.org/arcos/

Association of Southeast
Asian Nations (ASEAN)
http://www.asean.or.id/

Biodiversity Planning Support
Programme (BPSP)
http://www.undp.org/bpsp/

BirdLife International (BI)
http://www.birdlife.net

Botanic Gardens Conservation
International (BGCI)
http://www.bgci.org.uk/

CAB International (CABI)
http://www.cabi.org/

Centre for International
Forestry Research (CIFOR)
http://www.cifor.org/

Circumpolar Protected Areas
Network (CPAN)
http://www.grida.no/caff/
cpanstratplan.htm

Commission for Environment
Cooperation (CEC) (North
American Agreement on
Environmental Cooperation)
http://www.cec.org/

Commission on Genetic Resources
for Food and Agriculture (CGRFA)
http://www.fao.org/ag/cgrfa/
default.htm

Commission for Sustainable
Development (CSD)
http://www.un.org/esa/sustdev/csd.htm

Committee on Trade and Environment
(CTE), World Trade Organization
http://www.wto.org/english/
tratop_e/envir_e/envir_e.htm

Conservation International (CI)
http://www.conservation.org/

Consultative Group on International
Agricultural Research (CGIAR)
http://www.cgiar.org/

Convention on Biological
Diversity (CBD)
http://www.biodiv.org/

Convention on International Trade in
Endangered Species of Wild Fauna
and Flora (CITES)
http://www.cites.org/

Convention on Migratory
  Species of Wild Animals (CMS)
http://www.unep-wcmc.org/cms

European Centre for Nature
  Conservation (ECNC)
http://www.ecnc.nl/

European Community (EC)
http://europa.eu.int/

European Environment
  Agency (EEA)
http://www.eea.eu.int/

Forest Stewardship Council (FSC)
http://www.fscoax.org/index.html

Foundation for International
  Environmental Law and
  Development (FIELD)
http://www.field.org.uk/

Global Assessment of Soil
  Degradation (GLASOD)
http://www.gsf.de/UNEP/glasod.html

Global Biodiversity
  Information Facility (GBIF)
http://www.gbif.org

Global Coral Reef
  Monitoring Network (GCRMN)
http://coral.aoml.noaa.gov/gcrmn/

Global Forest Resources Assessment
  2000 (FRA 2000), UN Food and
  Agriculture Organization
http://www.fao.org/forestry/fo/fra/
  index.jsp

Global International Waters Assessment
  (GIWA), UN Environment Programme
http://www.giwa.net/

Global Invasive Species
  Programme (GISP)
http://globalecology.stanford.edu/DGE/
  Gisp/index.html

Global Resource Information Database
  (GRID), UN Environment Programme
http://www.grid.no

Inter-American Biodiversity
  Information Network (IABIN)
http://www.iabin.org/

Intergovernmental Oceanographic
  Commission (IOC), UN Educational,
  Scientific, and Cultural Organization
http://ioc.unesco.org/iocweb/

Intergovernmental Panel on
  Climate Change (IPCC)
http://www.ipcc.ch/index.html

International Center for Agricultural
  Research in the Dry Areas (ICARDA)
http://www.icarda.cgiar.org/

International Centre for Living Aquatic
  Resources Management (ICLARM)
http://www.cgiar.org/iclarm/

International Centre for Research in
  Agroforestry (ICRAF)
http://www.icraf.cgiar.org/

International Cooperative
  Biodiversity Groups (ICBG)
http://www.nih.gov/fic/programs/icbg.
  html

International Coral Reef
  Action Network (ICRAN)
http://www.icran.org

International Coral Reef
  Information Network (ICRIN)
http://www.environnement.gouv.fr/
  icri/index.html

International Council for the
  Exploration of the Sea (ICES)
http://www.ices.dk/

International Council for Science (ICSU)
http://www.icsu.org/

International Food Policy Research
  Institute (IFPRI)
http://www.ifpri.org/

International Fund for
  Agricultural Development (IFAD)
http://www.ifad.org/

International Geosphere-
  Biosphere Programme (IGBP)
http://www.igbp.kva.se/

International Institute of
  Tropical Agriculture (IITA)
http://www.iita.org

International Maritime
  Organization (IMO)
http://www.imo.org/

International Rivers Network (IRN)
http://www.irn.org/

International Union of
  Biological Sciences (IUBS)
http://www.iubs.org/

Man and the Biosphere Program MAB),
  UN Educational, Scientific, and
  Cultural Organization
http://www.unesco.org/mab/index.htm

Marine Stewardship Council (MSC)
http://www.msc.org/

Organization of African Unity (OAU)
http://www.oau-oau.org/

Organization for
  Economic Cooperation
  and Development (OECD)
http://www.oecd.org/

Ozone Secretariat Homepage
http://www.unep.ch/ozone/

Pan-European Biological and Landscape
  Diversity Strategy (PEBLDS)
http://www.strategyguide.org/

Program for the Conservation of
  Arctic Flora and Fauna (CAFF),
  Arctic Council
http://www.grida.no/caff/

Protocol Concerning Specially
  Protected Areas and Wildlife (SPAW)
http://www.cep.unep.org/law/
  cartnut.html

Ramsar Convention on Wetlands of
  International Importance (RAMSAR)
http://www.ramsar.org/

South African Development
  Community (SADC)
http://www.sadc.int/

South Pacific Regional
  Environmental Programme (SPREP)
http://www.sprep.org.ws/

Species Survival Commission (SSC),
  World Conservation Union
http://iucn.org/themes/ssc/index.htm

TRAFFIC (the joint wildlife trade
  monitoring programme of World
  Wide Fund for Nature and World
  Conservation Union)
http://www.traffic.org

United Nations Centre for
  Human Settlements (UNCHS)
http://www.unchs.org

United Nations
  Children's Fund (UNICEF)
http://www.unicef.org

United Nations Conference on
  Environment and Development
  (UNCED), Rio de Janeiro, June 1992
http://www.un.org/esa/sustdev/
  agenda21.htm

United Nations Conference on Trade
  and Development (UNCTAD)
http://www.unctad.org/

United Nations Convention to Combat
Desertification (UNCCD)
http://www.unccd.int/main.php

United Nations Convention
on the Law of the Sea (UNCLOS)
http://www.un.org/Depts/los/
index.htm

United Nations Development
Programme (UNDP)
http://www.undp.org/

United Nations Educational, Scientific,
and Cultural Organization (UNESCO)
http://www.unesco.org/

United Nations Environment
Programme (UNEP)
http://www.unep.org/

United Nations Food and
Agriculture Organization (FAO)
http://www.fao.org/

United Nations
Forum on Forests (UNFF)
http://www.un.org/esa/sustdev/
forests.htm

United Nations Framework Convention
on Climate Change (UNFCCC)
http://www.unfccc.de/index.html

United Nations Industrial
Development Organization (UNIDO)
http://www.unido.org/

World Agricultural Information Centre
(WAIC), UN Food and Agriculture
Organization
http://www.fao.org/waicent/search/
default.htm

World Bank (WB)
http://www.worldbank.org

World Commission
on Dams (WCD)
http://www.dams.org/

World Commission on Protected Areas
(WCPA), World Conservation Union
http://www.wcpa.iucn.org/

World Conservation
Monitoring Centre (WCMC)
http://www.unep-wcmc.org

World Conservation
Union (IUCN)
http://www.iucn.org/

World Health Organization (WHO)
http://www.who.int

World Heritage Convention (WHC)
http://www.unesco.org/whc/index.htm

World Resources Institute (WRI)
http://www.wri.org/wri/

World Summit on Sustainable
Development (WSSD),
Johannesburg, South Africa,
September 2002
http://www.johannesburgsummit.org/

World Trade Organization (WTO)
http://www.wto.org/

World Water Council (WWC)
http://www.worldwatercouncil.org/

World Wide Fund
for Nature (WWF)
http://www.panda.org/

WorldWatch Institute
http://www.worldwatch.org/

Index